Dance If Ye Can

Dance If Ye Can

A Dictionary of Scottish Battles

'I have brought you to the ring, dance if ye can'
– William Wallace, Falkirk, 1298

Malcolm Archibald

Copyright (C) 2016 Malcolm Archibald
Layout design and Copyright (C) 2016 Creativia
Published 2016 by Creativia
Paperback design by Creativia (www.creativia.org)
ISBN: 978-1536821796
Cover art by http://www.thecovercollection.com/
All rights reserved. No part of this book may be reproduced or transmitted in any form or by any means, electronic or mechanical, including photocopying, recording, or by any information storage and retrieval system, without the author's permission.

For Cathy

Contents

Introduction – Freedom Is a Noble Thing	1
Part One – Dance If Ye Can: The Scottish Soldier	4
Part Two – All Their Time in Wars, An Alphabet of Scottish Battles	16
Part Three – A Scottish Timeline	223
Select Bibliography	236
About the Author	241

Introduction
Freedom Is a Noble Thing

Freedom is a noble thing –John Barbour c 1360

Small nations often have to accept terms dictated upon them by more powerful neighbours. They have to adapt to survive and use political pragmatism as a tool to escape the consequences of their size; bowing to the dragon's will rather than chancing its wrath. There are some small nations who do not accept their role in life, but react to insult with insult and aggression with retaliation. It is almost inevitable that warfare punctuates their history. Scotland is one of these nations.

Even if left alone, the Scots would probably have developed into a contumacious lot. Living in a small country with a generally harsh environment and a climate that ranges from impossible at worst to temporarily pleasant at best, the Scots were always going to have a struggle to survive, but when fate added neighbours who were larger, more powerful and often aggressive, what developed was arguably one of the most bloody-minded, stubborn people on earth.

Scotland is bounded on three sides by the sea and has a single ninety-odd mile long land border with England. She boasts a population of just over five million people; some of the most diverse landscapes anywhere, world-class universities and an international outlook. A land of cool winters and damp summers, Scottish agriculture is nevertheless a world leader while her fishermen brave some of the world's most unpredictable seas. Scotland has produced a plethora of philosophers, a sheaf of innovative scientists, an array of explorers, engineers by the thousand and soldiers by the battalion. There is a measure of pride in her daughters and sons, but scarce understanding of her history; an acceptance of the inevitability of hardships, but a desire to help the less fortunate. The Scots are a unique people whose courage was whetted in the daily grind of wrestling a living from achingly poor soil, but illustrated by the conduct of Scotsmen on a hundred battlefields.

From the defiant Caledonians who forced Rome to withdraw behind its stone fortification to the warriors of Malcolm II that fought on two fronts against English and Viking, from Wallace's spearmen who danced at the rings of Falkirk to the men of Verneuil who died for the French allies that had deserted them, Scots soldiers have plied their trade. Yet the periods of peace that interrupted their history have shown that aggressive war was not intrinsically part of their nature. Fighting was something usually forced upon them, and when called upon, they did what they could, and sometimes they broke all the odds. If they had not, there would be no Scotland now.

This book is intended to give a brief account of every major battle fought for Scotland and in Scotland from 83 AD until 1746, augmented by a host of minor skirmishes and sieges. Although battles such as Flodden and Bannockburn are documented in a score of publications, most clan battles, ambushes and sieges are barely known. Hopefully this book may go some way to rectifying this situation.

The title, *Dance if ye Can*, is taken from a supposed statement of William Wallace at the Battle of Falkirk, when his force of spearmen, backed by a few score archers and a handful of unreliable cavalry confronted the army of Edward Plantagenet of England. The words, however, could relate to any body of Scottish soldiers, in any combat in the world. Once they were committed, the men at the sharp end had no choice but to do their best. Their opponents, Norse, Roman English, or fellow Scot, would probably feel exactly the same. There was no glamour in these wars, only desperate butchery, and few men were heroes by choice.

The book is split into three unequal sections. The first section is a brief overview of the type of weapons, tactics and equipment used. The second and largest section contains an alphabetical list of Scottish battles, sieges and skirmishes, while the last is a historical timeline intended to put the battles in context.

There is no doubt that some battles and many skirmishes will have been missed. While researching, the same battle was often found recorded in different dates, with different results and often in different localities. Wherever possible, these inconsistencies have been ironed out, or explained. It is hoped that the result should provide a rough guide to Scotland's battles, and a reminder that, however bad the modern world seems, things were probably much worse a thousand years ago.

Finally, a note that this book is not intended to be academic. It is a general guide that hopefully leads to some interest in the subject and some sort of understanding of the Scottish people who endured so much over such a long period of time to carve out the country in which they live.

Malcolm Archibald

Part One
Dance If Ye Can: The Scottish Soldier

I have brought you to the ring; dance if ye can – William Wallace, Falkirk, 1298

Romans, Picts and Vikings

Scottish soldiers have attracted respect, contempt, admiration, vilification and sometimes fear, but perhaps most of all there was fascination. Every enemy he encountered seemed to comment on the attire, attitudes and methods of fighting of the men of the north.

When Julius Agricola marched his Romans into Caledonia in the early 80s, his biographer, Tacitus wrote telling comments on the tribesmen that he met. The initial comments were hardly charitable, as Tacitus termed the Caledonians *"a pack of spiritless cowards"* but their practice of guerrilla warfare tested the mettle of even the professional Roman army.

Unlike the Celts of the south, before the Caledonians faced Agricola in pitched battle, they sent their women and children to safety. When battle was joined, Tacitus no longer slated his opponent:

The Britons wanted neither skill nor resolution. With their long swords and cetrae, they managed to elude the heavy weapons of the Romans, and at the same time to discharge a thick volley of their own.

The Caledonians used the chariot, which was an anachronism elsewhere, but were defeated by superior Roman tactics. However, even in retreat they:

had their moments of returning courage and gave proof of virtue and of brave despair. They fled to the woods, and rallying their scattered numbers, surrounded such of the Romans as pursued with too much eagerness.'

Other invaders met similar tactics: the Scots proved expert at the savage night raid, the battle, the retreat and ambush in woods or hills. Calgacus, who commanded the Caledonians, could almost have written the Rules of Engagement for future Scottish wars.

If one accepts that the Picts were a Celtic people, and that is by no means certain, then their way of life would equate with other societies across the British Isles. At the apex of Celtic life was a warrior aristocracy, whose exploits were lovingly recalled by bards. Unfortunately no bardic writings remain from any of the Pictish nations, but instead they left some of the finest stone carvings in Europe. A carved stone at Aberlemno, near Forfar, may refer to the battle of Dunnichen in 685, when the Picts repulsed the Northumbrians. The stone depicts a battle between two distinct groups of warriors, one with helmets and one without.

There are various scenes, but the Pictish tactics seem clear. When facing cavalry the infantry appeared to fight in three disciplined ranks. The front rank held a defensive shield, with a sword ready for retaliation, the second thrust forward his spear to cover his front rank man and the third waited in reserve. In effect it was a schiltron, the same tactic as Wallace used at Falkirk, and not too dissimilar to the squares of Waterloo or Ulundi, where Scots also fought.

The enemy carried swords and spears, with round shields and helmets of a type that the Northumbrians used. The horsemen used the spears for throwing, not couched as lances, and the level of Pictish horsemanship must have been high to control their animals in close battle. Weapons and tactics of the Dark Ages seem to have been broadly similar across Scotland. Pictish stone carvings from Orkney reveal men with spears that are not much taller than themselves, while their shields are small and square, with that of the chief the most ornate.

Other evidence comes from verse. The *Gododdin* is a bardic elegy that may refer to the battle of Cattraeth, although there is a strong possibility that some of the verses were tagged on at a later date. The story is of glorious defeat, and naturally all the warriors are heroes. Verses speak of men with names such as Hyfeidd the Tall, Caradawg and Gwawrddur; the *Gododdin* is about a British war band, the "retinue of Mynyddawg" that fought the encroaching Angles around 600 AD. They came from south of the Pictish lands, and were describes as: "*a force with steeds and blue armour and shields, javelins aloft and keen lances, and bright mail-coats and swords.*" There are echoes of Arthur in the words, inevitable defeat against insufferable odds, a Homerian tragedy enacted upon the damp lands of Britain.

To the west of the lowland British were the Dalriadic Scots, and if they fought like their blood brothers from Ireland, then they used shield and sword, the large spear known as a *sleg* and the smaller *bir* and *foga*. In the early days when Rome was the enemy, the heroes rode chariots to battle and fought for honour and cattle. They gloried in single combat and displayed the heads of their victims, but rather than chain mail they fought with armour of linen or even with no protection at all.

There is a work of the tenth century known as the *Senchus Fer nAlban*, the *History of the Scots*, which includes a military survey of Dalriada. This text reveals that the kingdom was split into three sub-kingdoms, with a combined fighting strength of around 2,100 men. As an island and coastal nation, it is not surprising that the warriors were expected to take their place at the oars of the ships in addition to fighting on land.

Such were the warriors of the Dark Ages. In the eighth century the Norse roared south, with large axes, long swords and coats of mail. Where other nations fell before the Viking menace, the warbands of the Alban nations fought back and in the Highlands at least, the men adopted many of the Norse battle tactics.

At the battle of Bruanburh, the Scots fought in similar style to their Norse allies. They fought on foot, behind a shield wall. It became a Scottish tradition to ride to battle but dismount before the fighting began.

Mediaeval and Renaissance

By the twelfth century the picture is clearer, as Scottish warriors faced more literate opponents. The Norman-English affected little respect for the native Scots as King David's expedition of 1126 combined Galwegian with men from Lothian, Norman with Celt. While the Norman lords huddled around the king, secure in grey armour and kite shaped shield, the Galwegians fought naked, or nearly so, with leather shields and swords, while the men from the lowlands had the small shield and the long spear that was to be Scotland's primary weapon for centuries. When they got close, the Scottish spearmen were ferocious opponents, but the English countered with the longbow that killed at a hundred paces.

At this period the Scottish host was composed of every fit man between sixteen and sixty. When the king commanded, they were duty bound to serve for forty days, unpaid. The local *maormor*, later known as an earl, led the men of his area, and in the Highlands, the status of clan chiefs depended on the number of men in their fighting tail. This method ensured that the king had the maximum of manpower with the minimum expense, but it also made for an untrained and short-term army. Like their Dark Age ancestors, most Scots fought on foot, and not until the statutes of Robert I in 1318 was there any official attempt to provide some protection from the killing hail of English archers. Even the quilted coat or chain mail of the wealthy was little defence, while the poorest, those worth less than £10, could only shelter behind their courage.

Save for a short war with Norway, rebellion in Moray and an invasion of Man, the Scottish knights had little opportunity to show their military prowess. They stagnated in relatively peaceful Scotland. The knights retained the appearance of martial skill, but when Edward of England mounted a challenge, all they knew was the conventional charge of chivalry, which failed before the experience and guile of veteran English commanders. Wallace and Andrew Moray used the power of the people, but it was King Robert I who returned to the old Celtic tactics of hit and run and ambush. His lieutenant, James of Douglas, became the commando fighter *par-excellence*, and generations of Borderers followed his lead.

By the late Middle Ages there was a degree of professionalism about the nucleus of the royal army, with full time artillerymen and perhaps a number of crossbowmen in the royal castles. In 1429 King James I ordered the Scots to learn archery, presumably with the hope they could beat the English at their own game. The Scots probably paid lip service to the idea, but retained their traditional arms. In the event, the king's idea was sound but outmoded; by the fifteenth century there were to be no more ritual slaughters of Scottish armies by Welsh and English longbowmen.

Each area of Scotland would have an annual *wappenshaw*, literally, 'weapon show', where in theory each man's state of readiness for war could be checked and maintained. The primary infantry weapon in the Lowlands continued to be the spear, sometimes termed a pike, and those who could afford it carried a sword. The Scottish spearmen, however, were not to be despised. They fought shoulder to shoulder in a compact hedgehog known as a *schiltron* that could advance on an appalled enemy or repel the charge of armoured chivalry. If a sufficient number of spearmen could reach the enemy, they were hard to beat.

While the gentleman class provided the heavy cavalry, the Borders produced a large number of light horsemen, known as *prickers*. These men were invaluable for scouting, irregular warfare and the fast, hit-and-run raids that were a Border speciality. Both William Wallace and King Robert I used the archers from Ettrick, while parts of the Highlands also sent archers, such as the contingent from Argyll at the battle of Pinkie.

Highland and Lowland fighting men evolved differently, probably due to their diverse cultural backgrounds. Writing in 1420, Andrew Wyntoun describes the Highland combatants at the Battle of the North Inch as fighting "with bow and ax, knyf and swerd." The bow was an important weapon in the north. In 1521 John Major said that the Highlanders:

Always carry a bow and arrows, a very broad sword with a small halbert, a large dagger, sharpened on one side only, but very sharp, under the belt. In time of war they cover their whole body with a shirt of mail of iron rings, and fight in that.

Major was obviously referring to the upper classes of Highland society, for he added that the:

Common people of the Highland Scots rush into battle, having their body clothed with a linen garment manifoldly sewed and painted or daubed with pitch, with a covering of deerskin.

In 1549, when the French were assisting to remove the last of the English from southern Scotland, the Frenchman John de Beaugue wrote that the Scottish army were:

Followed by the Highlanders, and these last go almost naked; they have painted waistcoats and a sort of woollen covering, variously coloured.

The Lowlanders were also light infantry, with a spear or pike, an iron or steel helmet and a leather jerkin or quilted jack. In the Borders, at least, firearms became popular in the sixteenth century.

Writing in 1583, another Frenchman, Nicolay d'Arfeville, wrote that the Highlanders used:

The bow and arrow, and some darts, which they throw with great dexterity, and a large sword, with a single-edged dagger. They are very swift of foot, and there is no horse so swift as to outstrip them.

In the early 1570s, Lindsay of Pitscottie termed the Highlanders:

Very rud and homlie kind of people... called the Reidschankis or Wyld Scottis... thair weapons ar bowis and dartis, with ane verie broad sword and ane dagger scharp onlie at the on edge.

Describing the Highlanders as 'redshanks' was common at the time, the name referring to their bare legs, and casting memories back to the Norwegian King Magnus who earned the title Magnus Barelegs when he adopted Hebridean dress after his campaigns in the west.

George Buchanan, who wrote in 1582, mentioned that the Highlanders wore:

An iron bonnet and an habbergion... even to their heels. Their weapons... are bowes and arrows. The arrows are for the most part hooked, with a bauble (barb) on either side, which once entered within the body cannot be drawn forth again, unless the wounde be made wider. Some of them fight with broad swords and axes.

The combination of light infantryman with armoured axe men was potent, causing major problems at Harlaw in 1411 and defeating a royal army at Inverlochy twenty years later. The axes seem to have been a speciality of some of the warriors from the far north and the Western Isles, the areas most influenced by the Norse. There was a traditional movement of warriors from western Scotland to Ireland from at least the thirteenth century. These men were known as *galloglaich*, or gallowglass, which meant 'foreign warrior.' Gallowglasses often settled in Ireland and featured in most Irish conflicts until the wars against Queen Elizabeth. They fought on foot, wearing long shirts of mail and wielding a long handled battleaxe. They were the elite fighting men of the Irish chiefs and kings.

Scottish Highlanders featured very strongly in sixteenth century warfare in Ireland. In 1545 Donald Dubh sent many of his men over, and an English observer reported that they were:

Very tall men, clothed…in habergeons of mail, armed with long swords and long bows but with few guns; the other thousand, tall mariners that rowed in galleys.

Peregrine O'Cleary, in his *Life of Hugh O'Donnell* described the Highlanders who fought Elizabeth as carrying:

Horn-hafted swords, large and military, over their shoulders. A man when he had to strike with them, was obliged to apply both his hands to the haft.

At the other end of the country, the Borders also created a distinctive type of warrior. Their light horsemen usually bore the brunt of any English invasion, and when not at war, were often involved in clan feuding or straightforward cattle reiving. In the fourteenth century Froissart had commented that the Scots rode to war, with *the common people on little hackneys and geldings.* By the sixteenth century the Borderers had evolved their own culture of the horse and their prickers were perhaps the most professional soldiers in Britain. The word professional means just that; they rode and fought for profit, not for glory or honour, and would leave a battlefield without a qualm if there was a chance of a quick buck. More like modern soldiers than their contemporaries, the Border 'licht horsemen' were supremely functional. From the steel helmet that protected his head, past his reinforced quilted jacket to the leather boots, everything had a purpose, and none more than the nine-foot lance, the backsword and the pair of pistols that they used with chilling skill.

The less favoured foot soldier that filled the ranks at Flodden, Hadden and a hundred forgotten skirmishes through the centuries, carried a long spear or a shorter bill, with the Jedburgh Staff or Axe being a local favourite. Knowing that they lived on one of the most volatile frontiers in Europe, the Borderer was good at his job. He had to be.

But how effective were the Scots as fighting men? In the sixteenth century, English armies triumphed in major battles such as Flodden and Pinkie, but failed in smaller encounters such as Hadden Rigg and Ancrum. Scotland seemed to drain the English desire for war, so that England thought it wise to wrap Berwick in some of the most impressive fortifications in Europe, while the expenditure in Scottish wars drained the English treasury. Warfare in Scotland cannot have been popular, given the climate, the uncertainty and the constant possibility that there was a Scottish retaliatory force waiting over the next hill.

Seventeenth and Eighteenth Century

The seventeenth century was a seminal period in the history of Scottish warfare. The last official war with England had finished, and excess Scottish manpower honed their skills fighting other people's wars. Not until the late 1630s did the horror return to Scotland, but when it did, it lasted for years.

The 1640s and early 1650s were bloody years with armies of the King and Covenant butchering each other in the name of religion or power. When the First Bishop's War erupted in 1639, the government of Scotland created a more professional army, yet retained some national characteristics. Religion created the war, as King Charles 1 attempted to impose the Episcopalian Church, of which he was head, onto the Presbyterian majority in Scotland. Instead of meek Scottish compliance he encountered the Covenanters and utter defiance. Musicians garnished the army that gathered at Duns in 1639, but the blue bonnets that Alexander Leslie led over the border the following year achieved their military objectives with little trouble.

Armies still comprised cavalry and infantry, but improvements in the musket had changed the face of the battlefield. In common with other European states, Scotland trained dragoons, which were little more than mounted infantry, and a force of armoured medium cavalry that David Leslie was to use with some effect. Strangely, pikemen were seen as more honourable than musketeers, and had to be strong to manage the eighteen-foot long pike. In the early years they outnumbered the musketeers by around two to one, and although musketry could thin the enemy's ranks, most battles were won by 'push of pike.' However, by mid century musketeers were more numerous, numbering over half the infantry. The fortitude of the infantryman remained as important at it had ever been.

The musketeer was unarmoured, firing behind a thin screen of stakes, much like the English archers at Crecy. He fired a matchlock, and was responsible for ensuring that bad weather or carelessness did not extinguish the match. At that period his musket was supported by a wooden rest, and fired a ball an ounce in weight with little accuracy and no speed. A good musketeer might fire every two minutes. Slow moving, slow firing and slow of manoeuvre, the seventeenth century musketeer was not a figure of grace, although his position improved when the lighter flintlock musket came into use.

In the early seventeenth century the musketeers fought in ranks ten deep to allow a continual roll of musketry. As each man fired, he fell back and his rear marker took his place. As the weapons improved, the ranks thinned to six, and eventually to three.

Montrose was said to be the first Scottish commander to use the Swedish *salvee* method of having all six ranks fire a salvo together. His *salvees* were usually enough to shake the enemy formation, so that the ensuing Highland charge would destroy it. Cromwell's New Model Army copied Montrose, but with far greater numbers of men.

Infantry tactics were relatively simple. A body of skirmishers, known as the *forlorn hope* harassed the enemy until the musketeers were in range. There was an exchange of musketry and then push of pike. The cavalry would fight each other and either hit the enemy flanks or chase a defeated opponent.

In the 1640s these slow moving infantry faced a terrifying enemy when the Marquis of Montrose united Alasdair MacColla MacDonalds Ulster veterans with the Highland clans. Fast moving, dedicated and relentless, the Gaels ducked when the opposing musketeers fired, moved forward rapidly and delivered a killing volley from close range before closing with the broadsword and Lochaber axe. William Cleland, veteran of Bothwell Bridge and Drumclog described the Highlanders of 1678 as carrying

Dance If Ye Can

A targe of timber, nails and hides;
With a long two-handed sword.

They killed him at Dunkeld, in 1689.

More conventional forces found such adversaries formidable opponents, so long as they were well led. It was the Camerons that gave Cromwell his biggest headache after he had defeated the Covenanting armies, and he thought so highly of the MacLeans that he sent five government warships to arrest their ten-year-old chief.

After the Restoration of King Charles II, legislation was put in place to raise a Scottish militia of 20,000 infantry and 2,000 cavalry. This manpower, backed by a handful of regular regiments, was used primarily for suppressing unrest at home. The later Covenanters, who resolutely opposed King Charles' attempt at imposing Episcopacy, were the main targets. At the battles of Rullion Green, Drumclog and Bothwell Brig redcoated Scottish troops face ill-armed Scottish Presbyterians.

By 1689 the situation had changed as religious intolerance saw the Catholic King James VII replaced by the Protestant William of Orange. Between that year and 1746, redcoated regulars of Scottish and English regiments faced Highland clans who supported the exiled Stuart kings. By that time the Highland tactics were anachronistic. They fought the same was as their grandfathers had under Montrose, but faced infantry who could fire faster and with more skill, backed by artillery. There was no doubting their ability or courage; in 1688 William Sacheverell, governor of the Isle of Man visited the Maclean lands of Mull and commented that the Highland soldiers had:

A round target on their backs, a blue bonnet on their heads, in one hand a broadsword, and a musquet in the other. Perhaps no nation goes better armed; and... they will handle them with dexterity

Highland courage and broadswords won the battle of Killiecrankie, albeit at great cost, but failed against the Cameronians at Dunkeld. Badly led, the Highlanders could only draw at Sherrifmuir in 1715, as they faced Argyll's regular forces. Their victory at Prestonpans came in a flank attack, and they fought hard and skilfully at Falkirk, but Culloden was a disaster. After enduring an artillery bombardment for half an hour, the Highlanders launched a piecemeal attack against twice their number of regular infantry. Bravery could not stop the massed volleys of musketry, nor honour save them from the Duke of Cumberland's spite.

After Culloden, there were no battles fought in Scotland, only civil disturbance and riot. There was no peace, however, for the manhood of the nation was siphoned off to fight Britain's wars.

Part Two
All Their Time in Wars
An Alphabet of Scottish Battles

The Scots spend all their time in wars, and when there is no war, they fight with one another – Don Pedro de Ayala, 1498

A

Abercorn Castle, 1455: West Lothian. When King James II realised that the Douglas family may have had ambitions for his crown, he murdered Earl William Douglas and began a military campaign against the Douglases. During this mini civil war, the king besieged Abercorn Castle. Douglas and one of his supporters, Hamilton of Cadzow, arrived with an army that seemed to tip the balance against James, until Hamilton changed sides. Douglas fled, and when the castle surrendered in May, James hanged the garrison.

Aberdeen, March 1644: Aberdeenshire. In March 1644 during the civil war that raged through Scotland in the middle of the seventeenth century, Royalists under Sir John Gordon of Haddo raided the city of Aberdeen. They kidnapped several important citizens including the Provost. The prisoners were held for a short while in the Castle of Strathbogie, but were freed when the Gordons learned that a Covenanting army under the Duke of Argyll was heading north.

Aberdeen; 13th September 1644. This battle was fought during the great civil war of the seventeenth century. A Royalist army under the Marquis of Montrose fought a force of Covenanters just outside Aberdeen.

After an earlier victory over Lord Elcho's Covenanters at the battle of Tippermuir outside Perth, many of Montrose's Highlanders left his army. Left with around 1500 men, mainly Alasdair MacDonald's Ulstermen and Highlanders, Montrose marched north. Lord Burleigh led a Covenanting force to meet the Royalists at the Justice Mills outside Aberdeen. Montrose sent a drummer boy to demand the surrender of the town, but an Aberdonian shot him. The resulting battle took place at Two Mile Cross, near the present retail park at Brig o Dee.

The Covenanters started the battle with a cavalry charge, which Montrose repulsed with his own force of mounted men. When the Covenanters flanks crumbled, Montrose ordered his infantry forward, driving back the Covenanters after a hard struggle of over an hour. The Ulstermen and Highlanders then sacked the town for three days. Perhaps 200 people were murdered, with much rape and looting. There is no memorial for this battle, which is also known as Justice Mills or Crabstane Rout.

Aberfoyle, Pass of, 1653; 20 miles (32 kilometres) west of Stirling, 25 miles (40 kilometres) north of Glasgow, in Stirlingshire. During Glencairn's rising against the Cromwellian invasion of 1653, there was a skirmish in the Pass of Aberfoyle. Graham of Duchray seems to have stalled a Cromwellian advance.

Achdalieu, 1654, situated about two and a half miles west of Corpach, near Fort William, Lochaber, Highland. Clan Cameron defeated Cromwellian forces. During the Cromwellian occupation of Scotland,

Clan Cameron, under Ewan Cameron, was probably the Royalist clan who did most damage to the invader. General Monck, Cromwell's man in Scotland, attempted to quell the Camerons. Five Cromwellian ships landed two thousand of Cromwell's troops at Inverlochy and set about building a fort that would later be Fort William. Ewan cleared the area of his people and observed Cromwell's forces with only thirty-two men.

According to Cameron history, when a force of Cromwell's men ventured out to cut timber and loot the local houses, Ewan Cameron led his men in a charge on around 150 of the enemy. An estimated forty or fifty Cromwellians were killed and the rest ran. It was in this fight that Ewan Cameron fought an English officer hand to hand and bit out his throat. When the Camerons offered quarter, an Englishman fired at Ewan, so the Camerons finished off the enemy. Only two English escaped, and five Camerons were killed. After the battle, the Camerons examined the bodies to see if the English had tails, as their behaviour made them more like devils incarnate than men.

Achintore c 1654: once a separate village but now part of Fort William, Lochaber, Highland. This was another battle between the garrison of Cromwell's fort at Inverlochy, now Fort William, and the Cameron clan, in whose land the Cromwellians were intruding. The Camerons ambushed and defeated a force of Cromwell's men that was gathering timber.

Achnashellach, c 1505: near Lochalsh, Sutherland, Highland. This clan conflict was fought twelve miles from the Castle of Strone in Lochalsh. It is one of the many battles in Scotland for which details are vague, but accounts suggest that a body of Camerons under their chief Ewan Cameron defeated the Munros and Mackays. It seems that Sir William Munro of Foulis was killed

Alitan-Beath, 1542, Sutherland; skirmish between Clan Mackay and Sutherland. Donald Mackay of Strathnaver had recently taken over as chief of the clan, and when Adam, Earl of Sutherland died, he invaded

Sutherland with a body of men. He burned the township of Knockartoll and plundered Strathbrora. Sir Hugh Kennedy of Griffen Mains, Gilbert Gordon of Garty and Hutcheon Murray of Abirscors gathered a force and attacked Mackay at Ailtan-Beath.

The Mackays lost the fight that followed, and John MacIan-MacAngus was killed, with many of the Mackays. Donald Mackay fought well, killing William Sutherland before he fled with the others. He was later captured and imprisoned in Fowlis Castle in Ross.

Airds Moss, 22 July 1680: near Muirkirk, East Ayrshire. Government forces defeated the Covenanters. On 22 June, 1680, the radical Covenanter Richard Cameron, known as the Lion of the Covenant, his brother Michael and twenty horsemen rode into Sanquhar and fixed a declaration to the Mercat Cross. It stated that the Covenanters intended to 'disown Charles Stuart, who hath been reigning, or rather... tyrannising on the Throne of Scotland.' On Thursday 22 July Captain Bruce of Earlshall, the commander of Claverhouse's troop of dragoons found Cameron and 40 followers on Airds Moss near Muirkirk in Ayrshire. Bruce led 120 government troopers to capture him.

Cameron led his men into battle with the call "Lord, spare the green and take the ripe." In the skirmish that followed, Richard and Michael Cameron were both killed, with seven of their followers. The remainder scattered. Cameron's named lived on when the Cameronian Regiment of the army was raised in 1689. There is a tall stone monument that remembers Cameron and his men.

Alcluith, 756: Dumbarton, Strathclyde. This battle was fought at the fort on Dumbarton Rock. At a time when Alcluith was the capital of the British kingdom of Strathclyde, the Britons defeated Oengus MacFergus and his ally Eadberht, King of Northumbria. The Britons had pretended to surrender ten days before the battle, and then attacked without warning, defeating the allies.

Aldy-Charrish, 1487, also known as Aldicharrish: Wester Ross. This was a clan battle in which the Mackays defeated the Rosses. Men of the clan Ross had killed Angus Mackay at Tarbat, and John Riabhach Mackay, the son of Angus, asked the Earl of Sutherland, his feudal superior, for help to avenge the death. Sutherland sent Robert Sutherland and a body of men to reinforce the Mackays.

The combined Mackay – Sutherland force ravaged Strathcarron and Strathoykel. The Ross chief, Alexander Ross of Balnagown brought his men and attacked the allies at Aldicharrish. There was a hard fought battle that the Mackays and Sutherlands ultimately won. Ross of Balnagown and seventeen gentlemen were among the Rosses killed.

Alford, 2 July 1645, 25 miles west of Aberdeen, by the River Don. This was a significant battle in the Civil War between the supporters of King Charles I and supporters of the Covenant. The Marquis of Montrose and Royalist army defeated the Covenanters under General William Baillie. The Covenanters had around 2000 foot, including a number of veterans, and around 300 cavalry. Montrose had an equal number of infantry but perhaps only 200 cavalry.

After defeating General Hurry at Auldearn, Montrose spent time feinting with Baillie's army, then the armies met at Alford in Aberdeenshire, with Baillie possibly intending to stop Montrose attacking Aberdeen. Although Montrose had marginally the smaller army, Baillie had his own problems. The Committee of Estates was a body of political ecclesiastics with no military experience, but they were in a position to overrule Baillie's decisions. The Committee had also ordered 1000 of Baillie's most experienced men to join the force of General Lindsay, instead offering him a number of inexperienced local levies. Montrose positioned himself in a low hill, possibly Gallows Hill overlooking the River Don, with his Highlanders in the centre. The Committee members urged Baillie to attack, and when the Covenanting army was split, with the horse on one side of the river and the foot on the other, Montrose put in a counter attack. He pushed away the Covenanting horse, and then hit the Covenanting foot with infantry and cavalry. Not surprisingly, the Covenanters gave way, with around

1000 casualties, but Montrose had lost Lord Gordon, who had charged in front to avenge the ravaging of his lands by the Covenanters.

Some early writers suggest that there was a commemorative stone known as the Gordon Stone, where Lord Gordon was killed. However, this stone, which may have been a prehistoric standing stone with no relevance to the battle, has now gone. To add to the uncertainty, there are conflicting accounts as to the exact whereabouts of the battle, but the action may have taken place on the northern side of Gallows Hill.

Allantonplains, May 1307 East Ayrshire, Strathclyde, sixteen miles north east of Ayr. This was a minor skirmish in the First Scottish War of Independence. Robert the Bruce attacked a force of English under Ralph de Montherner, Earl of Gloucester and chased it back to Ayr.

Allt Camhna 1586, Caithness. The Earls of Sutherland and Caithness were at feud with Clan Gunn, who they decided were the chief troublemakers in Caithness. The Earls sent two bodies of men against the Gunns in Caithness, one commanded by John Gordon of Backies and James MacRorie, the other by Henry Sinclair, cousin of the Earl of Caithness. Henry Sinclair's company were first to meet the Gunns at Allt Camhna. The Gunns were outnumbered, but had some of Clan Mackay with them and the advantage of a small hill named Bingrime. They seem to have fought without tactics, but Sinclair's men fired the first flight of arrows, which fell short. Clan Gunn waited until they came in range, and their arrows caused great devastation. Henry Sinclair and 120 of his men died and the rest fled, with some being killed as they ran.

Alnwick 13th November 1093: Northumberland, England. After the English increased the fortifications of Carlisle Castle, Malcolm III (Canmore) invaded. He had been waging intermittent war to stop the spread of English influence in Scotland. Malcolm's army looted Northumberland and camped near Alnwick, but Robert de Mowbray, the governor of Bamburgh Castle sallied out and attacked the Scots, taking them by surprise. Malcolm was killed in the fighting, as was his son Edward. There was a persistent legend that Mowbray attacked while a truce was in operation.

A monument, 'Malcolm's Cross', was erected in 1774 and marks the spot where the king was killed. It is one mile north of Alnwick.

Alnwick 1174: Northumberland. With England in turmoil due to civil war, King William 1 (the Lion) of Scotland joined the side of King Henry's son (the Young Henry.) In what could be seen as a precursor of the Auld Alliance, William invaded England to create a diversion for the French king, who also supported Young Henry. Uchtred and Gilbert of Galloway supported King William.

King William led a mixed army of Gaels, Norman-Scottish knights and warriors from Galloway into Northern England. The English accused them, perhaps justly, of various atrocities, but when the Scots failed to take Carlisle Castle, they raided right cross Northern England. King William led a small force to Alnwick and attempted to besiege the castle, but the larger English garrison, reinforced by another force under Ralf de Glanvil sallied out. It appears that there was a mist and King William approached a body of horse, thinking they were his own men. When he realised that they were English he couched his lance, shouted '"Now it will appear who knows how to be a knight" and charged. During the skirmish, Williams's horse fell and rolled on him and he was captured. The subsequent Treaty of Falaise was expensive, for William agreed to become the English king's liegeman for all of Scotland. The Treaty was not cancelled until 1189, when the Treaty of Canterbury restored Scotland's independence in exchange for 4000 marks. King Richard of England needed the money to finance his part in the Third Crusade.

Altimarlach, 13 July 1680. Tradition places this battle on a farm just outside Wick, Caithness. It was also said to be the last clan battle fought in Scotland, although some historians would disagree. The name may come from the Gaelic *Uilt na Muirleach*, the Burn of the Thieves, because the bodies of those killed were robbed.

Sir John Campbell of Glenorchy claimed ownership of the Girngoe lands and the Earldom of Caithness. It seems that the 6th Earl of Caithness had not repaid a loan made to Campbell of Glenorchy. In response, Glenorchy was later granted the title of Earl of Caithness, Lord of Berriedale and Glenorchy. George Sinclair of Keiss contested his claim, and after legal disputes the king granted Glenorchy permission to invade Caithness to take his lands.

Glenorchy gathered his forces in Perth and marched to Braemore in Caithness, then to the Hill of Yarrows. He may have had around 800 men, including Campbells and other auxiliary clans including MacGregors under John MacGregor. Glenorchy marched on Wick during a mist, but when the mist cleared Sinclair's forces saw Glenorchy coming and raised the alarm.

According to some accounts, Glenorchy marched to Stirkoke and Altimarlach, where he split his army in two, concealing some in the burn channel but leaving the remainder in open view on the haugh ground. As the men on the haugh land attacked the Sinclairs, those who were concealed rose in ambush. With the burn behind them and Glenorchy's men in front, the Sinclairs were badly mauled, losing around 300 men. It is said that Finlay Ban MacIvor composed the pipe tune *The Campbells Are Coming* as Glenorchy's army marched to Caithness, and *The Breadalbane Gathering* is also said to date from this campaign.

Although it was reported that the Sinclairs spent the night before the battle drinking in the hostelries of Wick, this can be discounted, as can the legend that claims the battle for Allt a Mhullaich in Argyll. There is a memorial cross at the site near Wick.

Ancrum Moor, January 27 1545: about four miles north of Jedburgh, Scottish Borders. The Earl of Angus defeated an English force under Sir Ralph Eure and Sir Brian Layton. This battle was fought during the so-called Rough Wooing, when Henry VIII attempted to make Mary of Scots marry his son Edward by destroying as much of Scotland as he could. Not surprisingly the Scots retaliated. Sir Ralph Eure commanded the 3000 strong English force that burned its way through southern Scotland. Eure had defaced the tombs of long-dead Douglas at Melrose Abbey, which annoyed the Douglas Earl of Angus. Eure had also burned Broomhouse Tower, killing an old woman and her family. Eure made a night foray from Jedburgh against the Earl of Angus and Scott of Buccleuch, who had about 300 men, plus some Fife cavalry under Norman Leslie of Rothes. Angus and his riders were in the hills and scouted Eure's force until it was on the moor just north of Ancrum, five miles from Jedburgh. Angus outflanked Eure's line of march, dismounted his riders and used the ground to conceal how many men he had.

The English and their Scots allies were heavy with plunder when Angus ambushed. The English charged forward, but Angus had positioned his men in the west, so the setting sun shone in the English faces. The wind also blew gun smoke into their eyes, so they could not see the extent of the Scottish force. The Scottish lances turned the English charge into a shambles.

As Eure fell back those Scottish Borderers, and possibly even some Highlanders, who had been fighting with the English ripped off the St George Cross signs that marked them as 'assured Scots' and attacked their erstwhile allies. Hundreds of English, including the leaders Eure and Laiton, were killed, and about a thousand were captured. Speaking of Eure, James Hamilton, the Earl of Arran said, "God have mercy on him, for he was a fell cruel man."

This battle had tremendous propaganda effect, raising morale in Scotland and France. Legends speak of a local woman named Lilliard who joined in the action, fighting even when her legs were cut off. A monument at the site, known as the 'Maiden's Tomb,' commemorates her part. There is a footpath along Dere Street that accesses the battlefield.

Annan, 17 December 1332: Dumfries and Galloway. Scottish patriots chased Edward Balliol and his pro-English supporters out of Scotland. After the death of Robert I, the English had again interfered with Scottish affairs by sending an army north to support their puppet king Edward Balliol. When Balliol decided to spend Christmas in Annan, central to his power base in southwest Scotland, the Guardian, Sir Archibald Douglas and the Earl of Moray gathered the patriots at Moffat. They rode south by night and attacked at dawn, overwhelming Balliol's men and killing many in their beds. Sir John Mowbray and Sir Walter Comyn were killed but Edward Balliol made a hole in the wall of his chamber and escaped, riding bare-backed into England.

Antonine Wall, c184: Scottish Lowlands between the Forth and Clyde. The tribes in Lowland Scotland rose against the Romans and overcame the Wall. A man named Corvus died in this campaign; he may have been an ancestor of the later kings of Strathclyde. Despite their superior tactics and weapons, the Romans under Governor Ulpius Marcellus had to campaign three times before he thrust the Britons back. This must have been quite a significant war, for Commodus gained the title *Britannicus* after his victory. However the Romans still abandoned the Wall before the end of the century.

Apardion, 1153: possibly Aberdeen. Around this time a Norwegian leader named Eystein attacked a Scottish town that he named Apardion in what was possibly the last significant Norse raid on Eastern Scotland.

Arbroath, 23 January 1445: Angus. This battle was fought for the control of Arbroath Abbey. It took place just outside Arbroath when the son of the 2nd Earl of Crawford defeated the Ogilvies and Sir Alexander Seton.

Sir Alexander Lindsay, Master of Crawford was Bailie of the Regality of Arbroath. He had retained a large number of armed followers, paid for by the monastery but his conduct had made him 'uneasy to the convent' so the Chapter appointed Alexander Ogilvy of Inverquharity as his successor. Crawford refused to surrender his appointment and took control of Arbroath and the abbey. The Earl of Douglas sent a hundred men from Clydesdale to support Crawford, and the Hamiltons also sent Crawford reinforcements. Meanwhile Sir Alexander Seton, Lord of Gordon, had arrived at Inverquharity on his way to Strathbogie. He travelled with the usual band of armed followers. By Scottish tradition the host's quarrel became the guest's quarrel. Seton and some other local lords joined the Ogilvy army as it marched on Arbroath.

The Lindsays, who were firm allies of the Crawfords, formed up in battle formation in front of Arbroath. With his wife an Ogilvie, the Earl of Crawford, father of the Master, ran between lines to try and make peace but an Ogilvie ran a spear through him, perhaps not knowing who he was. The Earl fell mortally wounded. The Lindsays charged and won the battle. There were about 100 Lindsay casualties and perhaps 600 Ogilvies. Inverquharity was wounded and captured; his brother and Seton fled. Inverquharity was carried to Finhaven Castle, the Earl of Crawford's seat, to be smothered with a pillow by the Earl of Crawford's wife. The Earl died of his wounds a week later.

Ardcorran, 627. The location of this battle is uncertain. It was fought either in Northern Ireland or in Kintyre at a time when the Scottish kingdom of Dalriada still maintained a foothold in Ulster. Conadd Cerr of Dalriada defeated Fiachna MacDemain, an Ulster king.

Ardde-anesbi or Airdeanesbi, perhaps in Argyll: 719; civil war. According to the *Annals of Tigernach – the battle of Ardde-anesbi, on the sea, between Duncan Bec, with the tribe of Gabran, and Selbach with the tribe of Loarn; and Selbach was defeated.* As the Cenel Gabrain (the clan or family of Gabrain) controlled what is now Kintyre and Cowal, and Loarn controlled Lorne, the battle might have been fought in the sea off Argyll, or in one of the sea lochs. This is the first recorded sea battle in British history, and concerns a dynastic struggle within Dalriada.

Ardnary, 1586, Ulster: this was a battle in the confused situation where Clan Donald was expanding into Ulster after losing lands and prestige in Western Scotland. The local O'Neills allied themselves with the English in a campaign to curb the MacDonalds and in this encounter they were victorious.

Ardoch, 83 AD; Strathearn, Perthshire; supposed site of an attack by the Caledonians on Agricola's invading 9th Legion. According to Tacitus, the Caledonians attacked at night: *surprising and cutting down* *the sentries, who were asleep or panic stricken, the enemy broke into the camp.* Agricola eventually repelled the raiders but they, *thinking themselves cheated not so much by our valour as by our general's skill, lost nothing of their arrogance.* Agricola did not advance further that year.

Ard Rannoch, 1685, Perthshire. This was a minor skirmish that occurred during Argyll's rising when a night patrol of Camerons accidentally killed some of Earl of Atholl's Perthshire Horse. Both units were on the royal side against Argyll.

Ardscull, 1316; near Athy, County Kildare, Ireland, This battle was fought during the First War of Independence. When Edward Bruce opened a new front against the English in Ireland, he had himself crowned High King of Ireland and won a series of victories. One such was at Ardscul, where he defeated the Anglo-Irish Lord Justice Sir Edmund Butler. Bruce was outnumbered but the Anglo-Irish force was riven by internal disputes.

Ardvorlich House, 1620. South of Loch Earn, Perthshire. A minor skirmish when a party of Glencoe MacDonalds raided the Stewarts of Ardvorlich on the south side of Loch Earn. The Stewarts repulsed the MacDonalds, killing seven. A stone marks the site of the encounter.

Ardvreck Castle, 1672: Assynt, Sutherland. Originally a castle of the MacLeods, in 1672 the Mackenzies attacked and captured it as they took control of Assynt. The castle is now a picturesque ruin in a splendid setting.

Argoed Llwyfain, c 588: location uncertain but possibly in south west Scotland. This was a legendary battle in which Owain of the British kingdom of Rheged apparently defeated the Saxon prince of a small state named Fflamddwyn. Rheged was based around the Solway Firth.

Arkinholm, 1 May 1455, Langholm, Dumfriesshire. Royal forces defeat the army of the Douglases. The Douglas family had gradually risen to power in southern Scotland since Sir James of Douglas had been instrumental in helping King Robert I maintain Scotland's position as an independent nation. By the middle of the fifteenth century the Douglases were powerful enough to threaten the Crown. In 1440 the young King James II, advised by Sir William Crichton and Sir Alexander Livingstone, enticed the head of the family, William Douglas to Edinburgh, where they beheaded him. Twelve years later, in 1452, the Douglases refused to break an alliance with the Lord of the Isles, and rode to Stirling to see the King under a safe conduct. The king murdered him. Not surprisingly, the Douglases, led by James, the 9th Earl, rose in rebellion against the king. The earl's three brothers, the Lords Moray, Ormond and Balvenie led the Douglas army.

The Scots kings traditionally had no royal army but asked loyal nobles to raise their men. The Laird of Johnstone called up his own men and some of the leading Border families and defeated the Douglases at Arkinholm on the River Esk near Langholm.

Balvenie escaped to England, the Earl of Ormond was wounded, captured and executed, Archibald Douglas, Earl of Moray was killed and his severed head sent to King as present. The defeat marked downfall of the Black Douglas branch of the family.

Arthuret, 573 AD, possibly fought in southwest Scotland or northwest England. This was one of the more interesting of the Dark Age battles, which may have had some bearing on Arthurian tradition, and could have marked a turning point for the victory of Christianity over paganism.

In one version, the Christian king Rhydderch Hael of Strathclyde defeated his pagan Briton rivals. Welsh tradition affirms that the battle was fought between the rival British princes Gwenddoleu and his cousin Gwrgi and Peredur and Gwenddoleu was killed. Tradition always claims that the battle was fought for "a larks nest", possibly Caerlaverock, a strategic harbour commanding the approach to the Solway. The battle site may have been near the village of Arthuret on the outskirts of Longtown.

It is also claimed that Myrddin, who may have been the domestic bard of Gwenddoleu and possibly a prototype for the legendary Merlin, fought in the battle and won a gold torque. Myrddin was said to have become insane in the battle and later lived as a wild man in the Forest of Celyddon in Scotland. There a lot of 'maybe's in this battle but if any mediaeval scholar can untangle the web, what a fascinating story could be found!

Asreth c 584: in Circinn, possibly in present day Angus. One of the early legendary battles where the Pictish king Bridei (Brude Mac Maelchon) was killed either in a civil war or in a battle with a rival Pictish dynasty or kingdom.

Athelstaneford: East Lothian. This was a legendary battle that possibly never took place. According to legend, Angus MacFergus king of the Picts, allied to the Eochaidh the Poisonous, King of the Dalriadic Scots, defeated the Angles. Legend says that Angus MacFergus and Eochaidh were returning from a successful raid into Northumbria, when an English army caught them on the banks of the River Tyne. Some accounts claim that King Athelstan (925 – 940) led the Angles. It is possible that there was a battle with an English force, but if so, the famous King Athelstan almost certainly was not involved. Perhaps a segment of his army was defeated, or a warrior with a similar name led the Angles.

There is no doubt that in the eighth and ninth century Lothian was a borderland, with the Picts to the north, the Strathclyde Britons to the West and the Angles in residence.

The most interesting part of this legend is the birth of the Scottish national flag. The Picts and Scots apparently prayed for victory and a white Saltire appeared in the blue sky. After the victory the allies replaced the traditional boar's head national flag with the Saltire, and St Andrew became the patron saint. As Athelstan died in the battle, the place was named Athelstaneford.

The Scottish Saltire flies permanently above the village, together with a monument showing the rival armies and a cross in the sky.

Dance If Ye Can

Auchencloy Moor, December 17 1684. Back Water of Dee, Kirkcudbrightshire. In the latter part of the seventeenth century, followers of the Presbyterian faith were in direct conflict with the official Episcopalian religion of the King of Scotland and England. The Presbyterians refused to agree that the King was head of their church, maintaining that only God held that position. Some of the more extreme Presbyterians were known as Covenanters, owing to the covenant that they had signed with God. The authorities fined, tortured, hanged and otherwise persecuted the Covenanters.
In 1684 a 100-strong party of Covenanters invaded Kirkcudbright, released the Presbyterian prisoners in the tolbooth and killed the sentinel. Graham of Claverhouse, a noted follower of the king, caught a small body of Covenanters on Auchencloy Moor and there was a skirmish. Five Covenanters were killed and three captured. There is a stone monument to the dead men.

Auchenreoch: near Brechin, Angus. According to legend, a twelfth century battle was fought here between the army of David I of Scots and the Mormaer of Moray.

Auchindoon or Auchindoun, 1640: two miles east of Dufftown, Moray. There was a minor skirmish here between the Covenanters and Royalists during the religious troubles of the seventeenth century.

Auchindoun Castle, 1592: two miles east of Dufftown, Moray. In 1592 the Mackintoshes captured and destroyed Auchindoun Castle in retaliation for the Gordon's murder of the Bonny Earl of Moray, who was their ally. There are ballads commemorating both events. The castle itself, an L plan tower house, stands as a ruin inside an Iron Age hillfort.

Auchtertool, 1316 or 1317: about two miles west of Kirkcaldy, Fife. The Scots defeated the English in this battle fought during the First War of Independence. A small English fleet sailed from the Humber and landed at Inverkeithing. A Scottish force under the Sheriff of Fife and possibly Earl Duncan of Fife retreated when the English landed. William Sinclair, the Bishop of Dunkeld and brother of Sir Henry Sinclair of Roslin was angry at the sheriff's behaviour and brought together a small force. When he saw the English he is reported to have grabbed a lance and immediately attacked. The English were driven back to the sea, many were killed by the Scots and others drowned as their boat capsized when they tried to escape.

Auldearn, 9 May 1645: about two miles outside Nairn, Highland. This battle was fought during the Civil Wars of the seventeenth century.
The Marquis of Montrose and his Royalist army defeated the Covenanters under Major General John Hurry. Montrose had marched along the East Coast, pillaging and looting, but Hurry and General Bailie led two Covenanting forces to trap him. Montrose, with around 1500 men, evaded Baillie, and hoped to defeat Hurry, who had around 3000 foot, and 300 cavalry. Many of the Covenanters were veterans of Marston Moor. The battle took place on marshy ground, which was perhaps better suited to Montrose's Highlanders and Ulstermen than to the heavier equipped troops of the Covenanters.
Montrose set his men west of Auldearn; Hurry attacked from the east with his infantry; his initial thrust pressed back the Ulstermen, until their leader, Alasdair MacDonald led them into the first charge.
At a time when the Highland charge was virtually irresistible, it says much for the Covenanter foot that their pikemen fought with great courage around the pigsties of the village. Only when Aboyne led the Gordons into the attack were the Covenanters defeated, although it is possible that an error by the Covenanter cavalry, who charged through their own infantry, also helped the Royalist cause. Around 2000 Covenanters were killed or wounded, to 200 Royalists, but Montrose, who had hoped to capture Inverness, turned to face General Baillie.
There is now an interpretation panel on a motte beside a dovecot on the north west of the village, with a small car park, and the Covenanters Inn stands where the two armies first made contact. The old

church at Auldrean also contains a memorial to those Covenanters who were killed.

Auldgown, 1586: also known as Aldgown. This clan battle was fought on the borders of Sutherland and Caithness when the Gunns and Mackays on one side faced the Sinclairs on the other.

In the later sixteenth century the Earls of Caithness and Sutherland were enemies, but in 1586 they agreed on a truce and decided to attack clan Gunn and force them out of the area. Fortunately, the Gunns learned that they were to be attacked and found a willing ally in William Mackay, the brother of Hugh Mackay of Strathnaver. The combined Gunn-Mackay force found the forces of the Earl of Caithness at Auldgown, and savaged them before the Earl of Sutherland could help. The allies killed Henry Sinclair, the cousin of the Earl of Caithness and an estimated 140 of his Sinclairs. In petty retaliation, the Earl of Caithness hanged John Gunn, one of the clan nobles who he held prisoner in Girnigoe Castle.

Ayr, 836 Ayrshire, Strathclyde. This battle is more mythological than historical, but the story says that the Britons of Strathclyde defeated a Dalriadan army.

Ayr, Barns of; May 1297. Ayrshire, Strathclyde. In the early stages of the War of Independence, William Wallace attacked and burned the barns around Ayr where the English garrison were sleeping. He is said to have acted in revenge for the English murdering a number of local gentlemen, including Wallace's uncle. Around 500 English are said to have died, which seems a very high figure, and according to legend, Wallace said "the Barns of Ayr burn weil." This event occurred roughly where Mill Street in Ayr is today and the Barnweil Monument allegedly marks the spot where Wallace stood to watch the fire.

B

Baingle Brae, 844; Tullibody, Clackmannanshire; legendary battle in which Kenneth MacAlpin is said to have defeated the Picts, thus beginning the process of Scottish unification.

If this battle actually occurred, it could be thought of as one of the most significant in Scottish history. Unfortunately, it appears more in tradition than in any historical document. In 843 Kenneth MacAlpin became king of Dalriada, possibly because the Picts killed his father. According to legend he gathered an army and marched against the Picts, whose king, Drustein, called up his men and marched toward Kenneth. The Picts camped on the north bank of the Forth, while Kenneth camped east of the River Devon at a place now known as Baingle Brae. The Scots swore not to lay down their arm until they were dead or victorious.

The following day the two armies met at the site of the future Cambuskenneth Abbey, and the Scots won the day. Again according to legend, this battle united the Scots and Picts into one nation that became known as Scotland. It is a nice story, but probably apocryphal. There is no hard evidence that Kenneth even ruled a united kingdom, but he did have both Pictish and Scottish blood, and he moved the headquarters of the Dalriadic kingdom eastward to what had been Pictish territory.

Ballyshannon, 1247: County Donegal, Ireland. This battle seems to have been fought between an alliance of Gaels from Scotland and Ireland on one side and the Anglo-Normans on the other. The Anglo-Normans killed the Scotsman Macsomairle as he fought alongside Mael Sechlainn O'Donnell, King of Cenel Conaill.

Balgillo, 1548; on the outskirts of Dundee; this was a small skirmish during the Rough Wooing when the English garrison of Broughty Castle captured the French soldier D'Estanges.

Ballindalloch Castle, 2nd November 1590: nine miles North East of Grantown-on Spey. During the religious struggles of the late sixteenth century, the Gordon Earl of Huntly besieged and took the Grant castle of Ballindalloch.

Bann, 733; the annals of Tigernach record –*Flaithbertach led the fleet of Dalriada to Ireland, and great slaughter was made of them...and many were drowned in the river that is called the Bann.* This entry seems to record a disastrous raid by Scottish Dalriada on Ireland.

Bannockburn, 23rd June 1314: near Stirling. Scots under King Robert 1 defeat English under King Edward II. This was the military climax of the Wars of Independence and one of the defining moments of Scottish history.

King Robert's brother, Edward Bruce had been besieging the English in Stirling Castle and had agreed with the garrison that unless relieved by Midsummer's Day 1314 the castle would surrender. Knowing that honour would compel King Robert to face him in open battle, Edward II gathered an army of an estimated 20,000 men and marched north. Robert could count on around 5000 men.

The English knights were backed by about 15000 foot; many of them Welsh archers. In contrast, the Scots had few armoured knights, and perhaps 500 mounted men under Keith the Marischal. The Scottish infantry probably represented all parts of the country, including the Highlands, Galloway and Hebrides. The few Scottish archers were from the Ettrick forest.

King Robert had attempted to equalise the odds by choosing a battlefield with ground too soft for the English cavalry and the forest of Torwood, at his back in case of retreat. His position also had the New Park for closer cover and the Bannock Burn in the centre. He ordered his men to dig pits between the New Park and the Bannock Burn as a cavalry trap. There were also caltrops, four pronged spikes that were designed to impale the hooves of horses and acted like a mediaeval minefield.

The Scots infantry formed into four spear rings, known as *schiltrons,* which were positioned between the boggy Carse of Stirling and Torwood. Cavalry could not penetrate the spears but the closely packed infantry provided perfect targets for archers. King Robert led the Scots in person, but was ably backed by Thomas Randolph the Earl of Moray,

Walter the Steward and James of Douglas. Edward Bruce, the king's last surviving brother also commanded a schiltron.

Edward II of England commanded the English army, with the Earls of Gloucester and Hereford in the English van. When they moved forward, the Ettrick archers withdrew, encouraging the English knights into a galloping charge. After Bruce defeated the leading knight, Henry de Bohun, in a single combat that must have astounded his men, Sir Robert Clifford led 300 knights over the Carse but Randolph's spearmen blocked their road to the castle. The English retreated, having lost the first round of the battle.

That night the English camped on the Carse. They held Mass early the next morning followed by a bread and water breakfast and watched as the Scots advanced across the Carse. When the Scots halted, perhaps to dress their ranks or receive a final blessing, the English king believed that they were asking for mercy.

Because of Robert's choice of battlefield, the English cavalry could not gather sufficient momentum for a charge and the Scots spearmen pushed back their horse. The Earl of Gloucester was only one of hundreds to die on the spear points. As the Scots infantry pressed forward, the English were compressed into an ever more limited space, but their archers began to take a toll of the Scots.

In perhaps the crucial point in the battle, Keith's light horse scattered the English archers, which had proved their major battle winners in previous encounters. After that the field became little more than a scene of slaughter.

With the archers removed Bruce used his Highlanders, but although the Scots were winning, they were still heavily outnumbered. The Scots pressed on, shouting "on them, on them, they fail."

There were no Scots reserves, but the camp followers, a motley crowd of women, tradesmen and the unarmed, swept into the attack. According to legend they shouted, "Upon them now; they shall all die." It was enough to break the English spirit and they began a general retreat.

Of all his thousands of men, only 500 remained to escort the fleeing King Edward to Dunbar, from where he grabbed a ship and sailed to the safety of England. A great number of English knights and lords were captured, 35 English nobles were killed, with over 200 knights and 700 lesser gentry and uncounted commoners. King Robert also captured Stirling Castle. It was arguably Scotland's greatest victory over the English, and certainly the best remembered.

There is a fine equestrian statue (by Pilkington Jackson) of Robert Bruce on what may be the battle site; and the National Trust for Scotland has an interpretation centre with a shop for the interested visitor. There are facilities for the disabled and children. However, despite the importance of Bannockburn, historians dispute the actual battle site.

Barry, 1010: near Carnoustie, Angus. In this alleged battle, the Scots under Malcolm II defeated the Danes under Camus. The Danes had anchored their fleet in Lunan Bay, north of Montrose and landed at Red Head. They failed in an assault on Brechin Castle but set fire to the town and church before they headed east. They burned the villages of Panbride and Arbirlot and camped at Carnoustie, from where they could threaten all of Angus and the fertile Strathmore.

King Malcolm II assembled his army at Dundee. He had many local knights and marched northward to Barry, where he formed battle formation a mile from the Danes. The fight was long and bloody, but eventually the Danes broke and ran. Local legend said that their leader, Camus, was killed on the heights of Monikie, near to the present Country Park, while the Lochty Burn was said to have run red with blood for days.

> 'Lochty, Lochty is red, red, red
> For it has run three days wi blood'

The Camus Cross, at Monikie on the Panmure Estate, four miles inland, is said to commemorate the grave of the Norse leader, but that interpretation is open to doubt.

Bass Rock, Siege of the, 1691: Firth of Forth. The Bass Rock lies about a mile off shore, two miles east of North Berwick. It has a castle that was used as a royal prison and was the subject of abortive attacks by the English in 1548 and 1549, but possibly its most dramatic years were at the end of the seventeenth century.

After King William of Orange mounted the throne in 1689, the Jacobites rose in rebellion. The garrison of the Castle of the Bass, under Sir Charles Maitland, was starved into surrender by 1690, but four Jacobites were thrown into the dungeons. In June of 1691, they escaped and shut out the garrison. When seventeen more Jacobites left East Lothian to join them, and the French supplied a couple of boats, the Bass became a notable menace to shipping on the Forth. The Hanoverians sent two warships to blockade the Rock, but not until 1694 did the Jacobites agree to leave, with a free pardon and a passage to France. The Scottish Birdwatching Centre at North Berwick has enviable observation points for watching the prolific birdlife on the Bass, and in summer there are trips around the rock. Weather permitting, landings are possible.

Batayle Dormag (Battle of the Casting Stones) 1334: Island of Bute. This skirmish was fought during the Second War of Independence. After Robert Steward captured Dunoon Castle from the English, John Gibson led his followers to attack Rothesay Castle on Bute. Alan de Lisle, the English sheriff, threw back the Scots first attack, but they only withdrew as far as Barone Hill. Gathering in the old Iron Age fort, the Scots gathered rocks and attacked again. A shower of stones scattered the English, then Gibson's men took the English weapons and also the castle.

Barone Hill is a prominent landmark in Bute, and if climbed, offers vast views, but there is no memorial to the skirmish.

Bauds, the, around 962: Findochty Moor, Banffshire. Indulf, King of Scots defeated Eric Bloodaxe and the Danes. It is possible that Indulf was killed or severely wounded during the battle for he died shortly after and was buried on Iona. The Kings Cairn on Findochty Moor is said to mark the spot where Indulf was slain, or at least, wounded.

Bauge, 21 March 1421, fought to the east of Angers, France. Scots and French defeat English. This battle was fought on Easter Eve; the Scots under John Stewart, Earl of Buchan, Wigtown and Sir John Stewart of Darnley, and the French under the Sieur de Lafayette. The Duke of Clarence, heir presumptive to the English crown, commanded the English. He was among the slain.

The English had around 3000 men but they had scattered to loot and plunder. One plundering party captured a lone Scots knight and brought him to the Duke of Clarence. Until then the English were unaware of the presence of the Scots. Clarence decided to attack at once, although it was nearly dark. The English army faced the Scottish vanguard at the bridge at Vieil-Bauge. The English tried to outflank the Scots, with Clarence leading a charge that made inroads into the Scottish flank and drove the Scots into the village of Bauge.

When the main Scottish body arrived, supported by the French, Clarence continued his attack, charging uphill. The Scots advanced to meet them, with Sir Alexander Buchanan killing the Duke of Clarence. The English army was badly defeated, losing Sir Gilbert Umfraville and Lord Ros, while the Scots captured the Earl of Somerset and the Earl of Huntingdon. The Earl of Salisbury retreated with the survivors.

When Pope Martin V heard the news, he allegedly remarked that the Scots acted as an antidote to the English. The Dauphin was said to have remarked to some detractors of the Scots "what think ye now of the Scottish muttoneaters and wine-bibbers?" The Earl of Buchan was made Constable of France, and John Stewart of Darnley was granted the Lordship of Concressault.

The Alliance France-Ecosse, an organisation dedicated to remembering the Auld Alliance, has erected a plaque at St Symphorium Church, Vieil Bauge.

Benburb; June 1646; fought in south Tyrone, Ireland. Irish Confederates defeat Scots Covenanting army.

In the 1640s, a Scottish Covenanting army was sent to Ulster to protect the Scottish Presbyterian settlers from Irish attacks. The Covenanters succeeded in pushing the Irish away from the plantations, but by 1646 there was a shortage of food.

The Papal Nuncio in Ireland, Giovanni Rinuccini, ordered the Irish army, led by the veteran Owen Roe O'Neill to move against the Scots. Colonel Robert Munro led the Covenanters on a foraging expedition and the two armies met at Benburb.

Both sides were looking for a fight, but while the Scots were worn out after a long march, the Irish were fresh. The battle began in the late afternoon, with Munro hammering the Irish with artillery. O'Neill was experienced in European warfare and had trained his troops well, so that his infantry repelled a Scottish cavalry attack. When the light faded O'Neill ordered his infantry forward and the Scots withdrew, being trapped on the banks of the Blackwater River. When the Scots infantry and cavalry became intermixed in the dark, the retreat became panic and they abandoned their artillery and many of their muskets. The Scots lost around 2,500 men to the Irish 300 with most of the Scots casualties occurring during the retreat.

The Pope and Giovanni Rinuccini were jubilant, expecting a Catholic revival in Ireland, but the remaining Scots in Ulster managed to consolidate their position. The Visitor's Centre in Benburb, in a weaving factory beside the Old Ulster Canal, has displays of this major Irish victory.

Benquhillin, 1601: Isle of Skye. In this clan battle the MacDonalds of Sleat defeated the MacLeods of Dunvegan. MacDonald of Sleat had married a sister of MacLeod of Dunvegan, but he divorced her in favour of a sister of Mackenzie of Kintail. Enraged at this slight on his kin, MacLeod raised his clan and harried MacDonald's lands in Trotternish. In revenge, MacDonald ravaged the MacLeod island of Harris, killing many people, and then attacked MacLeod's lands in Skye. The MacLeods met the MacDonalds at a mountain named Benquhillin. The MacDonalds defeated the MacLeods, and captured their leader, Alexander, the chief's brother, as well as thirty men.

Bealach Glasleathaid, around 1485, fought near Kintail, Highland, during a feud between the Mackenzies and the MacLeods of Gairloch. In this battle Hector Roy's Mackenzies and the Macraes defeated MacLeod of Gairloch. The battle is noted for the exploits of Donnacha Mor na Tuagh (Big Duncan of the Battle axe) and his son Dougal, both of whom were Macraes.

Bealach na Broige, both the date and place of this battle are disputed. It has been dated at 1299, 1369 and 1452, and the location has been given as near Loch Broom and to the north west of Ben Wyvis. The victor is also uncertain. Apart from these minor difficulties, there were different names, such as Bealach nam Broig, Bealach nam Brog, Beallighne-Broig and Bealach na Broige, but all seem to mean the Pass of the Brogue. It is possible but by no means certain that it was fought near Fodderty in the pass between Ben Wyvis and Carn More.
The contestants, however, are fairly constant. On one side were the clans of Wester Ross, on the other the Earl of Ross with the Munros and Dingwalls. There was a dispute between the western clans and the earls, who lived in the east, and the earls responded by seizing one of the chiefs of the western clans – who this is unclear although one account names him as Donald Garve MacIver. The western clans retaliated by capturing an important person, possibly the son of the Earl of Ross, and withdrew toward the west. The western clans may have been Mackenzies and Macraes. The Munros and Dingwalls pursued them and the two forces met at a place called Bealach na Broige. There was a terrible fight with high casualties; one account reported that William Dingwall of Kildun and 140 Dingwalls were killed, as well as eleven Munros of Foulis while the MacIvers, MacAulays and MacLeays were almost wiped out. The prisoner was rescued.
Another and much more romantic version claims that the battle was over a desire of Euphemia, Countess of Ross to marry the chief of the Mackenzies, with the usual additives of torture, intrigue, imprisonment and one brave man defending a pass against a pursuing army.

Benrig, 1382. This minor skirmish was fought near St Boswells, Roxburghshire, Scottish Borders. The Scots under George Dunbar, Earl of Dunbar and March, defeated the English.
At this period the English occupied Roxburgh Castle, one of the most powerful fortresses in Southern Scotland. Ralph Baron of Gaistock was marching from England to become installed as the new governor of the castle when the Earl of March attacked his convoy and took him prisoner. The Earl held the Englishman to ransom
Bern Bige, 1598 Islay: This battle occurred during a longstanding feud between the MacDonalds and MacLeans. Hector Mor Maclean of Duart led a combination of clans including Macleod of Harris, MacNeil of Barra and the MacKinnons to defeat Macdonalds of Dunyveg. This was part of the feud between the MacDonalds of Islay and MacLean of Duart.
Berwick upon Tweed Today Berwick sits a handful of miles south of the English frontier with a formidable ring of Elizabethan stone walls guarding its historic centre. The town has changed hands between Scotland and England fourteen times, making it arguably the most fought over mediaeval town in Europe. The Scots claimed it in 1018, and it became the most prosperous of all Scottish towns until 1296, when Edward I of England started centuries of warfare. In 1482, England claimed it for the last time. Although the railway station now sits on the site of the mediaeval castle, there are fragments of castle remaining beside the River Tweed, and Berwick's sixteenth century town walls are a reminder of the days when this town was on one of the most disputed frontiers in Europe.
Some of the more notable encounters are detailed below:

Berwick, 1216; King John of England captured and sacked the town. There had been trouble a few years previously when the English attempted to build a castle at Tweedmouth, opposite the Scottish town, so already Berwick was becoming a typical frontier settlement.

Berwick, 30 March 1296. Following a dispute over who should be King of Scots following the death of Alexander III, Edward Plantagenet of

England claimed that he was the Overlord of Scotland. When King John Balliol eventually disputed the claim, Edward invaded.

A veteran English army arrived before Berwick, the chief port of Scotland and the centre of the wool trade. At that period the Scots were unused to war and jeered at the English army. Edward Plantagenet rode Bayard, his favourite horse, across the flimsy defending ditch and through the timber palisade on the first assault. The English had no difficulty in overwhelming the Scots defenders. More serious resistance came from a group of Flemish merchants defending the Red Hall; they killed Edward's cousin Richard of Cornwall. Because Berwick had resisted, Edward gave his army permission to sack the town. At least 7000 civilians were killed and the castle, commanded by Sir William Douglas the Hardy, surrendered without a fight.

The slaughter at Berwick soured relations between Scotland and England for generations.

Berwick 1317/18; During the Wars of Independence, the Englishman Sir Robert Neville, known as the Peacock of the North said he would attack Sir James Douglas. Douglas brought a party of men to the outskirts of Berwick, and planted his banner as a challenge. Neville led his men out after dawn, but when he saw Douglas he moved to a nearby hill and waited for the Scots to attack. As Douglas advanced upward, Neville moved down hill and the two forces met. Douglas killed Neville, captured his two brothers and defeated the English, afterward going on a raid into England

Berwick, April 2 1318 During the Wars of Independence, the Scots recaptured the town from the English. Robert I blockaded Berwick so closely that the inhabitants were eating horses, while the Flemish engineer John Crabbe commanded Flemish privateers to fend off English supply ships. In the event an English burgess helped James Douglas and Thomas Randolph over the wall to take the town and the castle surrendered shortly afterward.

Berwick, July 1319, Edward II besieged Berwick but Walter Stewart and John Crabbe repulsed every attack. King Robert led a force into England with the rumoured intention of capturing Edward's queen, then at York. The Northern English withdrew from the siege to defend their lands, and Edward was left with too small an army to succeed, so he abandoned the siege.

Berwick, 1333. When the Second war of Independence started in 1332, the English again besieged Berwick. The siege was long; with the English aided by the Flemish engineer John Crabbe. A combined land and sea assault failed, although the English ships approached at high tide and an attempt to destroy them with fire only set part of Berwick ablaze. Only when a relieving Scots army was annihilated at Halidon Hill did the town surrender.

Berwick, 1482. On their withdrawal from another invasion of Scotland, the English captured Berwick for the last time. The town still remains in English hands.

Blackearnside, 1298: north Fife. This battle was fought during the First War of Independence. Edward I of England ordered a double invasion of Scotland after the English defeat at Stirling Bridge. One part of the army, under Aymer de Valance landed at Tentsmuir in Fife and marched toward Perth. According to Blind Harry, Wallace was sheltering near Lindores and called up the men of Fife to fend off the invasion. The Scots intercepted the English at Blackearnside and defeated them in what seems to have been a savage little encounter. Sir Duncan Balfour was killed on the Scots side.

Blackford, 1297, Fought in Strathearn, Perthshire. A supposed victory of William Wallace over a small English force who were crossing the ford of the Allan Water at Blackford

Blair Castle, 1746: Blair Atholl, Perthshire. This much-altered castle is the home of the Duke of Atholl and boasts the only private army in

Europe. Cromwell's men captured it in the early 1650s, but it is better known for its role during the 1745 Jacobite Rising. First the Hanoverians occupied it after Charles Edward Stuart marched south, and in 1746 Lord George Murray besieged it for the Jacobites. He is recorded as having fired seven cannonballs through the roof. Blair Castle has the accolade of the last castle to be besieged in Britain.
The castle is open to the public.

Blar- Tannie around 1438, Caithness. Tradition speaks of a clan battle in which the Keiths and Mackays defeated the men of Caithness, possibly the Sinclairs. The Keiths had a feud with the men of Caithness and asked the Mackays to help them. Angus Mackay of Strathnaver and John Mor MacIan-Riabhaich from Assynt led the Mackays as they joined the Keiths and invaded Caithness. The local men met them at an unknown location, known as Blar-Tannie and there was a battle with many casualties on both sides. The Keiths were victorious, and the Mackays claimed that John Mor MacIan-Riabhaich played a major part in the conflict.

Blar-na-Leine, 15 July 1544. The name translates as the field of shirts, so-called from the combatants fighting only in their shirts, but it is also known as Kin–Loch Lochy as it was fought at the head of Loch Lochy near Inverness, Highland.
The battle was fought between Clan Ranald and the Frasers in a dispute over land ownership. Clan Ranald won, killing Lord Lovat, and his son and heir, but Ranald Gallda of Clan Ranald also killed. Around 800 men were involved and, according to tradition, only fourteen were alive at dusk. Tradition also says that 80 pregnant widows were left, each of whom produced a son to replenish Clan Fraser. According to legend, all these eighty men were said to have mustered at Tomnahurich in 1574 when the Regent Moray ordered the new Lord Lovat to muster his clan against Huntly.

Blair na park 1491, although other sources say 1476 or 1488. This battle was fought about a mile to the west of Strathpeffer in Easter

Ross, near to present day Jamestown. As often in clan battles, different sources give different interpretations of the battle, but they agree that the Mackenzies defeated the MacDonalds.

The most consistent account says that after an Irish harper assassinated Angus Og MacDonald in Inverness, Sir Alexander MacDonald of Lochalsh, Alasdair Mac Gilleasbuig, raised a force and marched east to regain the Earldom of Ross. At that time there was also a feud between the MacDonalds and the Mackenzies, which had started after an exchange of insults between the chiefs and continued when Kenneth Mackenzie had sent his one-eyed MacDonald wife back to her father on a one-eyed horse and with a one-eyed servant.

Alexander MacDonald led 1500 men, including a contingent from Islay, to Kinellan in Strathpeffer, and burned the church of Contin. The congregation were inside at the time. Kenneth Mackenzie gathered 600 men and fought the MacDonalds at Blair na Parc, near Jamestown. Duncan MacRae, one of the Mackenzie champions, fought axe to axe with Lachlan Mac Thearlaich MacLean in a personal combat and the MacRae won. The Mackenzies won the battle and chased the MacDonalds as far as Strathconon.

Blathlvag, 12 August 729; north east of Pitlochry, Perthshire. This battle was between Oengus MacFergus and Drostan, who were contending for the Kingdom of the Picts. As usual with battles from this era, there is little information, but it seems that Oengus was victorious.

Bloody Bay, 1480 or 1481, fought off Mull. The date and exact location of this sea battle are disputed, but it was a power struggle between John, Lord of the Isles and his son Angus for control of the Lordship. It was also possibly the last large-scale galley fight in the Isles. At this time the Crown was beginning to erode the power of MacDonald of the Isles and John had been giving away land to other clans, who supported him, while Clan Donald supported his illegitimate son Angus Og.

Angus Og gathered his galleys but foul weather kept them on the northern coast of Ardnamurchan. When the weather cleared they rounded the point and sailed up Loch Sunart. They saw a galley that they believed belonged to MacLean, but was actually from Ardgour as John's fleet collected to support him. A general fight ensued, with unknown numbers of galleys. Angus Og had at least four, possibly more, and there were at least five on John's side. When John's forces broke, two galleys pursued the ship of MacNeil of Barra.

Angus Og MacDonald was victorious. His forces severely wounded the heir of MacLeod and killed MacLeod of Harris during the battle. Angus Og became the effective head of Clan Donald and John became a protégé of the crown. Angus Og was the last MacDonald Lord of the Isles as King James IV forfeited the title a few years later.

Bloody Mire, 1164: see Renfrew

Bloody Pits, 953 or 1004 near Gamrie, now known as Gardenstown, Aberdeenshire, Scots defeated Danes. After suffering defeat further south, a Danish raiding force was retreating toward Caithness. A storm forced them into Gamrie Bay, where they sent a force ashore to raid. Perhaps 600 men landed at the Braid Sands for an orgy of looting, before they withdrew to their ships. However the local landowner, Mermane, Mormaer of Buchan had gathered his forces and waited at Castle Hill. The Norse retreated to a safer distance and tried to draw the Scots into leaving their defensive position.

Knowing that most of his men were only farmers, while the Norse were professional raiders, Mermane is said to have prayed for help, vowing to build a church if he was granted victory. While he sent half his army around Mhor Head to remain above the Danes, he led the remainder in an attack across a shallow valley. The Danes withdrew to the top of Mhor Head as the Norse fleet landed reinforcements. The Danes charged, driving the Scots downhill, but news of the invasion had spread and Scottish reinforcements arrived. The Scots drove the Norse back, trapping them at the point of the Head, where they were cut down. After the battle the Danish bodies were thrown into pits, where wolves fed on them, hence the battle became known as 'Bloody Pits.' A church was built on the battle site, dedicated to St John but often known as the 'Church of the Skulls' after the skulls of three Danes were displayed there.

Bloody Vespers, 1st January 1555; fight in Elgin Cathedral, Moray, between followers of William Innes and those of Alexander Dunbar. About 80 Dunbars fought 120 men of clan Innes in and around the Cathedral. It appears that William, the 15th chief of the Inneses attempted to kill Alexander Dunbar, the prior of Pluscarden Abbey, which minor incident is alleged to have started the dispute

Bonnymuir, April 1820; near Falkirk. A body of radical weavers from Glasgow was routed near Falkirk by detachments of hussars and yeomanry.

Scotland had a long radical tradition, but the British government, always fearful of the spread of French revolutionary tendencies, cracked down hard on any hint of republicanism. During and after the Napoleonic War, conditions in Scotland deteriorated for many workers, but the handloom weavers in particular suffered. After a series of strikes, radicals who hoped for political reform met on a number of occasions. There were riots in Paisley and unrest throughout the country. Some men spoke of establishing a Scottish republic, but others only of a general strike. In April 1820 an order for a General Strike was made, either by the radicals, or by Government agitators. There was more unrest, and at Bonnymuir the Stirlingshire Yeomanry and a few of the 10th Hussars met a small party of radicals, and captured most.

In all there were 88 men charged with treason, but sympathetic juries acquitted most. Three men were executed, including the last beheading in Scotland, and twenty transported to Australia.

Boroughmuir, 30 July 1335, Edinburgh. During the Second War of Independence, the Earl of Moray's speciality was attacking English supply columns. He also had a network of patriots, one of whom told him that Guy of Namur, cousin to Queen Philipa, was leading a force to join the main English army in central Scotland. Moray, with the Earl of Dunbar, Sir Alexander Ramsay and Lawrence Preston intercepted the enemy at Boroughmuir. Sir William Douglas and his men, who had been sheltering in the Pentland Hills, joined Moray.

The Scots forced Namur back to Edinburgh Castle, which was then in ruins. Namur and the English killed their horses and made a barricade of the corpses but thirst forced them to surrender the following day.

Moray made Namur agree not to fight in Scotland again and chivalrously escorted him back to the border. On Moray's return to Edinburgh, the English ambushed him and he was imprisoned for five years.

Boroughmuir, 1571, Edinburgh, skirmish fought during the civil war between Kingsmen and Queensmen. The Kingsmen supported the young King James VI, and the Queensmen supported the Catholic Queen Mary.

Sir William Kirkcaldy of Grange, holding Edinburgh Castle for the queen, sent 200 men from the castle to attack Regent Morton's Kingsmen near the Powburn. Morton's men beat back the assault with losses.

Borthwick Castle, 1567: Midlothian, about ten miles south of Edinburgh. The Confederate Lords who supported a Protestant Scotland besieged the Catholic Queen Mary and Bothwell inside the castle. When Queen Mary married James Hepburn, Earl of Bothwell, she made herself even more unpopular. Bothwell was suspected of association in the murder of Mary's second husband, Lord Darnley. The newlyweds fled to Borthwick Castle. A force of around a thousand men besieged the castle, demanding that Bothwell surrender and Mary find yet another husband. Bothwell slipped to freedom, leaving Mary behind. Disguising herself as a boy, she lowered herself over the castle wall and escaped, but the tragedy of her reign continued.

Borthwick Castle, 1650: Midlothian. This short siege occurred during Cromwell's invasion of Scotland. The Cromwellian army besieged the castle, which surrendered after a brief artillery bombardment, but the scars can still be seen.

Bothwell Bridge, June 22 1679: south east of Bothwell, Lanarkshire, Strathclyde. In the later seventeenth century, King Charles II wanted all his kingdoms to be Episcopalian and ordered the persecution of Scottish Presbyterians. The Presbyterians of South West Scotland included a large number of dedicated Covenanters, men who had formed a Covenant with the Lord and refused to acknowledge that any king had authority over their church.

This battle was fought when the anti-Covenanter campaigns were at their height. The Covenanters had defeated a royal force under Graham of Claverhouse at Drumclog, and followed with a march to Glasgow. Claverhouse repelled their half-hearted attack on the town. Worried that the insurgency may spread, the government called up the militia. The Covenanters gathered at Rutherglen, as the Duke of Monmouth took control of the Scottish army. On the 19th June Monmouth marched into the Covenanter heartland of the West Country. Around 5000 Covenanters under Hackston of Rathillet waited at Bothwell Bridge. They were mainly infantry, with John Balfour of Kinloch commanding what horse they had. Monmouth had about 2000 soldiers.

When Hackston barricaded the bridge, Monmouth ordered a cannonade, to which the Covenanters single cannon could hardly reply. Nevertheless the Covenanters held their position until the Foot guards advanced, when the Covenanter horse broke and ran. The foot fought as best they could, facing Claverhouse's dragoons, as well as royal foot and artillery until they also broke. The royal army captured around 1200 Covenanters, sending many as slaves to the American Plantations.

There is a tall obelisk north of the bridge, marking the site of the battle.

Bothwell Castle, 1298-1299: Lanarkshire, Strathclyde. This strategically positioned castle commands one of the main crossing points of the Clyde. Built in the early to mid thirteenth century, it was reputedly intended to be one of the most beautiful castles in Christendom, and was not tested in war until the end of that century when Edward

Plantagenet of England initiated centuries of bitter fighting. In 1296 the English invaded Scotland and occupied most of the castles, including Bothwell. After the initial shock of invasion, the Scots gradually reasserted themselves with a slow campaign of reconquest. The Scots besieged the English in Bothwell for fourteen months before the castle was starved into surrender.

Bothwell Castle, September 1301. Lanarkshire, Strathclyde. Edward Plantagenet of England again invaded Scotland. He took an army of nearly 7000 men and the Belfry, one of the siege engines that he so enjoyed using, to attack Bothwell Castle. The Belfry was a tall machine that enabled the attackers to attack the top of the donjon without using external ladders. The English captured the castle within three weeks. They held the castle until 1314, when they surrendered in the wake of the Scottish victory of Bannockburn.

Bothwell Castle, October 1336. Lanarkshire, Strathclyde. With King Robert I and his band of veteran captains dead, the English again invaded Scotland. They captured Bothwell Castle once more and Edward III of England used the castle as his headquarters.

Bothwell Castle, 1337: Lanarkshire, Strathclyde. Andrew Murray of Bothwell recaptured the castle for the Scots. He destroyed much of the building to deny its use to the English.

Bourtree Church, 1390: Aberdeenshire. During the disturbed years of the 1390s, Robert Keith besieged his own aunt in Fyvie Castle. His uncle, Lindsay of Crawford raised an army of a reputed 500 men and marched to relieve Fyvie. The two forces met in battle at Bourtree Church in the Garioch and Keith was defeated with a loss of fifty men.

Borve, Castle of, around 1555. Strathnaver, Sutherland. After the Mackays ravaged in Sutherland, their chief was summoned to appear before the Queen Regent. When he failed to appear, the Queen Regent gave a commission to the Earl of Sutherland against him. The Earl invaded the Mackay country of Strathnaver, stormed Borve Castle and hanged the Captain of the castle. Mackay was also captured and imprisoned in Edinburgh.

Boyne: near Banff, Legendary battle between Scots and Norse on the coastal plain west of Banff. Possibly fought near Boyndie, at a little river called the Boyne; the Norse certainly raided this coast.

Braes, Battle of the, Skye; 19th April 1882. Crofters fighting for land rights. After a century of clearances and waste, by the 1880s the Highlands and Islands were bitter, demoralised, depopulated and resentful. In the Braes, an area south of Portree in Skye, the factor for Lord Macdonald had withdrawn common land to use for deer stalking. When several townships had been deprived of their grazing on Ben Lee the crofters withheld their rents in protest. They demanded that their grazings be returned and they destroyed Lord Macdonald's eviction notices.

Macdonald called in the police from Glasgow, but the crofters met them with a hail of stones and rocks. The police retaliated with a baton charge that was met by crofters and their wives with a barrage of poles and sticks, but the police injured some crofters. The police arrested five men from Braes, but there was nationwide support for the crofters and a subscription raised money to pay their fines.

An agreement was reached when the crofters returned their animals to Ben Lee, but now had to pay rent. Other crofters followed the example of The Braes by demanding fairer land tenure. With public opinion now on the crofters' side, the government was worried about a Scottish rebellion. A Commission of Enquiry eventually led to the crofter's holdings act of 1886, which aided security of tenure. There is a memorial to this incident about half a mile from Braes village hall.

Braes of Atholl, 17 March 1746: northern Perthshire. This episode is also known as the Atholl Raid. It occurred when the Jacobites were retreating northward after their attempted rebellion in 1745. Lord

George Murray and Cluny Macpherson attacked the Hanoverian militia posts in the Braes of Atholl at Strathtay. The Jacobites were completely successful as they killed a few of the Campbell militia and captured the remainder without losing a man.

Braes of Strathdearn, 1645: Strathdearn, Highland. A clan skirmish when a cattle raid by the Camerons on Moyness near Auldearn in Moray went badly wrong. The Grants, who owned the cattle, pursued the Camerons and caught them in Strathdearn. The Grants killed at least eight Camerons and badly wounded another twelve

Braemar Castle, 1689: Upper Deeside, 50 miles north of Perth. This castle was built in 1628 and during the Jacobite Rising of 1689 John Farquharson, the Black Colonel of Inverey attacked it, killing the governor, John Erskine.

Brander, Pass of, 1308: head of Loch Awe, Argyll. This battle was fought during the First War of Independence. In the process of defeating his domestic enemies so he could concentrate on the English, King Robert I was marching westward to subdue the MacDougalls of Argyll who were allies of the English. The MacDougalls, under John, son of the chief, took up position in the Pass of Brander, where Ben Cruachan meets Loch Awe. There was no other way through the hills and the MacDougalls waited on the hillside above the narrow road. John of Lorne was a sick man and watched the fight from a galley on the loch. King Robert sent James Douglas and a party of Highlanders to the crest of the pass above the MacDougall's position, while he marched his main force along the road. When the MacDougalls attacked the king's main body, Douglas brought down his Highlanders in an unexpected ambush. Robert and Douglas's men chased the MacDougalls across the River Awe to the walls of Dunstaffnage but John MacDougall of Lorne escaped down the loch.

Brechin, or Huntly Hill; 18 May1452; fought two miles north east of Brechin, Angus. There was Civil War in Scotland when King James

II heard that the Earl of Douglas had made a pact with the Lord of the Isles to divide Scotland between them. The king invited the Earl to meet him under a safe conduct, and murdered him. Earl 'Beardie' Crawford was on the side of the Douglases during the subsequent rebellion and called up his kinsmen and followers in Angus. The king ordered the Earl of Huntly to march south, while he led an army northward.

Crawford had the Lindsays and Collace of Balnamood in his force, and met Huntly's army at the Haercairn, two miles NE of Brechin. At first Crawford was successful, but he argued with Lord Collace, who promptly changed sides, along with his 300 followers. The betrayal cost Crawford the battle. Among the casualties on Crawford's side were Sir John of Brechin and the Laird of Pitcairlie. Earl Crawford retreated to Finhaven Castle, where he stated that rather than lose the battle "he wud be content to hing seven years in hell by the breers (lashes) o' the ee." The Lindsays also regretted the defeat. They had been dressed in green and a later rhyme stated that

> 'A Lindsay with green
> should never be seen'

After the battle Crawford devastated the lands of Collace.

Brechin, Bourd of 1572. Angus. During the civil war between the supporters of the Catholic Queen Mary and the Protestant King James VI, Adam Gordon of Auchindown fought for Mary. After defeating the Forbeses at Craibstane, Auchindoun took his men into the Mearns and began to burn and destroy. As he besieged the castle of Glenbervie, the Earl of Crawford, with Lord Grey, Lord Ogilvy and Lord Glamis gathered an army and marched to fight him.

Crawford camped at Brechin, but Auchindoun came at night, killed his sentinels and captured both the town and its castle. Crawford withdrew quickly, but when he realised that his army far outnumbered that of Auchindoun, he collected his men together. The armies fought for a second time, but Auchindoun's Gordons scattered Crawford's men at the first charge. Around 80 of Crawford's men were killed and many captured including Lord Glamis.

Bressay Sound, 13th June 1640: off Shetland. At a time when Spain and the Netherlands were at war, ten Spanish ships attacked a Dutch warship and three Dutch East Indiamen who were sheltering in Bressay Sound. The Dutch warship surrendered, two of the Dutch Indiamen were sunk and the other ran aground at Brunthamarsland.

Bressay Sound, 1665: off Shetland. During the Anglo-Dutch War, there was a minor skirmish between the English and Dutch navies in Bressay Sound. The English were victorious.

Bressay Sound, 1702, Shetland; during King William's War between the Dutch and French, six French warships attacked the Dutch herring fleet in Bressay Sound. Four Dutch ships escorted the herring fleet, but only one was a warship, the remainder being armed merchantmen. When the French sunk the Dutch flagship, the remaining escorts fled. The French burned at least 150 Dutch herring busses.

Brig o' Dee, 18th and 19th June 1639: outside Aberdeen. This was one of the earliest battles in the sequence of civil wars that racked Scotland in the middle of the seventeenth century. Ostensibly about religion, the wars were also fought to curtail to power of the king. In this opening skirmish, James Graham of Montrose, then fighting for the Covenanters, met the Marquis of Huntly and a Royalist force that were guarding the Brig o' Dee to block the road into Aberdeen. Neither commander realised that peace had been declared and Montrose scattered Huntly's men.

Brodick, 1306/1307: Island of Arran, Strathclyde. Tradition relates that there was a skirmish at Brodick during the First War of Independence. After the defeats at Methven and Dalrigh, King Robert and his supporters had withdrawn to the Western Isles or possibly Rathlin Island off Northern Ireland. Before their return to the mainland, they landed in Arran sometime in late 1306 and sent a force to reconnoitre

Ayrshire. Some of the Scots sheltered near Brodick Castle, which was occupied by the English.

Sir Robert Boyd and James Douglas concealed themselves between the castle and the shore and waited until the deputy warden of the castle and three shiploads of supplies arrived. The Scots attacked as the English were carrying up stores. The Scots drove back the guards and seized the goods. Men from boats put to sea so quickly that two of the English vessels capsized.

Brodick Castle, 1455: Island of Arran, Strathclyde. This was a skirmish during the rebellion of Clan Donald. Donald Balloch of Dunyveg captured the castle; he had 5-6000 men in ten galleys, plus John Douglas, illegitimate son of Archibald, 4th Earl of Douglas. The castle's troubles continued in the seventeenth century, with first the Campbells, then the Hamiltons, and finally Cromwell's army, capturing and occupying it. Today little remains of the old castle, as extensive modernisation in the nineteenth century created a stately home. However, there is one hidden room, rediscovered in 1977, and there are always the ghosts to look for.

Brora, c1588: Sutherland, Highland. This episode occurred during the feud between the Earls of Caithness and Sutherland. In this clan battle, Mackay of Strathnaver and John Gordon of Kilcolmkil, who were allies of Sutherland, defeated the Sinclairs, who supported Caithness.

Broughton 1571, Edinburgh; during the civil war between the Kingsmen who supported the Protestant King James VI and the Queensmen who followed the Catholic Queen Mary, Edinburgh Castle endured a long siege. It was common for sorties from the castle to clash with the besiegers, and one such skirmish encountered at the village of Broughton, now part of Edinburgh.

Broughty Castle, 1547 - 1550: Dundee. This series of encounters occurred during Henry VIII attempts to force Mary Queen of Scots to marry his son. He attempted to encourage the Scots by invasion, slaughter, devastation and murder. Perhaps it was not surprising that the Scots resisted his courtship. About the end of September the Englishman Sir Andrew Dudley occupied Broughty Castle when the owner, Lord Gray, handed it over. Attacks by the Earl of Arran and the Earl of Argyle both failed to retake it. The English also fortified the hill of Balgillo and occupied and ransacked Dundee. The French under d'Esse reoccupied Dundee but also failed to take Broughty Castle. The castle finally fell in February 1550, after a siege by Scots and French. Broughty Castle has no plaques telling of the siege, but is worth a visit for its situation and museum exhibits.

Brunanburh, 937: probably fought in north-western England. Athelstan of Wessex, the grandson of Alfred the Great seems to have been one of the first of the English kings to have visions of becoming ruler of all the nations in the British Isles. Constantine II, King of Scots had given asylum to Athelstan's wayward son, and the English king used that as an excuse to invade.

Allying himself with the Norseman Olaf Gothfrithsson and Owen of Strathclyde, Constantine marched to attack Athelstan, who had retreated to a place known as Bruanburh. It is likely that the allies were attempting to curb Athelstan's ambitions and drive him out of Northumbria.

As Athelstan won the battle, the allies failed but Athelstan's empire was weakened. The site of the battle is lost, but it may have been fought on or near the flat-topped hill called Burnswark, just south east of Lockerbie, but this site is by no means certain. This battle is known in Gaelic as *Dun Brunde*

Buittle Castle, 29 June 1308. This battle of the First War of Independence was fought near the castle on banks of River Dee, Galloway. Edward Bruce defeated the English and their Galwegian supporters, led by the former Guardian of Scotland Ingram de Umfraville and a knight named Aymer St John. The English commanders fled to Buittle Castle for safety. For this and his ferocious 'rape of Galloway' King Robert made Edward Bruce Lord of Galloway in place of John Balliol.

The original castle is now gone, and a sixteenth century tower house, splendidly restored, stands nearby.

Butts, the, 1544: Glasgow. This skirmish took place during the minority of Mary, Queen of Scots, when the Regent, James Hamilton, Earl of Arran and the Earls of Lennox and Glencairn disputed power in Scotland. At a place called the Butts at the Gallowmuir, then outside Glasgow, Glencairn and around 800 men attacked Hamilton's forces. At first Glencairn was successful, but Robert Boyd of Kilmarnock arrived with a small body of horse and supported the Regent. His attack turned the tide and Glencairn was defeated. It was said that the combined killed amounted to around 300 men.

Byland, Old, 14 October 1322; also known as Rievaulx; fought near Thirsk in Yorkshire during the First War of Independence. The English had invaded as far as Edinburgh, but King Robert had used 'burned earth' tactics to sweep the country clean of food. After an unknown number of English had died of hunger and dysentery, the remainder retreated, burning the Border abbeys and murdering priests in farewell. In response Robert I invaded England. A powerful English force led by John of Brittany, Earl of Richmond blocked the Scottish advance on Scawton Moor.

Moray and Douglas charged uphill at them while Robert I sent a party of Highlanders to climb up the cliffs on the English flank and attacked Richmond in the rear. At first the English under Sir Thomas Ughtred and Sir Ralph Cobham held Douglas's attack, but the Scots pushed Cobham back and captured Ughtred. When the English heard the noise of the Highlanders fighting in their rear they hesitated and broke.

The Scots captured Richmond and Henry de Sully, Grand Butler of France, Sir Ralph Cobham 'the best knight in England' and Sir Thomas Ughtred. King Edward II found a fast horse and fled to York, his Queen Isabella took ship at Tynemouth. The Scots also captured Seignior Sully, French envoy to Edward, but released him without ransom. This victory, deep in England, was one of Bruce's best.

There is a Roman Catholic chapel nearby, and beside that are stands of fir trees that are said to mark the last resting places of the Scots who died in the battle. The place is well named Scotch Corner. Within a short walk is a much larger tree covered mound that is said to hold the English dead.

C

Caerlaverock Castle 1300: Dumfries and Galloway. This siege took place during the First War of Independence. After the English victory at Falkirk, Edward Plantagenet, known as Longshanks, marched across Scotland, but found only wasted fields and hostility. He burned the religious centre of St Andrews and retreated. It was not until 1300 that he returned and attacked Galloway. He brought 87 knights and 3000 men to besiege Caerlaverock Castle, and ordered siege engines from Southern Scotland and Northern England. When Lord Maxwell and his 60 strong Scottish garrison surrendered, Plantagenet promptly hanged a number. The English remained in charge until 1312, when the commander, Sir Eustace Maxwell, switched allegiance to King Robert I. He survived a later English siege and the castle was destroyed to prevent the English from using it.
Owned by Historic Scotland, Caerlaverock Castle has a car park, shop and toilets. Although the castle has long been a ruin, the situation within a moat, and the building itself, are still impressive.

Caerlaverock Castle, 1356: Dumfries and Galloway. Unsure of the allegiance of Lord Maxwell who controlled this strategic Border fortress, a Scottish army besieged and captured the castle in case he joined the English.

Caerlaverock Castle, 1544 and 1545: Dumfries and Galloway. During the 'Rough Wooing' when Henry VIII of England was attempting to force the young Queen Mary of Scots to marry his son, the English captured the castle, only for the Scots to take it back the following year. There was a further English attack in 1570.

Caerlaverock Castle, 1640: Dumfries and Galloway. During the wars of religion and royal authority that disfigured the middle years of the seventeenth century, a Covenanting army besieged Caerlaverock. The castle held out for thirteen weeks before it surrendered.

Cairnburgh, 1504: Treshnish Islands, off Mull, Inner Hebrides. At a time when King James IV was determined to impress the Hebridean chiefs with his power, he sent a royal fleet to the islands. As well as capturing various chiefs, he bombarded Cairnburgh Castle until it surrendered.

Cairnburg Mor: 1691: Treshnish Islands, off Mull, Inner Hebrides. This skirmish was one of the last actions of the first Jacobite Rising. The Macleans had held out against King William's authority, but their last stronghold on the Treshnish Islands was reduced in that year.

Cairnwell, 1602, 1606, or possibly 1644: between Braemar and Glenshee, Perthshire. This skirmish was a confusing affair with more legends than hard facts. It seems that a group of cattle raiders came from Argyll and ravaged Glen Shee and Glen Isla. In at least one account these people were called the Cleansers, and the date was 1644. The local MacThomas clan gathered and defeated the raiders at Cairnswell. Legend says that during the fight an archer from Braemar known as the *Cam Ruadh* killed many of the Cleansers. However near the end of the fight an arrow struck Cam Ruadh in his bottom. When he returned to Braemar the people informed him "Cam Ruadh, there is an arrow in your backside." He replied: "I myself know this." When he reached home his wife pulled out the arrow.

Caislem Credi, 728. The location of this inter-Pictish battle is uncertain. During a period when there were rival claimants to the Pictish crown, Nechtan defeated Alpin, who lost his lands. Alpin was having a bad year, as he had lost his overlordship of the Picts to Oengus a few months earlier.

Calathros, 634 or 678: Callander, Stirlingshire, Central. Another of the many barely recorded legendary battles when the minor kingdoms of Dark Age Scotland were settling down. In this encounter, Oswald, king of Northumbria was said to have defeated Domnall Brecc of Dalriada. It is known that Oswald was a powerful king of Northumbria, but he seems to have been allied to, or even an overlord of Dalriada, so it is possible that this battle was actually fought between Dalriada and Strathclyde, if, indeed, it took place at all. It is, however, mentioned in both the *Annals of Ulster* and the *Annals of Tigernach*.

Camelon, legendary battle site near Falkirk, Central, where Medraut, King of the Picts defeated and slew King Arthur. There is a persistent legend that Arthur was based in Scotland, and there are certainly many Scottish sites that claim Arthurian connections. One version of the story says that Arthur was a prince of the Celtic Britons who tried to stop the Anglo-Saxon invasions in the sixth century. This particular Arthur was based at a Roman fort on the Antonine Wall that was then known as Ad Vallum or sometimes as Camelon, which is today a town near Falkirk. Some accounts have Arthur being killed at the battle of Camlann, which is another mythical battle sometimes thought to be near Stirling.

Camuston, 1010, legendary battle possibly fought at Camus Stone at Inverugie, 1mile south of Hopeman in Moray, in which Malcolm II, King of Scots defeated the Danes under Camus. Malcolm was one of Scotland's most successful military commanders, winning no less than five battles against the Danes and English. His victories ensured that Scotland was free of Danish conquest at a time when the Danish King Knut was empire building.

Carberry Hill, 1567: two miles from Musselburgh, East Lothian. More of a confrontation than an actual battle, James Douglas, Earl of Morton, led an army against that of Mary, Queen of Scots. Morton hoped to arrest Mary's third husband, Lord Bothwell, on suspicion of involvement in the murder of his predecessor in the marital bed, Lord Darnley.

After a period of negotiation, Mary agreed to hand over her current husband, but rather than walk into probable execution, Bothwell took ship to Orkney. Mary was arrested and imprisoned in Loch Leven Castle.

There is a monument to this battle, if you do not mind a search. There is a wall at the base of the hill, with a small opening marked by a plaque. The opening gives direct access to the monument. The alternative route is a half mile walk through the Carberry Woodlands. At the time of writing there is also an information panel in the woodlands.

Carbisdale, or Invercharron 27th April 1650: fought North West of Tain, in East Sutherland. Colonel Strachan defeated the Marquis of Montrose. After his defeat at Philliphaugh in 1645, the Royalist James Graham, Marquis of Montrose fled Scotland. By 1650 he had gathered a few hundred Danish mercenaries, added some hundreds of Germans and landed in Orkney, where around a thousand Orcadians joined his army. Sending General Hurry to capture Dunbeath Castle in Caithness, Montrose followed with the bulk of his army. He marched south, hoping for reinforcements from Royalist clans. He did not know that the local Munros and Rosses had just switched allegiance from the Stewarts to the Covenant.

The Covenanters had two armies searching for him. The Earl of Sutherland marched from the north while Colonel Archibald Strachan commanded a small force in the south. Montrose found a strong defensive position on a hill overlooking Carbisdale and drew up his 1200 foot and 40 cavalry. Colonel Strachan, with 220 cavalrymen but only a handful of musketeers and around 400 Rosses and Munros, allowed Montrose to see a single company of his horse and kept his Highlanders concealed.

When Montrose advanced against the cavalry, Strachan launched his own attack. The Orkneymen broke at once and then the Munros and Rosses joined in the fight. The Danes retired to a nearby wood, but soon surrendered to the Highlanders. Hundreds of Royalists were killed and only one Covenanter. Montrose fled but a few days later he was betrayed, captured and taken south to be executed.

Carham 1018: northern Northumberland, two miles west of Cornhill. Carham is one of the most important, and neglected, battles of Scottish history. Malcolm II, or Mael Coluim Mac Cinaeda, helped by Owen the Bald, last King of Strathclyde, defeated Uhtred of Bamburgh, King of Bernicia. Malcolm II was one of the most successful Scottish kings, and it seemed that he was trying to either extend Scottish influence into Northumbria, or maintain the Scottish position there.

The *Scottish Chronicle* says that Malcolm "fought a great battle at Carham" while the *History of the Church of Durham* claims the Bernicians had huge losses. Unfortunately there seem to be no details of tactics or numbers. By this period the King of Scots had controlled Lothian for at least a generation, so claims that Carham secured that area for Scotland appear incorrect. However, with so many Scottish historical documents being destroyed or pillaged by sundry invaders, the position is far from clear.

Carham, 1370: Northumberland. This was one of the many vicious little skirmishes that enlivened the Scottish-English border. After an English raid had ravaged his lands, Sir John Gordon retaliated with a plundering expedition to Northumberland. A large English army under Sir John Lilburn intercept the Scots at Carham, and the two forces met in a full day of slaughter. The Scots were victorious. Sir John Gordon seems to have been an excellent warrior, for he was active the following year, when he defeated another English force and captured Sir Thomas Musgrave, the English governor of Berwick. Gordon also took part in the victory at Otterburn, where he was killed.

Carnish, c 1603, fought in North Uist, Outer Hebrides, during a feud between Macleod of Harris and MacDonald of Skye. The MacLeods raided the MacDonald lands of Uist, landing near Kallin and plundering the island. MacIain Mic Sheumais led the MacDonald counterattack, ambushing the MacLeods with a preliminary volley of arrows. Around sixty MacLeods were killed in a battle that lasted for hours.

The ferocity of this clan battles is illustrated by one example. At one stage Donald Glas MacLeod, cousin of the chief, was fighting MacIain face to face and seemed to be winning, especially when two more MacDonalds joined in. However MacLeod killed them with a back flick of his sword, but another MacDonald stabbed MacLeod from behind.

Domhnal MacIain MhicShaumais was hit by several arrows during the fight. Tradition says that while the women pulled the arrows from his body, they composed a waulking song, which still survives to this day.

Carrickfergus Castle, 1315-16. Ulster. After their defeat by Edward Bruce at Conor, a party of English took refuge in Carrickfergus Castle. The Scots besieged the castle and eventually captured it.

The castle has a visitor centre, and is well worth a visit.

Cat Stone, c1652, near Corrie, Island of Arran, Strathclyde. During the Cromwellian occupation of Scotland, a garrison was placed in Brodick Castle, in Arran. There were a number of skirmishes with the local islanders including one at the Cat Stone, where the men from Arran were victorious.

Catacol, 1652, Island of Arran; this was another skirmish between Cromwell's men and the locals, although it is possible that this action, and the one above, are identical.

Cath Droma Deirg Blathug, perhaps around 746. The location is unknown. This battle was one of many fought when a number of princes disputed the overlordship of the Picts. In this encounter, Oengus defeated Drust. There is a possibility that this encounter is the same as the battle of Cato.

Cato, around 750. This was one of the many Dark Age battles about which there is little information. It seems that Oengus of the Picts defeated the Strathclyde Britons but lost his brother Talorgan in the fighting.

Cattraeth, c 600. This battle may have been fought at Catterick in Yorkshire. Unlike many Dark Age encounters, it was fairly well documented in bardic poetry known as *The Gododdin*. One theory suggests that British chiefs from the Christian court of Mynyddawg of Gododdin and Din Eidyn (Edinburgh) with warriors from Ayrshire, Elmet in Yorkshire and possibly Picts and men from north Wales combined to halt the pagan Saxon from expanding. There were possibly 300 selected warriors in the combined British army.

There was a battle at Cattraeth, which may be Catterick, a strategically important centre controlling the Yorkshire lowlands and threatening the British kingdom of Rheged that was centred around the Solway Firth. The British may have been defeated. However the historian John Koch has suggested that Urien of Rheged won the battle, which he believed was fought in the 570s.

Ceochan na Fola, around 1480: north side of Loch Rannoch, Perthshire. This minor skirmish allegedly helped establish the MacGregors in Rannoch.

Having been driven from Loch Lomondside by the Campbells, the MacGregors arrived in Rannoch around 1440. Forty years later an outlaw band known as Clann Iain Buidhe, (clan of John of the Yellow Hair) murdered two Stewarts. Stewart of Appin sent a party to seek revenge, and they collected some MacGregors in Glen Lyon as reinforcements. Together the Stewarts and MacGregors fell on the Clann Iain Bhuidhe at a small burn near Dunan. The allies massacred the murderers and the name of the burn was changed to *Ceochan Na Fola*, the stream of blood. The MacGregors liked the area so they settled in Rannoch in place of Clan Bhuidhe.

Chaseabout Raid: 1565. When Mary Queen of Scots married Henry Darnley, many in Scotland feared the royals would force Roman Catholicism on Scotland. The Earl of Moray said he wanted to maintain 'the true religion' of Protestantism and collected a force of like minded lords and their followers in Ayrshire. Queen Mary left Holyrood house and headed west with an army. In the meantime Moray and his thousand marched in the other direction and arrived in Edinburgh on 31st August. As they took over the town, the Queen's garrison in the castle opened fire on them.

Moray decided that it was best to leave, a few days before the queen marched her army in. Moray withdrew to Dumfries, Mary, now carrying a personal pistol, moved first to Glasgow and then to Stirling. Moray asked for help from the Protestant English. The English obliged by sending Captain Anthony Jenkinson. His ship *The Aide*, sailed into the Forth with a shipment of arms, but turned and fled when the queen's artillery on Inchkeith opened fire. He retreated to Berwick and apparently patrolled the coast, hoping to stop French vessels under Lord Seton bring arms to Queen Mary.

In the event Moray fled back to England and the rebellion was over with no bloodshed. Queen Mary soon invited Moray back to Scotland and he was on the Privy Council by May 1566. Such is the way of royals and politicians.

Chirchind, c600 AD. A legendary battle supposedly fought in northern Angus or southern Kincardineshire. Details are lacking, but what accounts there are say that the Picts defeated the Dalriadic Scots under Aidan.

Cindelgthen, 621: beside Loch Fyne, Argyll. Another Dark Age battle about which little is known. However accounts do say that Conal MacSuibne defeated Conaing, presumably in a clash between rival families in Dalriada.

Circinn, c 596 or 598, possibly in Angus or the Mearns; Aedan of Dalriada fought a battle, perhaps against the Miathi. His sons named Bran, Domangart, Eochaid Find and Artir were killed and Aedan was defeated. It is possible that Aedan was trying to expand Dalriadan control over the area. This may be another version of the battle at Chirchind. This battle is another of these encounters where mythology shrouds the truth. Some versions suggest that this battle was named Camlann or Manann and say that the legendary King Arthur fought against

Mordred. Adomnan, who wrote in the seventh century, calls this battle Miathi, which may be the name of the Pictish nation involved. It is possible that the Miathi lived around the Ochil Hills, where some authorities claim that Dumyatt is the fort of the Miathi

Clachnaharry; beside Kessock, Inverness, Highland. Various dates have been given for this battle between the Mackintoshes and Munros, from 1278, 1333, 1434; or most likely 1454. After their chief was insulted, 350 Munros from Easter Ross had made a cattle raid to Strathardle and returned through Mackintosh land. When the Mackintoshes demanded part of the spoil as 'road collop' tribute, the Munroes refused and kept moving. The Mackintoshes followed by a shorter route and ambushed the Munroes at Clachnaharry. Tradition claims that the Munro archers caused many Mackintosh casualties. Both sides suffered losses, with the Mackintosh chief killed in the battle but tradition states that Malcolm, their captain in the fight, eventually married Janet, sister of John who led the Munroes.
Major Hugh Duff of Muirtown erected a column topped by a statue beside the battlefield, with iron railings cast in the shape of battle-axes. Part of this monument survives.

Cleanse the Causeway, 1520 Edinburgh High Street. After the death of King James IV at Flodden, various factions attempted to control Scotland. Two of the main contenders were the Douglas Earl of Angus and the Hamilton Earl of Arran. In April 1520 the two factions faced each other in Edinburgh High Street. The Douglases won the vicious skirmish that cost seventy-two lives. James Beaton, Archbishop of Glasgow and leader of the Hamilton faction, ran down the Blackfriars Wynd to hide behind the altar of the church.

Clifton Moor, 18th December 1745: near Penrith, Cumbria, England. Famous as the last battle fought on English soil, Clifton Moor was fought between the Jacobites and the Hanoverians.
Prince Charles Edward Stuart hoped to claim the British crown for the Stuarts, and had brushed aside the Hanoverian forces in Scotland.

His small army had marched as far south as Derby but English Jacobites failed to keep repeated promises to give their support. When rumours of massive Hanoverian armies were heard, the Jacobites turned around.

The Duke of Cumberland led one of the pursuing Hanoverian forces and his vanguard clashed with the Jacobite rearguard at Clifton Moor. Lord George Murray led the MacPhersons in a charge on Kerr's and Bland's dragoons, sending the horsemen galloping in reverse, while the MacDonalds of Glengarry defeated Cobham's dragoons in an ambush. The Jacobites lost about twelve men to 40 dragoons and Cluny MacPherson was quoted as saying "this little action of my Regiment was a most gallant one and worthie to be Recorded if Done by the Oldest and Best Disciplined Troops." The Jacobites captured one man, who was one of Cumberland's servants, and sent him back unharmed. Contrast that with Cumberland's barbaric behaviour after Culloden.

Nearby St Cuthbert's Churchyard contains a stone to commemorate the battle, as well as ten of the victims.

Clitheroe 9 June1138; fought beside the River Ribble, Lancashire. King David of Scots had a blood relation to both sides in the bitter civil war that was tearing England apart, but he chose to fight for Matilda. The Scots invaded and won a victory at Clitheroe before losing at the Battle of the Standard at Northallerton.

William Fitz Duncan, the nephew of King David I led the Scottish army at Clitheroe, with the men of Galloway playing a large part in the victory. English accounts speak of the River Ribble running red with blood.

The site of the battle is now the Edisford picnic area

Clochmbenstane, see Sark

Clyne, 1589 or 1590, East Sutherland; this was a clan battle between the Earl of Caithness and men of Sutherland. This skirmish occurred during an on-going feud between the Earls of Caithness and Sutherland. After suffering losses the previous year, the Earl of Caithness gathered his forces, augmented them with a body of archers under

Donald Balloch Mackay of Scourie, and invaded Sutherland. After looting for a while, he retired and met a smaller Sutherland force at Clyne. There were around 400 Sutherland men led by Patrick Gordon of Garty and John Gordon of Embo. The Mackay archers were effective in the brisk action that followed. John Murray and sixteen Sutherland men died, while the Earl of Caithness lost Nicholas Sutherland, Angus MacTorMoid and thirteen others. Many more were wounded.

Cnuicc Coirpri, or Twini Onirbre, 736 or 739. This legendary battle was possibly the same in that in which Talorgan defeated Muredhach. It is just another incident that swirls out of the Dark Age mist to tantalise with a name and meagre details.

Cockburnspath, March 1400; East Lothian; the eldest son of the Earl of Douglas defeated Henry Percy in this incident in a campaign that saw Percy raiding into Lothian before being soundly defeated by the Douglases and chased back into England.

Coire ne Creich 1601 (Corrie of the Spoil): Cuillin Mountains, Island of Skye. This clan battle was fought between the Macdonalds and MacLeods. According to legend, when the famous MacLeod chief, Rory Mor MacLeod was absent, possibly in Ireland, the MacDonalds raided MacLeod lands. Rory's brother Alexander gathered the MacLeods and camped near the corrie where the battle was to be fought. The next day saw the two forces meet. The MacDonalds won, but at great cost, although they did capture Alexander MacLeod and thirty of the most important MacLeods. Coire ne Creich was supposedly the last clan battle fought in Skye.

Coltbrig, Canter of, 16 September 1745: Edinburgh. This was a minor incident during the 1745 Jacobite Rising. As the Jacobite army approached Edinburgh, the town gathered a very weak defence including Gardner's Dragoons. When Prince Charles came as close as Corstorphine, the dragoons were stationed at Coltbridge. Prince Charles ordered a few of his mounted youths to reconnoitre the dragoons. When the Jacobites came close, they fired a few pistol shots, which was enough to panic the dragoons. Turning their horses, they retreated at speed, galloping along the Lang Dykes, where Princes Street now stands, to Leith and Prestonpans. Some continued as far as Dunbar. This encounter became known as the 'Canter of Coltbridge' and the Jacobites occupied Edinburgh.

Connor, or Conagher, 10th September 1315: Country Antrim, Ireland. Edward Bruce defeated the Earl of Ulster and English army.
During the First War of Independence, Edward Bruce, brother to King Robert, took a small army to Ireland. He may have been opening a second front to distract the English, or possibly, in view of events, pursuing his own ambition, as he was to declare himself High King of Ireland.
When the Scots invaded, the Anglo-Irish lords, Richard de Burgh and Sir Edmund Butler raised an army and marched to meet them. Felim O'Connor, King of Connaught supported the English, but had to leave the army to deal with a rebellion. Bruce attacked De Burgh at Connor near Ballymena and sent him flying back to his allies in Connaught. Others of the English ran to Carrickfergus Castle, where the Scots besieged them.

Copeland Islands, Belfast Lough, 1595. The English Captain George Thornton defeated a flotilla of Hebridean and Highland galleys.
During the Elizabethan conquest of Ireland, many Scottish Highlanders helped the Irish. On this occasion a force of Highlanders had crossed by galley to aid of the Ulster chiefs. Captain Thornton commanded *Popinjay* and Gregory Rigges commanded *Charles*, which were on patrol to prevent Scots landing in Ireland. The Hebrideans set out from Arran on 22 July, perhaps with 100 vessels of all sizes carrying as many as 3000 men from Skye, Harris and Lewis. English warships met many as they came into Belfast Lough. The galleys were open rowing boats with no cannon and were hopelessly outclassed.
Two or three galleys were sunk, two captured and the rest driven ashore on Copeland Islands; the majority of Highlanders returned home; only around 1200 men led by the Tutor of Harris and Angus Og, son of Macdonald of Dunyveg got through to help the Irish.

Corbridge 914: fought on the Tyne in Northumberland. The Norse king Ragnall defeated the Scots and Bernicians. After the battle the Norse ravaged Bernicia. Ragnall was building up his kingdom around the Irish Sea, from the Mersey to Galloway and was probably attempting to extend it east of the Pennines. The area known as Bloody Acres is reputedly where this battle took place.

Corbridge 918, Tyne, Northumberland. This was another battle between the Norse King Ragnall and King Constantine II of Alba. The Scots were pursuing the Norse after they had sacked Dunblane and hoped to help Ealdred, son of Eadwulf, ruler of Bernicia. The victor is disputed, but Scots defeated three of the four Scandinavian divisions, slaying the leaders called Otter and Crowfoot, while all the Scottish leaders survived. Toward nightfall Ragnall managed to ambush the victorious Scots. The Bernicians fared badly and had to allow the confiscation of Lindisfarne church lands between the Derwent and the Wear. The north of Bernicia was then ruled by Ealdred, but possibly under Alban (Scottish) protection.

Corgarff Castle, Strathdon, Aberdeenshire, Grampian. Situated on the direct route between Deeside and Speyside, Corgarff Castle was once of major strategic importance. Thought to have been built by the Forbes family around 1550, the castle was attacked by the Gordons in November 1571. Adam Gordon chose a time when the men were elsewhere, but Margaret Forbes responded to a call to surrender by shooting and wounding one of the attackers. The Gordons burned the castle down, killing Margaret and another twenty-seven women and children. In 1689 the Jacobites burned the castle to prevent its use by Williamite forces and in 1715 the Hanoverians torched the castle, which had been used by the Jacobites. In 1746 the Jacobites used Corgarff as a weapons store, but the Hanoverians captured the castle and all the weapons. The 300 muskets they found might have been invaluable for the Jacobites at Culloden. The castle was used as a government fort and held a garrison in the period when the Hanoverians repressed the Highlands, and again in the early nineteenth century as a base to stamp out whisky smuggling.

Restored in the 1960s, Corgarff Castle now contains a permanent exhibition and a reconstructed eighteenth century barrack room.

Cornaigmore, c 1190, also known as the "Battle of the Sheaves", it was fought between Loch Bhasapol and Cornaigmore beach, Isle of Tiree, Argyll. When the people of Tiree were busy plucking their corn, a force of Vikings landed and attacked them. While some of the men ran to fetch weapons, the remainder faced the Vikings armed only with sheaves of corn. At first the Vikings were victorious, but the Tiree men fought furiously and gradually gained the upper hand. The Vikings fled to their boat.

Corrichie, 28 October 1562. This battle was fought on the southeast slope of the Hill of Fare, five miles north of Banchory in Aberdeenshire. When Queen Mary imprisoned the Gordon Fourth Earl of Huntly, the Gordons promptly rebelled. The Queen rode to Inverness but the Gordon Captain of Inverness Castle refused her admission, so she had him hanged. The Queen's army, led by James Stewart, Earl of Moray defeated the much smaller force of the Earl of Huntly. Huntly died on the field and his son John was carried prisoner to Aberdeen and beheaded. According to legend, Mary watched the battle from a granite rock on Berry Hill, which was later named the Queen's Chair. There is a granite pillar to commemorate the battle, just beside the B977.

Corinnie, around 600; fought in Aberdeenshire, this legendary battle saw the Picts defeat Aidan of Dalriada.

Corpach, 1439, or 1474: near Fort William, Highland. One version of this clan battle gives the date of 1439 and sees Donald Dhu, Captain of Clan Cameron defeat Hector Bui MacLean and his followers. It seems that Alexander MacDonald of the Isles had given the Cameron lands to John Garve Maclean of Coll. During the battle, a young chieftain named Ewen Abrach MacLean was killed

Coupar Angus, 1186, this was a massacre rather than a battle. At a time that kings sat uneasily on their thrones, Donald MacWilliam, was a claimant to the throne and in rebellion against King William. A man named Adam, son of Donald, who was known as *Uthlagus Regis*, the King's Outlaw, was on the run in the Mearns area. Earl Malcolm of Atholl chased him and sixty of his men into Coupar Angus abbey, where he killed them all. Adam may have been the son of Donald MacWilliam.

Coylton, around 420: Ayrshire. This battle is another of the obscure conflicts of the Dark Ages. Not much is known, and even that is more likely to be apocryphal than fact. The legend is interesting as it contains references to Coel Hen, better remembered as Old King Cole. Coel Hen may have been a ruler of Rheged, around the Solway Firth, or of Kyle, but he fought against another nation, possibly the Picts in a battle at Coylton in north Ayrshire and Coel was defeated. He is said to have died a few years later when he drowned in a bog at Tarbolton. It is possible that he was an ancestor of the Britons of Alcluid, capital of Strathclyde.

Craibstane, the; November 1571; fought near Aberdeen during the feud between the Gordons and Forbeses, which itself was part of the wider struggle between Catholic Queensmen and Protestant Kingsmen. Adam Gordon of Auchindown defeated the Forbeses. Accounts speak of the Master of Forbes being captured, together with 200 of his men.

Craig an Airgid, 1518 or 1519, location disputed, may be in the Island of Lewis, Morvern or more likely at Caig an Airgid about three miles from Kilchoan in Ardnamurchan. This was a clan battle in which Donald MacDonald of Lochalsh and Alexander MacDonald of Islay killed MacIain of Ardnamurchan and his two sons. MacLeod of Lewis also seems to have been involved.

Craig Cailloch, or Craig Caillog, 1441: possibly in Lochaber. The MacDonald Lord of the Isles encouraged the Mackintoshes of Clan Chattan to invade Cameron lands. It seems that the Camerons defeated the Mackintoshes at this spot, killing one of the chief's sons and wounding another

Cravant, 31 July 1423 Burgundy, France; English and Burgundians defeat Scots and French. This battle was fought during the Hundred Years War, when England tried to conquer France. As France's ally, Scotland had many troops involved. The Treaty of Troyes had given the English control of France north of the Loire, but when the English king Henry V died, the French resumed hostilities.
Sir John Stewart commanded a Franco-Scottish army about 9,000 strong that advanced into Burgundy toward Borges. The Earl of Salisbury commanded a joint Burgundian- English force that opposed them at the village of Cravant, where a bridge crossed the river Yonne. There was a standoff for some three hours, and then Salisbury ordered his men forward, covered by the fire of English archers. A second English force under Lord Willoughby de Eresby crossed the bridge and cut through the Scots, dividing the Franco-Scottish force.
Although they still outnumbered the English, the French fled, leaving the Scots to fight alone. Thousands were killed and many captured, including John Stewart.

Crawford Castle, 1297: South Lanarkshire, Strathclyde. During the First War of Independence, William Wallace, John Graham and forty men captured Crawford Castle from the English. There are ruins of a castle at Crawford, but this particular building was erected at a later date. The site, however, is ancient.

Cree, 1300: Galloway. This battle was fought during the First War of Independence. After capturing Caerlaverock Castle and hanging many of the garrison, Edward Plantagenet advanced westward. He sent an advance party forward to the Cree, where they captured Sir Robert Keith the Marischal. Next day the main English army also reached the

Cree, probably between Creetown and Newton Stewart. After an exchange of arrows at high tide, the English infantry crossed over and engaged a defending Scottish force. The English had their cavalry in three brigades, which they kept back for fear of Scottish traps, while the Scottish chivalry seemed to have reluctant to do much. When the English cavalry crossed the Cree, the Scottish horse, commanded by Buchan, Comyn of Badenoch and Umfraville, fled. Many of the Scottish nobility dismounted and ran into the moors where the English could not follow. The English had won an easy victory with little loss on either side, and they also managed to capture Robert Baird of Strathaven.

Crichton 1337, south of Gorebridge, Midlothian. While returning from a raid into England during the Second War of Independence, Sir Andrew Murray besieged John de Stirling and the English garrison in Edinburgh Castle. The English under Lord Dacre, the Bishop of Carlisle and Edward Balliol moved north to raise the siege. Leaving Edinburgh, Murray headed south and met the English in battle at Crichton. The battle was indecisive, but the English had the greater losses and withdrew south.

Crichton Castle, south of Gorebridge, Midlothian. This castle is now a ruin, but enough remains to show the splendour it once enjoyed. The original keep was built around 1370 but was added to over the years. In 1445 John Forrester, an ally of the Douglases, attacked the castle which was held by the rival Crichton family. When William Crichton conspired against James III, the castle was again besieged and Crichton fled, and in 1559 it suffered during the religious struggles. Now in the care of Historic Scotland, the castle has a small car park and interesting architecture.

Cromdale, Haughs of, 1st May 1690: north of Grantown on Spey, Moray. Colonel Sir Thomas Livingstone, King William's General, defeated what was left of General Buchan's Jacobite army. Most of

Buchan's army came from the Highlands, including Macleans, Macdonalds, Camerons, Macphersons and Grants of Glenmoriston.

After their defeat at Dunkeld, the few hundred men who were all that remained of the Jacobite army were camped on the Haughs of Cromdale. They made an occasional raid into Strathspey but no longer constituted a real threat to the Williamite government. Sir Thomas Livingstone's force at Inverness was ordered to stop the raids. The Grants, who were loyal to King William, led his army of Scots Dragoons and a regular infantry battalion to the Jacobites.

Early on the morning of the 1st of May 1690, the Jacobite outposts saw Livingstone's troops fording the Spey but the dragoons attacked before the majority of those in camp were prepared. Some Jacobites retired to the Hill of Cromdale, where they were defeated, with 400 killed and prisoners. Most of the Highlanders had no time to lift their weapons. Some fled stark naked up the Cromdale hills. A few were captured at Lethendry Castle or near Aviemore, while those that stood were killed or captured on the spot. There were few, if any, Williamite losses.

The skirmish at Cromdale marked the end of the first Jacobite Rising. After that King William ruled unchallenged in Scotland. He proceeded to bleed Scotland of her manpower for his war with France but also created the first genuine parliamentary government Scotland had known.

There is a stone near the Conglass Water, a few miles from the battle, marked with the date 1690. This stone traditionally marks the spot where a soldier died after fleeing the battle.

Culblean 30 Nov 1335: east of the burn at Marchnear, west of Lochhead in Deeside, Grampian. In this crucial battle of the Second war of Independence, the Scots defeated a pro-English force.

David de Strathbogie, Earl of Atholl and one of the Disinherited Scots that supported the English, was laying siege to Kildrummy Castle with around 3000 men. Lady Christian Bruce, the aunt of King David, defended the castle. Sir Andrew Murray, husband of Lady Christian and Regent of the nation, broke off negotiations with the English at

Bathgate to raise the siege. Murray, together with the Earl of March, William Douglas, Alexander Ramsay and Lawrence Preston, gathered about 800 men and hurried north. When he became aware of the threat, Strathbogie raised the siege and faced the Scots in the forest of Culblean.

A local man known as John of the Craig joined Murray with another 300 men, and guided the Scots around Strathbogie's force. Murray advanced on the Disinherited early on the 30th November, but a sentry warned Strathbogie that the Scots were coming and the Disinherited prepared for battle. Murray's force was divided in two, with William Douglas commanding the forward unit.

When Douglas saw that Strathbogie drawn up in battle array he halted his men. Believing that the Scots were wavering, Strathbogie led a downhill charge but when they broke ranks to ford a burn, Douglas ordered his men to attack. When these two forces were engaged, Sir Andrew Murray attacked Strathbogie's exposed flank, and the Disinherited and English army was defeated.

While his men fled in all directions, Strathbogie showed that he had courage, if no patriotism. He stood with his back to an oak tree and was killed in a last stand with a small group of followers. Some survivors took refuge in the nearby island castle of Loch Kinnord but surrendered the next day.

Sir Andrew Murray was the son of the Murray who had held joint command at the battle of Stirling Bridge. After Culblean he used guerrilla tactics to remove the English.

In 1956 the Deeside Field Club erected a 13 foot high stone near Oldhall, Aberdeenshire, to commemorate the battle.

Cullen, around 961, Moray; Indulf, King of Scots defeated the Danes. As in so many battles of this period, information is scanty and vague. It appears that a fifty strong Danish fleet was seen off the Firth of Forth, but a Scottish force waited for them so they sailed north. The Scots followed, which seems unlikely given the comparative ease of sea travel compared to land. However, when the Danes landed at Cullen on the

Moray Firth, a few miles east of Buckie, Indulf attacked and defeated them.

Culloden, 16 April 1746. This decisive battle was fought on Drumossie Moor a few miles east of Inverness. It closed the series of struggles between the Hanoverian and Jacobite dynasties that were competing for the British crown. It was also the last major battle on Scottish soil, and one that had terrible consequences for the Highlands.

The Jacobites had penetrated as far as Derby in England on their hopeful march to replace Hanoverian King George with James Stuart. With only a few thousand men in their army, and not knowing that the Hanoverians were panicking, they decided to withdraw in the face of much superior Hanoverian armies.

On their march north the Jacobites won victories at Clifton and Falkirk. When the armies reached Culloden there were about 9000 Hanoverians, with artillery, Campbells and 500 dragoons, opposed to around 4500 Jacobites. The previous night Prince Charles had attempted a march to Nairn to surprise Cumberland's army, without success. The march had exhausted many of the best men in the Jacobite army.

The armies drew up on Drumossie Moor, on ground totally unsuitable for the mainly Highland Jacobite army, but which favoured Cumberland's regulars. The Duke opened the battle with a barrage from his artillery, so that cannon balls ploughed into the unprotected Highlanders, who were ordered to close ranks after each hit. The few Jacobite cannon, with no trained gunners, fired for only nine minutes.

The Jacobites were in two ranks, with the Macdonalds at the left, rather than their favoured right flank. Unable to retaliate and with their ranks being decimated, the clans demanded the order to charge. At last they surged forward, without orders, in an uncoordinated piecemeal charge led by Clan Chattan. Although they charged into grapeshot and musketry, some still reached the bayonets and a few penetrated the front rank. The Camerons and Stewarts broke through Munro's and Barrell's Foot to be hit by flanking fire from Campbell's foot, the 25th foot and Wolfe's Foot. The survivors drifted back. Some threw stones in an attempt to make the redcoats break ranks and come forward.

As the Highlanders retreated the second Jacobite line of Franco-Scottish infantry held back the dragoons before also withdrawing. Perhaps 1200 Jacobites were killed, most by artillery. Hanoverian casualties were disputed; they claimed only fifty killed and around 300 wounded. In the aftermath of battle, the Duke of Cumberland gave orders to slaughter the wounded, earning his name of 'Butcher Cumberland.'

Culloden is one of the most easily accessible battlefields in Scotland, hard by the B9006 five miles to the east of Inverness. The National Trust for Scotland runs a fine visitor centre on the field itself, with a wide range of books and souvenirs. There is also a coach and car park. The actual battle site has been partially restored to the condition it was when the Jacobites and Hanoverians squared up to each other that April day in 1746.

There is a multi-language audio-visual programme, with a self service restaurant, a raised map, induction loop and guided tours.

D

Dail-Riabhach, 1576. This clan battle was fought in Sutherland. After the death of the chief of the Mackays, there was a dispute over who should be his successor. John Mackay, son of the chief, challenged his uncle, Neil, who many believed should claim the honour. When John grabbed the chieftainship, Neil said that he was illegitimate, but withdrew to Caithness, where the Earl allowed him to raise men to pursue his claim.

Neil's force took over the Mackay lands of Strathnaver, so John fled south and sought sanctuary with Clan Chattan. While he was in Badenoch his brother Donald launched a night attack on his uncle at Dail-

Riabhach and dispersed them. The two brothers then executed their uncle Neil.

Dalchosnie, around 1307; Loch Rannoch (The Winning Field) This field at the mouth of Loch Rannoch is the traditional site of a battle in which King Robert I defeated the MacDougalls. Perhaps the story is a garbled version of the battle at Dalrigh, where the MacDougalls defeated Bruce, or the site of a minor skirmish.

Dalhousie Castle, Midlothian, 1400. During the English invasion of 1400, Sir Alexander Ramsay held Dalhousie from a siege by Henry IV of England for six months. Much modernised, the castle is now a luxury hotel.

Dalnaspidial July 1654; fought in the Drumochter Pass, 15 miles north of Blair Atholl, Perthshire, this encounter ended the Royalist rising against Cromwell when General Morgan defeated the Earls of Middleton and Glencairn.

After his hard fought victory at Worcester, Cromwell planned to incorporate Scotland into his Commonwealth. Naturally the Scots were not consulted, and equally naturally they fought back. Augmenting the local resistance, William Cunningham the 8th Earl of Glencairn led an army that initiated a guerrilla campaign against Cromwell's forces. Huntly, Mackenzie of Seaforth and MacDonald of Glengarry as well as the Campbell Lord Lorne joined Glencairn. In 1654 Major General Middleton took command of the army, which was around 5000 strong, but a duel between Middleton's second in command, Sir George Monro and Glencairn gave strong evidence of a divided command.

The Cromwellian commander, Colonel Lilburn contented himself with limited patrolling in the Highlands in 1653. In April 1654 General Monck took command in Scotland and sent columns into the Highlands, while also establishing strategic garrisons. Cromwellian troops plundered the lands of suspected Royalists. Monck sent Colonel Morgan north, and he met Middleton at Dalnaspidial. Morgan outnumbered the Royalists, who had allowed their horse and foot to become separated. The Royalist horse ran, and when Morgan advanced on the foot, they ran too.

Dalnaspidial ended organised Royalist resistance in Scotland, although guerrilla warfare continued.

Dalry or Dalrigh; July or August 1306; Strathfillan near Tyndrum, Stirlingshire, Central. This battle was fought during the First War of Independence. The MacDougalls of Lorne supported the Comyns against King Robert I. As King Robert retreated westward after his defeat at Methven, the MacDougalls ambushed him and virtually destroyed his army.

King Robert was outnumbered about three to one in this, his second battle and his second defeat. At one point a MacDougall seized the king's plaid and attempted to drag him from his horse. Bruce knocked the man down, but the MacDougall tore the plaid, which was fastened with a brooch, now known as the Brooch of Lorne. After the defeat at Dalrigh, Bruce split his forces, sending his women to the supposed safety of Kildrummy Castle while he took to the hills.

The battle field has a simple stone marked with the words 'The Field of the Battle of Dalrigh, 1306'

Dalswinton, 1297: six miles North West of Dumfries. This battle was fought during the First War of Independence. The initial English assault had taken Scotland by surprise, and the feudal host had been badly defeated at Dunbar. The Scots, however, responded with a number of resistance movements, including that of William Wallace.

Captured at Berwick Castle but subsequently freed, Sir William Douglas declared for the cause of freedom and captured Sanquhar Castle in the South West. The English promptly besieged Sanquhar, but Wallace moved against them and won an encounter at Dalswinton. Accounts tell of 500 English dead, which is certainly an exaggeration.

Darnick, 24 July 1526; fought at the western portion of Melrose, Scottish Borders. After the death of James IV at Flodden left Scotland with an infant king, different factions sought to control the crown. In 1526 the still young James V hoped to escape from the power of the Douglas Earl of Angus and enlisted the assistance of Scott of Buccleuch, a leading Border landowner. Buccleuch collected 600 light cavalrymen from Liddesdale and Annandale and ambushed Angus's party at Darnick but Angus dispersed Scott's men, killing around 100. During the pursuit an Elliot in Buccleuch's service killed Kerr of Cessford and started a feud that lasted 25 years. This site of the battle is sometimes known as Skirmish Hill. The Turn Again Stone is said to mark the spot where Elliot turned to kill Kerr.

Delgon, c574; fought in Kintyre, Argyll, Strathclyde. *The Annals of* Tigernach and the *Annals of Ulster* both mention this battle. There are few details, of course, but it is possible that Aidan defeated Duncan son of Comgall in a competition for the kingship of Dalriada. The *Annals of Ulster* has this to say about the battle: "In which fell Dunchadh son of Conall son of Comgall and many others of the followers of Gabran's sons fell."

Degastan, Dexastan or Degsastan; around 603: Scottish Borders, perhaps Dawston in Liddesdale. There are various accounts of this battle, but many historians have accepted the version given by Bede, who said that "Aedan, king of the Irish living in Britain" (the Scots of Dalriada) "marched against him (Aethelfrith of Northumbria) with an immensely strong army; but he was defeated and fled... almost all his army was cut to pieces in a very famous place called Degastan. In this fight Theobald, Athelfrith's brother was killed. From that day until the present no King of the Scots in Britain has dared to make war on the English race."
However, Bede may be mistaken, and he certainly has a Northumbrian bias. *The Annals of Ulster* do mention a battle around 600 AD where the Angles defeated Aedan, but the *Annals of Tigernach* are more ambiguous about the outcome. If this battle was fought at this time and place, it seems that the initial Dalriadan charge destroyed the Anglian van, killing Theobald, brother of Aethelfrith and the Angles also sustained heavy losses.

Even more confusingly, the entire battle may have been fought around 613, between Aethelfrith and some British princes, without Aedan even being present.

Dingwall, 1411: Easter Ross. This was a clan battle between Donald MacDonald of the Isles and Angus Dubh Mackay. The Lord of the Isles had formed an alliance with England and hoped to resume his claim to the Earldom of Ross. He collected an army of some ten thousand men and marched across Ross. Angus Dubh Mackay of Farr with his brother Rory Gald gathered the men of the north and opposed MacDonald at Dingwall. MacDonald won, taking Angus Mackay prisoner and killing Rory Gald. MacDonald continued to march south, toward Aberdeen.

Dirleton Castle, 1651: East Lothian. This fine castle was prominent during the Wars of Independence, with the English capturing it in 1298, and the Scots taking it back in 1311. During Cromwell's invasion of 1651, mosstroopers used the castle as a base from which to harass the invaders. In response, the Cromwellians besieged the castle and damaged it by cannon fire. Run by Historic Scotland, the castle has a car park, shop and gardens

Dirlot, 1464: south of Westerdale, Caithness. The Clan Gunn seems to have been the most powerful in Caithness until the fifteenth century, when the Keiths and Sinclairs gradually took over their land. Gunns and Keiths were traditional enemies. Although the rivalry was over fertile land, which was in short supply in Caithness, the excuse was a woman named Helen Gunn, who was the daughter of Gunn of Braemore. In 1415 she was engaged to be married, but Dugald Keith of Ackergill murdered her fiancé and kidnapped her, taking her to his castle. Rather than submit to her captor, Helen killed herself by jumping herself from the walls, and the feud began; or so the story goes.

In this encounter at Dirlot, the more numerous Keiths were victorious, but lost many men to the archery of the Gunns.

Dirlot Castle, 1464, south of Westerdale, Caithness. This incident took place during the clan feud between the Gunns and the Keiths. Following their defeat at St Tears, the Gunns followed the victorious

Keiths to Dirlot Castle, shot their chief through a window and ambushed the Keiths as they came out to seek revenge. It is quite possible that this battle is merely another version of the previous one, with the outcome reversed. Even although the castle is now a complete ruin, the situation remains impressive.

Dollar; 875 or 877; Central, Norsemen, possibly led by Halfdan Haarfarger of York defeated Constantine I, King of Scots and for the next year occupied much of what is now southern Scotland. It seems that the Danes from York or the Tyne had invaded Scotland. The *Scottish Chronicle* stated that there was a battle at Dollar and "the Scots were annihilated at Atholl." The *Annals of Ulster* gave a similar account, saying that "The Picts encountered the dark foreigners (the Danes) in battle and a great slaughter of the Picts resulted." Constantine was killed in a further battle with the Vikings at Inverdofatha, which may possibly be Inverdovat in Fife.

Dornoch, 1570: Highland. This battle was fought in and around Dornoch, during a clan dispute between the Murrays and the Earl of Caithness. When Hutcheon Murray and the Murrays seized the town, castle and cathedral of Dornoch, the Earl of Caithness sent a force to remove them. After a few days of intermittent skirmishing, the Master of Caithness burned the town and church and besieged the castle. The Master of Caithness eventually persuaded the Murrays to leave the church, and they travelled to help the Gordons in their feud with the Forbeses.

Douglas Larder, 7th April 1308: Douglas, Lanarkshire, Strathclyde. This incident occurred during the First War of Independence. The English had occupied the strongholds of southern Scotland, including Douglas Castle, home of Sir James Douglas.
King Robert I sent Douglas into the area to strike back at the English. On Palm Sunday 1308 the Captain of the English garrison led his thirty men to Mass in the Church of St Bride, thus weakening the garrison inside the castle. A battle broke out inside the church with Thomas

Dickson, tenant of Hazelside apparently striking the first blow. Happily Dickson survived as King Robert later granted Symington in Lanarkshire to a Thomas Dickson, whose family held it for centuries. Douglas's men wiped out the garrison, captured and burned the castle and threw the bodies of the slain on top of the fire. This incident was known as the Douglas Larder.

The ruined remains of Douglas Castle (sometimes known locally as Castle Dangerous after a book by Walter Scott) are signposted from the town. It is a pleasant half mile walk to the castle.

Dromnaderg Blathug/Blathmig, or Druim Derg Blathug 729-30, possibly fought in Angus. This battle seems to have been the culmination of a sixteen year long war between three rivals for the kingdom of the Picts. In it Oengus, also known as Angus, Hungus or Ungust defeated and killed Drust to become king of the Picts.

Drum Castle, around 1640, near Banchory, Aberdeenshire. In 1640, Alexander Irvine of Drum supported King Charles at a time when most of the area supported the Covenanters who were rebelling against the King's imposition of Episcopalianism on Scotland. When Drum left home to go to war, the Covenanters besieged Lady Irvine in her Castle of Drum. Lady Irvine surrendered, and also said that her husband would lay down his arms. A Covenanter garrison took over the castle. There was a second siege in 1645 when the Marquis of Montrose captured Drum for the royalists. His forces looted the castle.

The National Trust for Scotland presently owns Drum castle.

Drum a Chaitt or Drumchatt (the Cat's Back) possibly 1501; this clan battle was fought on the western slopes of Knockfarrel, near Strathpeffer. It is also known as Tobair-nan-ceann, the Well of Heads. William Munro of Foulis led a small army of Munros, MacCullochs and Dingwalls in a raid on Hector Mackenzie of Gairloch. When Munro was returning, the Mackenzies and MacRaes ambushed him at Drum a Chaitt. The legend says that in one place, the Mackenzies killed nineteen men, whose heads rolled into a well above Fodderty churchyard.

The well came to be known as Tobar nan Ceann. The Mackenzies are said to have chased William Munro as far as Ferindonald.
There are splendid paths up Knockfarrel from Dingwall and Strathpeffer, but no memorial to the battle.

Druim na Corpa; March 1746, near the Kyle of Tongue, Sutherland; fought during the Jacobite Rising. After the Jacobites captured HMS *Hazard* at Montrose, they renamed her *Prince Charles* and cruised off Scotland. The Royal Navy forced her ashore in the Kyle of Tongue and some Jacobites fled inland. A force of Hanoverian Mackays met them at Druim na Corpa, killed a few and scattered the remainder.

Druim–a-Lea around 1031; fought near Creich in Sutherland. This legendary conflict was between Allan, Thane of Sutherland and the Norse. The Norse had taken the castle of Nairn and sent out parties to ravage other parts of Scotland. Allan, Thane of Sutherland is said to have raised an army and when the Norse invaded he faced them at a place called Creich on a river which formed the boundary between Ross and Sutherland and defeated them after a long fight.

Drumchatt, 1493 or 1497; Knockfarrel, Strathpeffer; this was a clan battle in which the Mackenzies defeated MacDonald of Lochalsh during the rising of Donald Dhu MacDonald. Hector Roy Mackenzie commanded the force loyal to King James IV while Alexander MacDonald of Lochalsh led the MacDonalds.
The MacDonald rising came about after King James IV revoked Clan Donald's right to be Lord of the Isles – a title that the son of the king still claims. Clan Donald were not happy, particularly when some of the smaller clans realised they were no longer legally obliged to be under the rule of the MacDonalds. MacLeod of Dunvegan and Harris was one such clan, although MacLeod of Lewis followed Donald Dhu when he raised rebellion.
The King summoned the clans to pledge loyalty to him in Glasgow. The Mackenzies and Munros were amongst those that complied. It is

possible but not certain that the Munros fought alongside the Mackenzies in this battle at Drumchatt. The MacDonalds lost and withdrew back to the west. It seems that Alexander MacDonald was later murdered by MacIain of Ardnamurchan.

Drumchatt, 1501: this battle may have never taken place. Alexander Mackenzie in his 1898 *History of the Mackenzies* claims there was a battle here when a small force of 140 Mackenzies under Hector Roy Mackenzie of Gairloch defeated 900 Munros, Dingwalls and MacCullochs. It may also be a garbled reflection of the battle listed immediately above.

Drumclog, 1st June 1679; fought in Lanarkshire, Strathclyde. At the end of the seventeenth century the King and government were determined to force the Presbyterians to accept the Episcopalian faith. The Covenanters, the more extreme of the Presbyterians, met in secret prayer meetings, or *conventicles*, which were often guarded by armed men. A large conventicle was arranged for the end of May 1679. John Graham of Claverhouse was sent with three troops of Life Guards and dragoons to find and break up the meeting. Claverhouse advanced over the moor near Loudon, climbed the hill and saw about 1500 Covenanters to the north.
George Hamilton, leading the Covenanters, sent the women and children in the company to the rear, before he led the men in a line toward the government forces. Characteristically, the Covenanters sang a psalm as they advanced. Claverhouse sent a party around to take the Covenanters in flank. The Covenanter William Cleland waited until the dragoons were in bog and attacked. Around 36 troopers were killed and Claverhouse withdrew.
There is a tall stone monument to mark the encounter, enclosed within a fence.

Drumcrob, 965, possibly fought in Strathearn, Perthshire. This battle saw Duffus or Dubh, the king of Scots, defeat Cuilean. There is very little more information about this possibly mythical encounter.

Drumderg-Blathmig; 728/729; fought in the parish of Lunan, Angus, possibly at Kinblethmont, near Arbroath. The *Annals of Ulster* said that Drosten, King of the Picts was slain. This was one of the battles in which three rivals for the Pictish kingship butchered each other's forces.

Drumlanrig, 1548; Dumfries and Galloway; this forgotten encounter occurred during the later stages of Henry VIII's Rough Wooing. The Earl of Angus led a party of mounted men over the Cheviot Hills to attack an English invading force at Drumlanrig. The Scots won and the English eventually lost control of Southwest Scotland.

Drumlui, around 1337, fought near Loch Arkaig, Highland. This clan battle was between the Camerons and the Mackintoshes in a dispute over land rights at Glenlui and Loch Arkaig. The Camerons claimed to have occupied the lands for some time, until William Mackintosh, 6th chief of the clan brought a force of men to claim the area. Donald Alin Mhic Evin led the Camerons, but Mackintosh won after a hard fought battle. This battle seems to have started a long-term feud between the clans

Drumnacoub, around 1427: near Tongue, Sutherland. This was another northern clan battle with a very tangled story that reads like the fiction much of it possibly is. Thomas Mackay of Creich had murdered Mowat of Freswick inside the chapel of St Duffus in Tain. When he heard of the murder, the king outlawed Thomas Mackay. A local man named Angus Murray made a pact with the brothers of Thomas that if they helped him capture the outlaw, they could marry his daughters, and he would help them obtain the lands of Strathnaver.
The brothers Morgan and Neil Mackay agreed and captured Thomas. The king later executed him and handed Murray a parcel of land at Polrossie and Spanzedell. Murray arranged with the Earl of Sutherland for a force of men to accompany the two brothers to take over Strathnaver.

However, Angus Dow Mackay, who was in possession, did not want to lose his lands. His son, John Aberigh led a Mackay force that faced the invaders at Druim-nacoub. Angus Murray and his two sons-in-law were both killed, while John Aberigh was left badly wounded. There were few survivors from either army. Angus Dow Mackay came to search for his relatives, but was also killed.

There are other versions of this battle.

Drury's Peace, 16 June 1571: near present day Easter Road, Edinburgh. This minor skirmish occurred during the 'Long Siege' of Edinburgh Castle in the early 1570s. The Queensmen, who supported Mary, Queen of Scots, were facing the Kingsmen, who fought for the young King James VI. There was an apparent truce arranged by English ambassador, Sir William Drury, but both sides had armed parties out. A group of Kingsmen dispersed some of the Queens men in a single charge in this simple encounter.

Dryfe Sands, December 6 1593, near Lockerbie, Dumfries and Galloway. This clan battle was between the Maxwells and the Johnstones, whose respective chiefs were rivals for the wardenship of the West March. The families had been at feud for decades when in 1593 John, the 7th Lord Maxwell gathered 2000 of his followers and rode into Annandale, the home of the Johnstones.

Unable to call upon so many men, Sir James Johnstone raised an army of around 800 Johnstones, Grahams, Scotts, Irvines, Elliots and Carruthers, including the 11-year old Robert Johnstone of Raecleuch. It was said that both chiefs offered a reward for the head of their opposite number. As Maxwell came near to Lockerbie, at a place called Dryfe Sands, Johnstone kept most of his men hidden, but teased his vanguard with a force of 'prickers' or light horsemen.

The Maxwells took the bait and broke ranks to pursue the supposed handful of their enemy, and then Johnstone launched his men in a mass charge. Unprepared, the Maxwells broke almost at once, and the Johnstones pursued them through the streets of Lockerbie. There was a slaughter, with the Johnstone's horsemen slashing many of the enemy across the face in a sword stroke that was known as a 'Lockerbie Lick.'

Lord Maxwell was killed in the battle, along with around 700 of his men. The Johnstones fixed Maxwell's head and right hand to the battlements of Lochwood Tower as a trophy.

Duart Castle, 1647, Mull, Fought during the great Civil War, a body of Campbells, fighting for the Covenanters, besieged Duart Castle, but the Royalist MacLeans repelled them. In a later war, the Macleans surrendered the castle to government forces in 1691. Today it has been restored and is open to the public.

Duffus Castle, 1297; five miles North West of Elgin, Moray. This siege took place during the First War of Independence. Andrew Moray and the Scots patriots besieged and captured the castle from Sir Reginald Cheyne, who held it for Edward 1 of England. Run by Historic Scotland, there is a car park and open access to the ruins of this castle.

Duffus Castle, 1308; five miles North West of Elgin, Moray. During the First War of Independence, Andrew Moray had captured and burned the original wooden castle of Duffus. After being rebuilt by Sir Reginald Cheyne and again held for the English, King Robert I recaptured the castle for the Scots.

Duffus Castle, 1452: five miles North West of Elgin, Moray. Archibald Douglas, Earl of Moray, burned the castle during the Douglas rebellion against the Crown. The castle was again destroyed in 1645 during the religious struggles. The ruins of this fine motte and bailey castle are open to the public

Dumbarton, Strathclyde. This rock is one of the most significant historical sites in West Central Scotland. It stood at what was the highest navigable point of the Clyde, before the river was extensively deepened in the eighteenth century. The name means 'fort of the Britons' but the rock was originally known as Alcluid or Alcluith, and was the power base of the British of Strathclyde. As well as withstanding a siege by Oengus MacFergus, the impressive Pictish leader, Dumbarton saw a number of notable encounters, the most interesting of which are detailed below. Today Historic Scotland runs the castle, which is well worth a visit, although most of the buildings are from a comparatively recent period.

Dumbarton, 870: Strathclyde. In the Dark Ages, Dumbarton or Alcluid was a rich prize and in 870 the Norsemen Ivar the Boneless, who had just captured York, and Olaf the White from Dublin combined forces to besiege the town, then capital of Strathclyde. The siege lasted for four months, which was highly unusual for the period, and only when the Danes cut off the town's water did it surrender. A fleet of two hundred ships carried the prisoners as slaves to Dublin.

Dumbarton Castle, 1489: Strathclyde. When Lord Darnley rebelled, King James IV besieged the castle. The first siege failed, so King James returned with the large bombard Mons Meg and captured the castle. He later used Dumbarton as a base when he sailed on expeditions against the Hebridean chiefs. Mons Meg can be seen in Edinburgh Castle.

Dumbarton Castle, 1514: Strathclyde. After the death of King James IV at Flodden, there was a period of instability in Scotland. As the Queen Mother and the Earl of Arran fought each other for control of the country, Arran sought to capture Dumbarton Castle. The Earl of Lennox dug a tunnel under the North Gate of Dumbarton Castle and captured it from the sitting garrison.

Dumbarton Castle, April 1571: Strathclyde. In May 1568, when Mary, Queen of Scots fled Scotland for captivity and eventual execution in England, a civil war gripped Scotland. Supporters of the queen fought the men who followed the infant King James VI. The Governor of Dumbarton Castle, Lord Fleming, supported Mary. The Kingsmen began a siege in January 1570, but it was not until April of the following year that they captured the castle. Captain Thomas Crawford of Jordanhill led 100 men in a daring assault up the north side of the rock. The castle was again captured in 1639, when the Covenanters took it, and in 1654, when a surprise Royalist assault overwhelmed

Cromwell's garrison. Even as late as 1941 it was under attack when the Luftwaffe favoured it with a stick of bombs.

Dunphail Castle, 1330: seven miles south of Forres in Moray. The Scots burned this castle during the Second War of Independence. Dunphail was a stronghold of the Comyns, who were supported by England in their quest for the Scottish throne. The ruins still exist.

Dunadd, 683: Kilmartin, Argyll, Strathclyde. This dramatic rock with its hill fort was the site of the capital of Dalriada, the original kingdom of the Gaelic Scots. There are a number of carvings in the rock including footprints and a boar, with the blue boar being an early Scottish symbol.
The *Annals of Ulster* records state that there was a siege of Dunadd at that date, but details are sadly lacking. The site was excavated in 1980 and 1981 and produced some impressive metalwork that helps prove this fortress was a major European workshop for metalwork. There was also a vast collection of pottery that had been imported from Continental Europe. The actual citadel of the stronghold was at the apex of a number of terraces, making it extremely defensive.

Dunadd, 736: Argyll, Strathclyde. Hungus, son of Uurgust, otherwise known as Oengus or Angus MacFergus, King of the Picts, defeated the Dalriadans in an ongoing campaign which may have been for supreme power in what is now Scotland. One highlight of Oengus's victory was the capture of the citadel of Dunadd. The Picts also seem to have devastated Scottish Dalriada and captured two sons of the Dalriadan king. Oengus MacFergus was probably the most successful of the Pictish kings.

Dunaverty Castle, 712: Mull of Kintyre, Strathclyde. Situated on the south tip of the peninsula of Kintyre, Dunaverty has a long history. It seems to have been a stronghold for many centuries, and the *Annals of Ulster* recorded that in 712 Selbach, King of the Cenel Loarn besieged the fort, which at that time was known as Aberte. After he captured it, Dunaverty became a principal stronghold of the Gaelic kingdom of Dalriada.

Dunaverty Castle 1248: Kintyre, Strathclyde. In 1248 the Englishman Walter Bisset captured Dunaverty Castle, but within a few months Alan, the son of Thomas of Galloway retook the castle and imprisoned Bisset. It seems that the English King Henry III sent Bisset to take Dunaverty in revenge for an earlier act of King Alexander II in sheltering some English pirates.

Dunaverty Castle, 1306: Kintyre, Strathclyde. During the First War of Independence, King Robert I spent some time in the castle, but in the autumn 1306 the English used miners, crossbowmen and masons to capture it. Sir Henry Percy, John de Botetourt and the Scotsman Sir John Menteith led the besieged, hoping to find King Robert inside. Apparently the men of Kintyre were not friendly to the English.

Dunaverty Castle, 1493: Kintyre, Strathclyde. James IV took the castle from Clan Donald, Lord of the Isles but as soon as the Royal fleet sailed away, Sir John MacDonald of Dunyvaig recaptured it. The Gaelic version said that John of Dunaverty stormed the castle and killed the royal keeper, displaying the corpse outside the walls in view of the departing fleet.

Dunaverty Castle, 1558: Kintyre, Strathclyde. In this year the Earl of Surrey subjected the castle to a short and pointless siege during his campaign against the MacDonalds of Ulster.

Dunaverty Castle, June 1647: Kintyre, Strathclyde. During the religious wars of the middle of the seventeenth century, Sir Alastair MacDonald, otherwise known as Alasdair MacColla Chiotach, had led a force of MacDonalds and Ulstermen in support of the Marquis of Montrose. When the two forces split, MacDonald was defeated at Rhunahaorine in Kintyre and retreated down the peninsula with General David Leslie leading the Covenanters in pursuit. Before he sailed to Islay for reinforcements, Alasdair MacDonald left around 300 men in Dunaverty under Archibald MacDonald of Sanda and John MacDougall of Dunollie. The Covenanters laid siege to the castle and cut off its water supply, which forced its surrender. Leslie had initially offered 'fair conditions' but when the water was cut off the defenders had lost their chance of humane treatment.

General Leslie, possibly persuaded by a fanatical minister named John Nevoy, hanged or shot some of the prisoners. Others were thrown off the cliff into the sea and only a few left alive, to be sent as prisoners into France. The dead were interred in a nearby stone enclosure, which can be reached by walking through the golf course, but be careful of flying golf balls.

Dun Eidyn, 638: Edinburgh. Oswald of Bernicia besieged and probably captured the fortress and township of Edinburgh; this event may mark the extinction of the small British kingdom of Gododdin. It almost certainly marked the expansion of the Angles into what is now southern Scotland. There is a possibility that the *Goddodin* mentions this event in the line:

> '*They lay hid before Eiddyn, the lofty hill;*
> *And of as many as he found none returned.*'

Dunbar, 27 April 1296: East Lothian. Dunbar was the first real battle of the First War of Independence, when the English under King Edward Plantagenet defeated the Scots.

After sacking Berwick-upon-Tweed, Edward Plantagenet sent John de Warenne, Earl of Surrey to invest Dunbar Castle. Although the castle's owner was the Earl of March, a firm supporter of the English, his sister Marjory supported the Scots. Now the defenders asked for help from King John Balliol at Haddington.

The Scots army moved to occupy strong position on high ground and faced the English. De Warenne took most of his force to face the Scots, while the defenders of Dunbar yelled: "Tailed dogs, we will cut your tails off," to the English. At that period some in Scotland believed that

Englishmen had tails. Warenne's cavalry tried to advance by crossing the gorge of the Spott burn; the inexperienced Scots believed they were retreating, broke ranks and charged.

There was no contest. The English calmly reformed and advanced into the ragged Scots army. One attack was enough. Most Scots lords fled, but Sir Patrick Graham fought to the death beside the doomed infantry. He was the only Scottish nobleman to gain honour that day. Dunbar Castle surrendered as the English scooped up three earls and 130 knights and squires.

Dunbar, 1560: East Lothian. In the 1550s, Scotland was occupied by French forces, which had originally helped the Scots repel an English invasion. By 1559 a Protestant group, the Lords of the Congregation, resented the Catholic French presence and, aided by the English fought a bitter little war to expel them. The main action was around Leith, but when English force-marched to help the Lords of Congregation against the French in Leith, the French garrison of Dunbar Castle attacked them.

Dunbar 3rd September, 1650: East Lothian. This battle was fought during Cromwell's invasion.

Cromwell had led around 11,000 English into a Covenanting Scotland that had helped him win his own war in England. When King Charles II recognised the Covenant, Scotland remained loyal to the crown, although riven by religious differences. General David Leslie had an army of around 12,000 men, most of whom were ill-trained and inexperienced recruits. All the same he was a brilliant strategist, outmanoeuvred Cromwell and repulsed him from Edinburgh, then occupied an excellent site that trapped Cromwell between Doon Hill and the sea. As Cromwell wrote to the Governor of Newcastle:

We are upon an engagement very difficult. The enemy hath blocked up our way at the pass of Copperspath, through which we cannot get without almost a miracle. He lieth so upon the hills that we know not how to come that way without great difficulty; and our lying here daily consumeth our men, who fall sick beyond imagination.

Unfortunately a group of Covenanting ministers had shorn the Scots of some of their best and most experienced soldiers, and now gave orders that turned the tide of battle.

The ministers allegedly urged Leslie to abandon his strong position. He did so, and Cromwell's dawn attack won the day, killing about 3,000 Scots and capturing around 6,000 more. The Roundheads sang the 117th psalm as they slaughtered the fleeing Scots. Never renowned for their clemency in victory, the English sent those prisoners that survived the death march to Durham as slaves to the New World. Cromwell's men occupied Scotland, massacring many in Dundee and being faced by guerrilla warfare that lasted years.

There is a monument to the Battle of Dunbar beside the old A1 road.

Dunbar Castle, 1338, East Lothian; fought during Second War of Independence. When the English captured the patriot John Randolph, 3rd Earl of Moray in 1335, he informed his sister, Black Agnes, Countess of Dunbar, that the English would kill him unless he surrendered Dunbar Castle. "Let them," Agnes said, for then she would inherit the Earldom of Moray. The English besieged the castle unsuccessfully for months, leading to the traditional Scottish rhyme attributed to William Montague, 1st Earl of Salisbury, the English commander:

> 'She makes a stir in tower and trench,
> That brawling, boisterous, Scottish wench,
> Came I early, came I late,
> I found Agnes at the gate.

The Earls of Salisbury and Arundel commanded the 4,000 strong English army, while Agnes had a garrison whose numbers were estimated at around forty. The English also hired two Genoese galleys, which attempted a naval blockade of the castle. Agnes was assisted by guerrilla warfare by Sir Alexander Ramsay of Dalhousie, who led a series of attacks on English supply lines from his base at Hawthornden near Roslin. Ramsay also dodged the naval blockade and supplied

Agnes through the sea-gate of the castle. When the besiegers began to starve Agnes send them a mocking gift of bread and wine.

The siege began on 13 January and ended on 13 June when Salisbury decided he could not succeed. Today the castle remains, although in a ruined state.

Dunbeath Castle, 1650: 20 miles south of Wick, Caithness. The Marquis of Montrose, on his last campaign to try and win Scotland for King Charles, landed from Orkney with 500 Danish mercenaries and 1000 Orcadians. The short siege and capture of Dunbeath Castle was to be his last victory, but the garrison he left were besieged in turn. They surrendered when the water ran out. Dunbeath castle still exists, a spectacularly sited building high on a cliff.

Duncrub, c946 or 965; fought in Perthshire, just to the north of Dunning. Also known as the battle of Knowes, Gray Man, or Maormar, this was a legendary battle between Duff and Calene or Colin for the Scottish throne. After the death of Kenneth Macalpin and Donald, his brother, Kenneth's sons Constantine and Aodh succeeded in turn to the throne. Their descendants formed rival houses that competed for the kingdom. In the battle of Duncrub, Duff of the House of Constantine defeated Colin, of the House of Aodh. There are two standing stones, one to the north east of Dunning, and one to the south, that legend claims mark where Donchathe Abbot of Dunkeld was killed, and where the Maormar of Atholl died of wounds.

Dundalk; 14th October, 1318: County Louth, Ireland. This battle is also known as Faughart. John de Bermingham and a large Anglo-Irish army defeated and killed Edward Bruce, whose body was beheaded and quartered.

This battle ended Edward Bruce's short reign as the High King of Ireland. He had defeated the English and Anglo-Irish in a series of encounters, but also laid the country waste, so he was disliked as much as the English invaders. The Anglo-Irish force outnumbered Bruce's army, but with characteristic courage Bruce fought. An Anglo-Irish knight named Sir John Maupas charged into the Scottish-Irish ranks to kill Bruce, and the Scots were defeated. Far from home in a hostile country, there was no quarter. Bermingham quartered the body of Bruce and displayed the pieces in various Irish towns, sending the pickled head to King Edward as a trophy.

Edward Bruce's campaign may have acted as a second front to the First War of Independence, but it cost valuable Scottish lives and added to the chaos of a famine-hit Ireland. However, it succeeded in clearing the English from large tracts of the country, allowed the Irish chiefs to repossess some of their lands and shook the English establishment in Ireland. If there is any moral to the story, it is to avoid interfering in other countries.

What was left of Edward Bruce was buried in nearby Faughart Cemetery.

Dundee, 4th April 1645. During the wars between the King and Covenanters of the mid seventeenth century, the Marquis of Montrose and his Royalist Highland army of 150 horse and 600 infantry arrived at the town walls of Dundee. Montrose ordered Dundee to surrender in the king's name but the Dundonians refused, and imprisoned the herald in the Old Steeple. Lord Gordon and the MacDonalds overwhelmed the defenders with little difficulty and plundered part of the town. When General Baillie and a Covenanting army approached, Montrose withdrew.

Dundee 1st September 1651. When King Charles signed the Covenant and agreed to impose the Presbyterian religion on all the nations of his kingdom, Scotland stood by him. Oliver Cromwell and his Parliamentary army had conquered England and now moved against Scotland. General Monck led the invading army into Scotland, captured Stirling and marched against Perth and then Dundee.

On 26th August, Monck ordered Dundee to surrender, but General Lumsden of Montquanie, who commanded the garrison, replied with a counter request for Monck to lay down his arms and "conform to the King's Majesty's Declaration." Monck sent his artillery and siege ladders to Dundee. On August 30th Monck began his bombardment, but a planned assault was cancelled. At four in the morning of the 1st September, Monck again began a cannonade, with the defenders replying as best they could. The cannon made large breaches in Dundee's walls and Monck ordered an attack with the password "God with us" and, in an age of no uniforms, a recognition signal of a flapping shirt tail.

The garrison defended themselves but were forced to withdraw into the Old Steeple. General Lumsden and his men surrendered on a promise of quarter, but were murdered and Monck allowed his men to sack the town. Monck allowed no quarter until he reached the market square. One source said there were 200 women and children among the dead.

The Old Steeple remains a significant Dundee landmark.

Dundee Castle, 1297. During the First War of Independence, an Englishman named Morton held Dundee Castle. William Wallace began the siege but it was the local man Alexander Scrymgeour who captured the castle. It was destroyed to ensure the English could not hold it again. However, Wallace also issued a charter confirming Scrymgeour as 'Constable of the Castle of Dundee.'

Dundee Castle is long gone, but is supposed to have stood at the head of Castle Street, where a statue of Admiral Duncan now stands.

Dundee Law, 834: Dundee. According to legend, the Lawhill that glowers over Dundee was the site of a battle between Alpin, King of the Scots and Brude, King of the Picts. When the Pictish king Oengus died, Alpin of Dalriada appears to have claimed the throne, but the Picts objected and fought Alpin at Restenneth in Angus, and again near Dundee. Henry Maule of Melgund stated that Brude was camped beside a hill "thirteen furlongs" from Dundee. When the battle began, Alpin was watching from his dun on the Law. The battle lasted several hours, until the Picts captured Alpin as he left his dun to lead a wing of the army in a charge on the Picts. The Dalriadic Scots army broke. The Picts beheaded Alpin at Pitalpy, three miles from Dundee, and then carried the head to their capital at Abernethy. Another legend states that the Picts beheaded Alpin on Dundee Law, while yet another claims that a Norse army attacked the victorious but weakened Picts and defeated them, leaving a vacancy for a king of both nations that Kenneth MacAlpin later filled. In other words, this is a tangled mess of legends with little historical fact, but it does make a good story.

The Law is still a favourite place in Dundee, for visitors and locals alike.

Dundurn, 683: Strathearn, Perthshire. The *Annals of Ulster* noted that there was a siege of this fortification. It is possible that it was recording a Dalriadic attack on a Pictish stronghold.

Dundurn, 889: Strathearn, Perthshire. Evidence of burning at this fort may relate to the death of Giric, son of Dungal. Giric was a king of Scotland between 878 and 889. It is known that he killed his cousin Aed to take the throne and he invaded Northumbria, and he may have ruled jointly with Eochaid. It is possible that he died in a siege of Dundurn.

Dunkeld, 21st August 1689: fifteen miles north of Perth, Perthshire. This battle was fought between the Jacobites, who supported King James VII, and Williamites, who supported King William of Orange.

When the Scottish parliament chose the Protestant William as their king, the supporters of Catholic King James gathered their forces for a civil war. They won a fine victory at Killiecrankie, but lost their military leader, John Graham of Claverhouse, also known as Bonnie Dundee.

When the Irishman Colonel Alexander Cannon took over command some of the Highlanders were incensed as they had expected the veteran Sir Ewan Cameron of Lochiel to be chosen. Sir Ewen left the army, taking some of his clan with him. Now led by Cannon, the Jacobites attacked the village of Dunkeld. Twelve hundred newly recruited Covenanters had been formed into the Cameronian Regiment and they held the town. Led by William Cleland, a veteran of Drumclog and Bothwell Bridge, they held off charge after Highland charge in a battle that lasted at least three hours and perhaps as long as sixteen hours.

The Jacobites gradually pushed the Cameronians back through the village to Dunkeld House, with both sides setting fire to Dunkeld and some Jacobite snipers screaming as they were burned to death. With ammunition running low the Cameroonians prepared to die where they stood but Cannon inexplicably withdrew. Three hundred Highlanders were killed, but the Cameronians lost William Cleland and around fifty men.

The Cameronians defence of Dunkeld is one of the turning points in Scottish history. If the Jacobites had been successful they might have gathered support and swept to the poorly defended Lowlands.

Although there is no memorial in the town of Dunkeld, there is a memorial to Colonel Cleland within Dunkeld Cathedral, which also boasts a small museum that mentions the battle.

Dunnichen, Saturday 20th May 685; near Forfar, Angus. This battle is also known as Nechtansmere, Duin Neachtain or Lin Garan (Pool of the Heron). It was a major Pictish victory over the Northumbrians as both sides struggled for control of Northern Britain. Northumbria had been gradually expanding by marriage and conquest; they seemed to have some control over the Picts and suppressed a Pictish rising in the early 670s. A new Pictish king, Bridei, son of Bile and brother of the king of Strathclyde rose and instigated a major resistance movement. In 685 Ecgfrith, King of Northumbria invaded, possibly through Strathmore. The Picts seemed to have lured him eastward toward Dunnichen and possibly ambushed him near the marshland of Nechtan's mere. The Picts won a major victory, with even Bede admitting that the Northumbrian bodyguard all died in a vain attempt to save their king. The Northumbrian frontier was pushed south of the Forth.

According to Bede: *From that time the hopes and strength of the Anglian kingdom began to ebb and fall away for the Picts recovered their own lands, which had been held by the English and the Scots that were now in Britain, and some of the Britons regained their liberty.*

This battle may be one of the most significant ever fought in Scotland, for if the Northumbrians had remained as overlords of the Picts, the later boundary of England may have been much further north. Scotland in her present for may never have existed.

There is a memorial cairn in the village of Dunnichen, and a replica Pictish stone, while the nearby Kirk of Aberlemno holds a marvellous sculptured stone that seems to show the actual battle. In itself it is worth a visit.

Dunnottar Castle, 1297: two miles south of Stonehaven, Grampian. This promontory castle has an interesting history. As early as 681 there was a siege here, and another in 693, but the participants are shadowed by time and a lack of evidence. Around 900 King Donald was killed here while fighting the Danes, while King Constantine faced the might of Athelstan of Wessex at Dunnottar as well.

During the First War of Independence the English had garrisoned Dunnottar, but in 1297 William Wallace recaptured it for Scotland. It seems that English casualties were high, although one reported figure of 4000 deaths is clearly an exaggeration. It is said that the English garrison and their supporters fled into the church but Wallace's men were incensed and slaughtered them despite the sanctuary of the holy place. After the death of Robert I the English again interfered with Scottish internal affairs with their support of Edward Balliol. By 1336 they were openly trying to conquer Scotland again in the Second War of Independence. They re-captured Dunnottar that year, only for Sir Andrew Murray, Regent of Scotland to take it back. He destroyed the castle to prevent any further English occupation. It was later rebuilt under the Keiths.

The castle has a car park, toilets and a small shop, but few facilities for the disabled.

Dunnottar Castle, 1645: near Stonehaven, Grampian. During the religious troubles in the seventeenth century, the Marquis of Montrose besieged Dunnottar.

Dunnottar Castle, Siege of, May 1652: near Stonehaven, Grampian. During Cromwell's invasion and occupation of Scotland, his troops besieged and eventually starved out the garrison. Sir George Ogilvy of Barras was the defender. Cromwell's men hoped to steal the Honours of Scotland (the crown and supporting jewellery,) which had been hidden inside the castle, but Mrs Grainger, the minister's wife smuggled them to safety in a nearby kirk. Cromwell's men are said to have tortured Ogilvy and the Graingers to discover where the regalia was hidden, but discovered nothing.

Dunoon Castle, 1334: Cowal, Argyll, Strathclyde. During the Second War of Independence, the pro-English Comyn faction held Dunoon Castle. Robert Stewart, the rightful owner, and Dougal Campbell of Lochawe attacked by sea and recaptured the castle. Although Dunoon was not a major victory, it was significant as it marked the beginning of the Scottish fight back after the defeat at Halidon Hill.
Today only fragments remain of this castle.

Dunoon Castle, 1544: Cowal, Argyll, Strathclyde. During Henry VIII of England's attempt to force his son on the infant Queen Mary, Henry sent a fleet under the Scottish Earl of Lennox into the Clyde. The English destroyed Brodick Castle but were repulsed at Dumbarton. They took Dunoon Castle after a short fight.

Dunshelt, around 877: near Auchtermuchty in Fife. Local folklore claim the name comes from Dane's Hold, after a battle on Falkland Moor where the Danes were defeated.

Dunsinane Hill; 27th July 1057 (or 1054,) Sidlaw Hills, Perthshire, Malcolm III and English forces commanded by Earl Siward defeated MacBeth, King of Scots This battle is also known as the Seven Sleepers. It would appear that Malcolm III marched from Birnam Hill near Dunkeld and assaulted MacBeth on his dun on the hill. There are no concrete details of the battle, but there is a very small car park at the foot of the hill, which can be climbed. The view from the fort on top makes it obvious why MacBeth chose such a strategic site for a stronghold.

Dunstaffnage, 1463: three miles north of Oban, Argyll, Strathclyde. Tradition states that in this clan fight, Sir John Stewart of Lorn was caught up in a power struggle between the MacDonald Lord of the Isles and the King of Scots. The Lord of the Isles believed that Sir John was loyal to the king and hoped to remove him. When Sir John was on his way from Dunstaffnage to the nearby chapel to marry a daughter of MacLaren of Adrvrech, a body of men under Alan MacCoul attacked the party. The Stewarts won the fight, but Sir John was mortally wounded. He died just after his marriage, but the son he had already fathered to his fiancé became the first of the Stewarts of Appin.

The castle of Dunstaffnage was built sometime prior to 1275, but as a MacDougall stronghold it was on the losing side during the Wars of Independence. Robert I captured it in 1309 and held it for some time. Owned by Historic Scotland, there is a car park and facilities for visitors.

Dunyveg: 1615; Lagavulin Bay, Island of Islay, Strathclyde. This tragic encounter between Clan Donald and the Campbells was one of a long drawn out feud in which Clan Campbell extended their territories at the expense of all their neighbours. The MacDonalds were perhaps the main sufferers, and Sir James MacDonald of Islay was condemned to death by the machinations of the Campbells. Escaping from Edinburgh Castle, he retaliated in what historians know as Macdonald's Rebellion. When King James VI ordered that anybody who took Dunyveg Castle from Angus Og MacDonald should receive a free pardon for past misdeeds, Campbell of Calder and Sir Oliver Lambert combined forces. They landed on Islay with 200 men, with another 140 arriving shortly afterward. They captured Dunyveg in early February, with some of the MacDonalds escaping. The rebellion continued for a short time, with around 7000 men scouring Kintyre and the southern Hebrides for such MacDonalds as still resisted.

There are interesting, if fragmentary ruins that can be visited.

Dupplin Moor, 12 August 1332; near Perth, Perthshire, somewhere on Dupplin Moor although the exact site is uncertain. This battle was the first of the Second War of Independence.

With Robert I and his chief captains dead, the English again revived their interest in making Scotland a puppet kingdom. Edward Balliol, son of King John sailed from the Humber with eighty-eight ships and a force of English archers and spearmen. His fleet contained English Lords such as Ralph de Stafford, Fulk Fitzwarren and Thomas Ughtred, who wanted Scottish lands, German mercenaries and the Disinherited, who were Scots lords whose lands Bruce had confiscated. Balliol and his men landed in Fife in August and marched toward Perth. The regent, Donald, Earl of Mar, raised an army and met them on Dupplin Moor. At midnight on 10th August Sir Alexander Mowbray led a force of English and Disinherited across a ford of the Earn showed him by a Scots traitor, Murray of Tullibardine. After outflanking the Scots, he took up a strong position. The English formed a line, with the deadly longbowmen at either flank. Mar led the Scots into an undisciplined charge, with Lord Robert Bruce racing him for the honour of being first to engage the enemy. Both died in the ensuing massacre.

Traditionally, the battle started at dawn and lasted until noon. The English won with some ease, primarily because of their archers, although many Scots were trampled to death by the pressure of their own men. There were a reported thirty-three English dead, and perhaps two thousand Scots. Within six weeks Balliol was crowned King at Scone.

There is no monument to this important English victory.

Durham, 1006 or 1008, England. During a period when Scotland was facing enemies on both its northern and southern extremities, the new king, Malcolm II, marched south to besiege Durham. Uchtred, Earl of Northumbria defeated him and the *Annals of Ulster* mention the 'slaughter of the good men of Scotland', which would suggest that there were many casualties among the Scottish nobles.

Durrisdeer (near), February 1548: Dumfries and Galloway. This skirmish was a Scottish victory during Henry VIII's war. When the English Warden Sir Thomas Wharton led 3000 men on a raid into the Scottish West March, he sent an advance party toward Durrisdeer in the Lowther Hills. The Earl of Angus led a Scottish force that faced the English, and Johnny Maxwell, 4th Lord Herries and other 'assured Scots' changed sides and wiped out their erstwhile allies. As more assured Scots joined Angus, Wharton had to retreat with his main force.

E

Edinburgh; 638; see Dun Eidyn

Edinburgh, 1544; During the 'rough wooing' when Henry VIII of England tried to force Scotland to marry the young Queen Mary to his son, an English army of 10,000 men under English under the Earl of Hertford landed at Granton. Henry's orders have been quoted as: 'to put all to fire and sword; to burn Edinburgh, raze deface, and sack it; to beat down and overthrow the Castle; to sack Holyrood and as many towns and villages as he could; to sack Leith, burn and subvert it, and all the rest, putting man, woman and child to the sword, without exception.'
The English were repulsed at the Leith Wynd Port, but forced through the Water gate and the Nether Bow Port. There was street fighting as the English fired the town, until the smoke from burning buildings forced them into the countryside.
Once the vastly outnumbered Scottish defenders were removed, the English looted all they could find. They returned to England laden with plunder, destroying every village and sinking every ship and boat they could on both sides of the Forth and as far south as Dunbar. Henry VIII had a strange method of making friends and influencing people.

Edinburgh Castle is one of the premier fortresses of Scotland, and one of the most impressive. A royal castle, it sits on top of its rock in the centre of Edinburgh and fulfils the double function of garrison and tourist centre. There are numerous facilities for visitors, including a number of military museums, the Honours of Scotland and fascinating displays. However, it has been involved in a number of battles and sieges, some of which are below.

Edinburgh Castle, 1296. During the First War of Independence, Edward I of England advanced to Edinburgh after his victory at Dunbar. When the English laid siege to the castle, the governor appealed to King John Balliol for help, but he ordered them to fend for themselves. After a siege that may have lasted a week, the wells ran dry and the castle surrendered. In his usual manner, Edward Plantagenet murdered the garrison and placed Walter de Huntercombe as governor. Wallace retook the castle the following year.

Edinburgh Castle, March 14 1314. During the First War of Independence the ownership of every Scottish castle was contested. Edinburgh Castle had already changed hands a number of times, but in 1314 the English were firmly in possession. It was Thomas Randolph, Earl of Moray who recaptured the castle in a surprise attack, and according to legend a soldier named William Frank led him up the rock. Frank had once been a soldier in the garrison and had often left the castle to meet a girl in the town. The Scots destroyed the castle to make sure the English could not use it again.

Edinburgh Castle, 1341; during the Second War of Independence Edward III of England refortified Edinburgh Castle. The Scots had been conducting an extremely effective guerrilla campaign until this date, avoiding most major encounters but hitting supply columns and small forces. Now Sir William Douglas and William Bullock disguised themselves as English merchants and jammed their wagons under the castle portcullis. With the English unable to close the gates, the Scots assaulted the garrison and captured the castle. Those English who survived were treated as reasonably as prisoners were at the time. Unfortunately the English later caught Bullock and starved him to death.

Edinburgh Castle, 1544; During Henry VIII's Rough Wooing, the Earl of Hertford had landed his English army at Granton and burned Edinburgh, but the Earl of Arran had fortified the castle effectively and had added artillery. Hertford spent four days in a sustained attack, losing a reported, but surely exaggerated, 500 men. The governor, Sir James Hamilton of Stanehouse made a sortie that cleared the English from the Castle Hill. The English were forced to abandon their single piece of mobile siege artillery in the High Street. The Scots later captured it. Hamilton of Stanehouse was still in command three years later when the English won the battle of Pinkie and asked him to surrender. Ironically, the English also had the same commander, although he was now known as the Duke of Somerset, but Stanehouse gave the same response and again the English retreated.

Edinburgh Castle, February 1573. When Mary, Queen of Scots fled to England, she left behind a country in turmoil. There was civil war between the largely Catholic Queensmen and the largely Protestant Kingsmen. Sir William Kirkcaldy of Grange held Edinburgh Castle for the queen and endured the longest of all its sieges. Kirkcaldy of Grange was a veteran of European warfare with a reputation as 'the bravest soldier in Europe,' and he strengthened the castle and its garrison. He sat there in March 1571 and breathed defiance at the Kingsmen.

Regent Morton, who led the Protestant faction, sought help from England and after the expiry of a truce on the first of January 1573, Kirkcaldy was first to open fire, but the besiegers replied vigorously. Kirkcaldy sallied and the besiegers met his men. When massive English cannon arrived to help the besiegers, a cannonade began that had the women of the garrison shrieking in fear and knocked down David's Tower. When his water supply was captured, Kirkcaldy surrendered on the 28th May. Morton hanged Kirkcaldy of Grange and imprisoned the survivors of the garrison.

Edinburgh Castle, 1640. The Castle was busy during the Civil Wars of the middle seventeenth century. Sir Alexander Leslie captured it by blowing up the barrier gate with cannon fire, but a restored Royal governor, Sir Patrick Ruthven held it against the Covenanters for five months before surrendering.

Dance If Ye Can

Edinburgh Castle, 1650. After Cromwell won the Battle of Dunbar he entered Edinburgh and besieged the castle. As both sides exchanged shots, Cromwell hanged an old gardener who had given information to Governor Dundas. When Cromwell pressed miners into digging a tunnel for a mine, Dundas surrendered. Many Scots accused him of treason as they watched the 'English blasphemers' take up residence. Of more importance than the loss of a castle, the Scottish records were sent down to London, from where most never returned.

Edinburgh Castle, 1689, When the Scottish parliament declared for King William, the Jacobite defenders of Edinburgh castle refused to surrender. The Duke of Gordon, with a small garrison, withstood a long siege. At its height the garrison was 86 strong, with only 30 barrels of powder, and the besiegers were many times that number, yet the castle held from the 18th of March until 13th June. It only had to endure one more siege, when the Jacobites of Bonnie Prince Charlie held Edinburgh in 1745, but there was no serious attempt at attack on that occasion.

Edryford, 1307: near Kilmarnock, Ayrshire, Strathclyde. Sir James Douglas was the victor in this skirmish during the First War of Independence. When the English knight De Valence sent Sir John Mowbray and a large force into Kyle to quell Scottish resistance. Sir James Douglas intercepted them at Edryford near Kilmarnock. He waited until the English leaders were crossing the ford, and then ordered his archers to fire. With the English in disarray, Douglas charged with 60 men. Although Mowbray escaped, most of the other English were killed or scattered into the moors.

Eilean Donan Castle, 1539: Kintail, Highlands. The Macraes traditionally held this castle for the Mackenzies. In 1539 the Mackenzies and MacLeods were at feud when Donald Gorm MacDonald, allied to the MacLeods attacked Eilean Donan with a reputed fleet of fifty galleys and a force of 400 men. The Acting Constable of the castle,

Duncan MacRae, killed Donald Gorm and ended the siege. It was said that it was MacRae's last arrow that killed MacDonald.

Eilean Donan Castle, 1719: Kintail, Highland. After the Union between Scotland and England in 1707, the Jacobites, who hoped to put a Stuart king back on the throne, fermented rebellion. One of the least remembered Jacobite risings occurred in 1719, when a few hundred Spanish soldiers landed in the Highlands. When the Spanish made their headquarters at Eilean Donan Castle, the Royal Navy send three warships, *Worcester, Flamborough* and *Enterprise* to attack the fort. The forty-eight Spanish defended themselves, but the castle's ancient fortifications were no match for modern artillery and they soon surrendered. Eilean Donan was seriously damaged. It remained in a ruinous condition until 1912 when Colonel John Macrae-Gilstap began to restore the castle. The arched bridge that today provides access was erected at this time, and in 1983 the Conchra Charitable trust was created to care for Eilean Donan.

Elgin Castle, 1297: Moray. When Edward I invaded Scotland, the Scots at first put up only limited resistance. It was not until the English had completed their occupation that a guerrilla campaign began. William Wallace engaged the invaders in the south and Andrew Murray took castle after castle in the north. One such recapture was of Elgin Castle in 1297.

There is little to see of the castle. It stood on Lady Hill, which is now dominated by the 1839 statue of the 5th Duke of Gordon.

Enterkin Pass, July 1684: Lowther Hills, Dumfries and Galloway. This skirmish occurred during the Covenanter disturbances when the government of the day attempted to crush the Presbyterian religion. When a party of soldiers was escorting Covenanter prisoners through the Enterkin Pass between Thornhill and Sanquhar, the Covenanters ambushed them. James MacMichael, known as the Black MacMichael, led the Covenanters. MacMichael waited until the soldiers reached the narrowest part of the pass before demanding that they give up their prisoners. When the soldiers refused, MacMichael shot Sergeant Kelt. One soldier was killed, some others wounded and fourteen prisoners were released.

Embo, around 1260: north of Dornoch, Sutherland, Highland. This battle must have been one of the last on the North East coast between raiding Vikings and the Scots.
A party of Danes landed at Little Ferry and marched to Embo, where they camped. The Earl of Sutherland ordered Richard de Moravia to keep the invaders occupied until he could raise his men. De Moravia, brother of the founder of Dornoch Cathedral, did so, but was killed in the fighting. When the Earl arrived he defeated the Vikings. Legend says that the Earl killed the Viking leader with the leg of a horse. A large stone near the village is said to commemorate the event.

Essie, 17th March 1058; fought in Strathbogie, Aberdeenshire. This battle seems to have been the culmination of a dynastic struggle that put Malcolm III (Canmore) on the Scottish throne.
Malcolm Canmore had defeated MacBeth with English help, yet when MacBeth was dead, it was his stepson Lulath the Fatuous that claimed the throne. It is possible that Malcolm and Lulach had combined to defeat MacBeth, but whatever the reason, Malcolm ambushed him at Essie in Strathbogie and killed him. On year later Malcolm was crowned king, the third to bear that name. The battle of Essie, however, did not end the issue, for there was a further two centuries of rivalry between descendants of Macbeth and those of Malcolm.

F

Falkirk, 22 July 1298, Central. In one of the most comprehensive battles of the First War of Independence, Edward 1 of England defeated William Wallace.

After Wallace's victory at Stirling Bridge, Edward Plantagenet gathered over 2000 cavalry and 12000 infantry including many Welsh archers. He marched north in July, with English and Welsh bickering between themselves and the English suffering from the Scots' scorched earth policy. Wallace withdrew before the English army. As Edward was about to retreat, two Scots traitors, the Earl of March and Earl of Umfraville informed the English that Wallace was in the Wood of Callender near Falkirk. Edward advanced toward Scots.

Wallace must have known that he faced a nearly impossible task, and he spoke to his people. Setting the Scots in four schiltrons of spearmen, he addressed his men. 'I have brought you to the ring,' he said, 'dance if ye can.' The Scots would understand. They may have danced around the ring in happier times, but now they had to hop to a martial tune. Between the schiltrons were Wallace's few archers under Sir John Stewart, while the horsemen sat between.

The English cavalry were in three battalions. Edward I sent his heavy cavalry forward first, but the Scots spearmen repulsed them. Unfortunately the Scots cavalry ran and the bowmen were overrun. Edward resorted to the archers. Genoese mercenaries and Englishmen joined the Welsh longbowmen in pouring volley after volley of missiles into the Scots lines. The Scots had no reply but their stubborn courage, and only when the Scots ranks had been thinned did the English cavalry attack again.

The archers had done their work well and the Scots were overrun with many casualties. Falkirk was the first major victory for archers fighting for England, but Edward still had to retreat as the Scots' scorched earth tactics had spread hunger and disease.

There is a memorial in the village of Wallacestone, where Wallace is reputed to have made his stand.

Falkirk, 17th January 1746, Central. This battle was fought during the last Jacobite Rising. After reaching Derby, the army of Prince Charles Edward Stuart retreated to Scotland. It fought a neat little skirmish at Clifton, and faced the Hanoverian army of General Hawley at Falkirk.

The Hanoverians were trying to relieve the Jacobite siege of Stirling Castle and the Jacobites hoped to block them. It was approaching the evening of a sleety day as both armies raced for a strategic ridge on Falkirk Moor, to the south west of the town. The Jacobites won the race, and their army of around 7500 outnumbered the 7000 Hanoverians. However Hawley believed that Highlanders could not face cavalry, and he had three dragoon regiments in his line as well as artillery. When the cannon became bogged down in the mud, Hawley ordered his dragoons forward, but rather than break, the Highlanders waited until the horsemen were close, and then fired a volley that scattered them. When the dragoons ran, the Highlanders charged forward at the Hanoverian foot. Only three regiments, Price's Barrel's and Ligonier's stood; the remainder ran in panic.

The Jacobites had taken twenty minutes to defeat the Hanoverians, killing between three and four hundred, to a loss of fifty Highlanders. Two hundred Hanoverians were captured.

A monument at the south of the battlefield commemorates the action.

Fenton, December 1558: Northumberland, England. In 1558 the last official Scottish English war was dragging itself to a close in horror and butchery. When the Queen Regent appointed the Earl of Bothwell as Lieutenant of the Border, he led a raid against Henry Percy's stronghold of Norham castle. At Fenton, nearby, he encountered an English force under Percy and defeated it soundly, sending the English running and capturing over one hundred men.

Fetteresso, 950 or 954: south of Stonehaven, Grampian. The men of Moray defeated and killed Malcolm I.

Fideoin, 630: Ireland. Maelcaich of the Irish Cruithni defeated Conadd Cerr, king of Scottish Dalriada in this Irish battle.

Finglen, 719: possibly Dunbartonshire or Glen Fyne. Selbach defeated his brother Ainbhceallach in this battle between Dalriadic rivals

Flodden, Friday 9th September 1513: Northumberland, England. English under Howard, Earl of Surrey defeat James IV of Scots in perhaps the worst defeat in Scottish history, with the king, many nobles and perhaps 10,000 Scots killed, but the English also lost a large proportion of their army.

With the Papacy, the Holy Roman Empire and England allied against France. Louis XII of France asked Scotland for help. Knowing how chivalrous the Scottish king was, the French queen appealed to James to advance 'one yard for her sake' into England. As an ally, James IV could not refuse and invaded England with probably the largest army Scotland had yet produced.

The Earl of Surrey had added southern levies to his army and marched behind the sacred banner of St Cuthbert. Surrey challenged James to fight it out on Friday 9th September. James accepted and occupied Flodden Ridge, near Coldstream. James had the larger army, with fine artillery and a splendid position, but he refused to use these advantages as they were not chivalric. When Surrey asked James to fight in the open ground, the Scottish king left his position to meet him and they fought through the wet afternoon, English bills and bows against Scottish pikes.

The Scottish Borderers on the left wing overran the English that opposed them but Surrey held the King's battalion. James advanced on foot as the English bills cut away the flanks of his army. James hacked his way into the centre of the English, where they seem to have become the target of English bowmen, as the English border riders harassed the rear. While Home's borderers plundered the English camp, both sides took off their shoes to get a better foothold on the blood-greasy grass.

In the evening the survivors of both sides withdrew to see who had won. With James dead, the Borderer Lord Home took command and withdrew with sixty English prisoners and as many English horses as the Borderers could get their hands on. Left in possession of the battlefield, the English claimed victory.

The magnitude of the loss of King James is highlighted by the belief among many ordinary Scots that four horsemen had carried him away to fight in the Crusades. An archbishop and two abbots had also been slain, together with eleven earls and fifteen lords.

There is a monument in the shape of a cross, which was erected in 1910, as well as a few interpretation panels on a minor road off the A697 just north of Wooler. Etal Castle also has a number of weapons that may have been used in the battle.

Ford of Arkaig, September 1665, Highland. This clan battle occurred between the entire forces of Clan Cameron under the redoubtable Ewan Cameron, and the chief of Mackintosh. The two forces, each allegedly over a thousand men, faced each other across the Ford of Arkaig, with Cameron planning a pincer movement, but the John Campbell, later of Breadalbane, appeared with a large force and said he would attack whoever started the battle. Nobody fought and the two rival chiefs agreed to end a feud that had lasted for over 300 years

Forfar, 1673: Angus. This clan battle was between the Farquharsons and the McComies of upper Glen Isla. The Farquharsons won and what remained of the McComies fled to Aberdeenshire

Forfar Castle, Christmas 1308: Angus. During the First War of Independence, small resistance movements accompanied the major operations of the kings and great nobles. In this instance, Philip the forester of Platan led a small group who climbed the walls of Forfar Castle and massacred the garrison. Nothing now remains of this castle.

Forres, 966 or 967: Moray. Cullen, son of Indulf defeated King Dub (Duffus), the son of Malcolm I in an attempt to take over Moray. This battle was part of the long lasting feud between the sons of Kenneth MacAlpin, Aed and Constantine. Alfred Smyth in *Warlords and Holy Men* suggests that Culen should have been king of Strathclyde in place of Donald, son of Owen, and tilted for the Scottish throne instead.

A superb Pictish stone stands on the eastern outskirts of Forres, with carvings that depict a battle. Although these carvings were originally thought to depict a victory by Sueno over the Scots, it is possible that they show the victory of Culen over Duff, or even of Malcolm II over the Danes. To add to the confusion, the *Orkneyinga Saga* mentions a victory by Sigurd the Powerful over the Pictish Mormaer Maelbrigte in this area.

Fortrose, around 1570: Black Isle, Easter Ross, Highland. The Munros and Mackenzies disputed possession of the lands of the Chanonry of Ross, so when Regent Moray gave the castle to Andrew Munro of Milton the Mackenzies decided to take direct action. Together with some Mackintoshes, they took control of the Cathedral Church and besieged the Munros in the Bishop's Palace and Irvine's Tower. The standoff lasted some time, but when the Mackenzies killed twenty-six Munros who were attempting to get supplies, the remainder of the Munros surrendered.

Fort William, 1746: Highland. During the last Jacobite Rising, the Camerons besieged the Hanoverian garrison of the fort from 20th March until early April. The mixed regulars and Campbell militia within the fort held firm.

Forter Castle, 1640: Glen Isla, Angus. This incident inspired the ballad *The Bonnie Hoose of Airlie*. It was also the climax of a feud between the Ogilvies of Glenisla and the Campbells. The Ogilvies had built Forter Castle around 1562, stopping the local Campbells from having easy access through Glen Isla to their lands in the west. The Campbells waited their chance, and the religious troubles of the mid seventeenth century gave them the perfect opportunity. When the royalist Earl of Airlie left his lands to join King Charles at York, the Covenanting Earl of Argyll brought his men to destroy the Ogilvie properties of Airlie and Forter.

Forth, Firth of, around 1489. Sometime around 1489 an English flotilla of five ships had been pirating Scottish shipping in the Forth. Andrew Wood of Leith sailed out with his ships, *Flower* and *Yellow Carvel* and captured the English vessels. The following year the English sent up the Londoner, Stephen Bull, with three powerful ships to capture Wood.

According to tradition, Bull waited in the lee of the Isle of May and ambushed Wood as he entered the Forth on his return from a trading voyage to the Low Countries. There were two days of close quarter fighting until Wood prevailed and towed his English prizes into Dundee. Wood was granted lands at Largo, from where he could watch the approaches to the Forth.

Forth, Firth of, 16th October 1939. During the Second World War the first air action in British air space took place above the Firth of Forth as Scottish RAF squadrons defeated a Luftwaffe attack on the Royal Navy. The German air force sent 12 Junkers 88 of 1 Squadron Kempfgschwader 30 Eagle Wing to attack HMS *Hood* and other Royal Naval vessels in the Forth.

About noon on the 16th the German aircraft were over the Forth. *Hood* was in Rosyth and the Germans had orders not to attack ships in port. The concept of bombing British civilians only came about later in the war. Obeying their instructions, the German pilots attacked the cruisers *Southampton* and *Edinburgh* and destroyer *Mohawk*. A Junkers hit *Southampton* with a 1000-pound bomb, and then 603 City of Edinburgh and 602 City of Glasgow RAF squadrons of Spitfires arrived. After the first aerial dogfight over Scotland, the Germans were chased away, leaving at least one of their aircraft downed.

Fulhope Edge, September 1400: Northumberland, England. In this skirmish between Scots and English, Sir Ralph Umfraville defeated a Scottish force that had already destroyed Wark Castle. Umfraville had followed the Scots and caught them in upper Coquetdale.

Fyvie, 28th October 1644, Aberdeenshire. This interesting little battle shows the strengths of the Marquis of Montrose as a leader of a small force when facing a much larger army. It was fought during the campaign of the Marquis of Montrose in the great civil war between the Covenanters and Royalists. After the sack of Aberdeen, Alasdair MacColla MacDonald, Montrose's second in command, left for the west, ostensibly to recruit from the MacDonalds. He took a large part of the army with him, leaving Montrose with barely 800 foot and around

50 cavalry. Montrose marched toward Aberdeen, hoping to raise men from the Gordons. He gained only 200 and marched to the Ythan valley, near Fyvie Castle. A Covenanting army of around 3000 foot and 1000 horse, led by the Earl of Argyll, found him and marched against his position.

Rapidly moving into agricultural enclosures above the Parkburn Glen, with a wood protecting his left flank, and a steep slope his right, Montrose prepared for battle. Argyll led his men up the boggy slope, and halted just out of musket range before launching an attack. The Earl of Lothian's Foot attacked first, supported by cavalry, and then Montrose's Gordons ran. Montrose's Highlanders and Ulstermen fired their muskets but the Lothians pushed them back, killing an officer named Robert Keith and about fourteen men. Montrose ordered a counter attack and pushed the Lothians back. Flank attacks also failed and when his attempts to lure Montrose from his position the following day failed, Argyll withdrew. The Ballad of the *Bonnie Lass of Fyvie* is said to have a connection with the battle.

G

Gallow Lee, 1571, Between Edinburgh and Leith. This skirmish occurred during the Long Siege of Edinburgh Castle, when Kirkcaldy of Grange held the castle for Queen Mary against Regent Morton and the supporters of King James VI. On this occasion the Kingsmen defeated the Queensmen.

Carbharry, about 1556, Beinn Mhor, Berriedale, Caithness, Highland. After the Mackays had ravaged in Sutherland and burned the chapel of St Ninian's, a body of Sutherland men caught them in Berridale, beside the Garbharry Water. The Sutherland men won the battle, killing a reputed 120 Mackays and scattering the remainder.

The back story started when the Queen Regent, Marie of Guise expected the Chief of Clan Mackay to meet her in Inverness. She ordered the Earl of Sutherland to punish him, so the Earl demolished the Mackay stronghold of Borve Castle, which, coincidentally, had been used as a base to raid Sutherland territories. The Earl then captured Mackay in Strathbrora and had him imprisoned in Edinburgh. The raid on St Ninian's was Mackay's cousin, John Mor Mackay's retaliation.

Garrison, the, c 1712: Inversnaid, Loch Arklet, Argyll, Strathclyde. In the early eighteenth century the Hanoverian government attempted to contain the Jacobite Highlanders with a series of forts and roads. The fort at Loch Arklet was known as the Garrison and it was intended to control the MacGregors. Soon after it was built, Rob Roy MacGregor and his men captured it. The Garrison was rebuilt and again garrisoned but taken again in 1745 by Rob Roy's son, Seumas Mor and 12 men. The Garrison was rebuilt a second time and manned until 1792. One of the garrison commanders, sometime after 1745, was General Wolfe, who later captured Quebec with the aid of Scottish Highlanders.
The ruins of the Garrison may still be visited.

Gartloaning, 12 October 1489, west of Stirling; this was a minor skirmish during the Civil War of 1489. With James III killed at Sauchieburn, the victorious nobles tried to secure Scotland, but others objected that power was held by only a few individuals. The Earl of Lennox and the Earl of Huntly rose in rebellion but Royal forces won a small victory at a place called Gartloaning and ended any armed dissent.

Gasklune, around August 1392: possibly two miles North West of Blairgowrie, Perthshire. The 1390s were a turbulent era in Scotland, when the king was weak and Alexander Stewart, the Wolf of Badenoch, ran rampant in the north. After the Wolf had burned Elgin Cathedral, another force of Highlanders from Badenoch and Atholl, possibly led by his son Duncan Stewart headed south to ravage Strathmore. Sir Walter Ogilvy, Sheriff of Angus, along with Sir David Lindsay of Glenesk and Sir Patrick Gray, raised a force to meet them. The two armies met at Gasklune on the Water of Isla, where the ferocity of the Highlanders charge shocked the Lowlanders. Ogilvy's men lost a reported sixty killed, with more among the Highlanders, who withdrew. There does not seem to have been a clear victor.

Girnigio, 1588: near Wick, Caithness. This incident occurred incident during the feud between the Earl of Caithness and the Earl of Sutherland. The men of Sutherland including a force of Mackays invaded Caithness. While the Earl of Sutherland took part of his army to burn Wick, the remainder besieged Girnigio Castle, with the Earl of Caithness inside. After twelve days, the Sutherland men raised the siege and embarked on a plundering return home. Girnigio later changed its name to Castle Sinclair, and this affair became known as La-na-Creich-Moire.

Clan Sinclair Trust presently owns the castle, and is trying to restore what is a most interesting ruin that sits on a rocky promontory on the coast of Caithness. It is the only Scottish castle to be listed by the World Monuments Fund.

Glasgow, 1679: Strathclyde, fought during the Covenanting disturbances.

After the skirmish at Drumclog, the Covenanters marched against Glasgow. Ross's Life Guards and three independent troops commanded by the Earl of Airlie, Claverhouse and the Earl of Home defended the town. On the approach of the Covenanters, the soldiers withdrew to the town centre. The Covenanters attacked in two groups with Sir Robert Hamilton of Preston advancing up the Gallowgate and another force moving in from the direction of the university. Accounts speak of horses stumbling on the cobbles as the defenders fired down narrow streets. The defenders were victorious and the Covenanters withdrew with perhaps six dead.

Glen Boltachan, 1522 or 1612: near Loch Earn, Perthshire. In this clan fight, Finlay MacNab, the 8th chief of the MacNabs led a force from his lands beside Loch Tay to attack the MacNeishes at Glen Boltachan.

However the MacNeishes came to meet them and the clans fought in the glen. The battle site is supposed to be around a distinctive boulder. As the MacNabs rushed downhill they threw away their plaids and, naked apart from their brogues, attacked the MacNeishes, who were similarly attired. The MacNab chief fought hard, putting his back to the boulder and using his sword until he was killed, along with his three sons. Legends claim that the unusual red lichen that covers the stone is still stained with the blood of the chief. The clan bard and relation of the chief, Maccallum Glas escaped with 20 survivors to their island refuge on Loch Earn.

The island of the MacNeish can clearly be seen from St Fillans. It is a tiny place, a man-made crannog, which suggests it was a refuge rather than a permanent residence. There was once a causeway from the shore to the island.

Glen Eanaich, Highlands, date uncertain. This clan skirmish followed the traditional pattern of one clan indulging in a cattle raid and being pursued and caught by the victims. In this case the Camerons had raided the lands of Tulloch when the local men had gone to Forres for a millstone. When the Tulloch men returned they found that all their cattle had gone. They raised their kin from Rothiemurchus, chased the Camerons and defeated them near the head of Glen Eanaich. As always, there are various versions of the fight.

Glen Fruin, 7th February 1603: by Loch Lomond, Argyll, Strathclyde. This battle is one of the better recorded and better known of the clan fights, possibly because of the repercussions. One version says that after the Colquhouns hanged two MacGregors, Alastair, 17th chief of the MacGregors had ravaged Luss and killed some Colquhouns. When a party of Colquhoun women showed King James VI the bloodstained shirts of their dead, along with others that they had dipped in sheep's blood, the king promptly gave the Colquhouns authority to attack Clan Gregor with fire and sword.

Colquhoun gathered a sizeable force of his own clan plus some Buchanans and a body of burgesses from Dumbarton, but Alasdair

MacGregor of Glenstrae returned to Luss with either 300 or 400 men, possibly with the encouragement of the Earl of Argyll who played his own double game. The MacGregors were backed by MacIains, MacLeans and Camerons, and carried 'halberschois, powaixes, twahandit swordis, bowies, bowis and arrowis, and with hagbuts and pistoletis.' The Colquhouns had a reported 300 horse and 500 foot, which sounds a bit excessive. The true numbers were probably around 200 MacGregors and the same or slightly more of the Colquhouns.

Crowds gathered to watch the ensuing battle, which the MacGregors won with some ease topping their victory with a fine massacre. Alasdair MacGregor was executed and on the 3rd April 1603 and the MacGregor name proscribed, with the king giving the order to 'exterpate Clan Gregor and ruit out their posterity and name.' The Privy Council abolished the name of Macgregor and ordered the adoption of other surnames on pain of death. All who were at Glenfruin were forbidden to carry a weapon in future other than a knife without a pint for eating their food. There were further proscriptions in an attempt to eradicate clan name, so that by 1633 it was no longer a crime to kill a MacGregor. There is a boulder commemorating the battle beside the B 832 road at the head of the glen.

Glendale, 1492 or after 1513: Loch Pooltiel, Isle of Skye. A large cairn is said to mark the spot where the dead from this clan battle were buried. On one side were the MacDonalds of Sleat and of Clanranald, while their opponents were the Macleods of Harris and Dunvegan and the MacLeods of Lewis. According to legend the MacDonalds were winning until the MacLeods unfurled their talisman, the famous Fairy Flag, which inspired the MacLeods with extra courage and they surged forward to victory. The MacLeod version, held in the Bannatyne MS also says that Donald Grumach MacDonald led a MacDonald raiding force that was robbing the lands of the MacLeods as far as Dunvegan. The MacDonalds had come when the MacLeod chief, Alasdair Crotach, was in Harris, but as soon as he learned of the attack he gathered the MacLeods of Harris and Lewis and brought their galleys to Glendale.

If Crotach was chief, then the battle post dated 1490, for he was not chief until years later.

Rather than attack the MacDonalds, the MacLeods drew up in battle formation on the crest of a hill, with a river in front, and waited for the MacDonalds to come to them. The MS states the MacLeods waited ten days for reinforcements, which seems a long time when their lands were being harried, but apparently Donald Mor of Meidle joined them with his men. After obligingly waiting until their enemies were at full strength, the MacDonalds attacked, killing Donald Mor and many of his men.

So many MacLeods were falling that their entire combined force was about to flee when a woman – the MS states it was Alasdair Crotach's mother – suggested that they unfurl the Fairy Flag. As soon as that happened the MacLeods rallied. As in most clan battles, there was great slaughter and episodes of heroism. At one point Allan MacDonald of Moidart led an attack that threatened MacLeod of Dunvegan and the Fairy Flag, but one of MacLeod's followers, Murdo MacCaskill killed Donald Grumach MacDonald and displayed his head on the end of a spear while a piper played a lament. With their leader killed, the MacDonalds broke and ran.

Unfortunately for a good story, Donald Grumach did not die until at least 1534, so was certainly not killed at that battle, nor was he chief of Sleat in 1490.

The area is also noted for the stand in 1882 of John McPherson of Milovaig, who fought against the clearance of the glen by the then landlord. The Government sent a gunboat, HMS *Jackal*, MacPherson was arrested and imprisoned, but the agitation helped lead to the Napier Commission and security of tenure for crofters in the Highlands. There is a monument to the Glendale Martyrs on the B884 at the entrance to Glendale.

Glenlivet, 1592: near Allanreid, Moray. When the Earls of Huntly and Errol continued to hold to their Roman Catholic faith, King James VI ordered them to renounce their religion or forfeit their estates.

When Huntly also murdered the Bonnie Earl of Moray and was suspected of Catholic plots, the 7th Earl of Argyll, nineteen years old and Protestant, marched to capture Huntly. Argyll had an army of around 7000 Campbells, MacLeans, Grants, MacNeils, MacGregors and Mackintoshes and advanced toward Huntly's lands. He spent some time besieging Ruthven Castle, held by the MacPhersons for Huntly, but failed to take it.

Huntly raised a much smaller army of around 2000 men including Gordons and Camerons and 300 cavalry under the Earl of Errol, but he also had a battery of six cannon. The two armies met in Glenlivet and Huntly won a decisive victory. The battle was notable for Huntly's use of cannon and cavalry against Argyll's irregular foot.

The Crown Estate has created a walk to the battlefield.

Glen Mairison, around 638. Both the *Annals of Ulster* and the *Annals of Tigernach* record a battle in a place named Glen Mairiston where Domnall Brecc was defeated, but neither suggest either his adversary or his opponent. It is possible that Mairison was Glen Moriston near Inverness, or even the Muriston Water about ten miles from Edinburgh.

Glen Shiel, 10 June 1719: about five miles east of Shiel Bridge, Ross-shire, Highland. After the Union between Scotland and England in 1707, the Jacobite supporters of the Stuart dynasty raised several risings to regain the throne. In 1719 the Spanish sent two fleets to aid the Jacobites; one fleet was led by the Duke of Ormonde and had 3000 men, the other was smaller and was led by George Keith, Earl Marischal of Scotland. Storms forced Ormonde's fleet back to Spain, but both Keith's frigates reached Scottish waters off Lewis.

Clanranald and Cameron of Lochiel joined the Spaniards and together they attempted to cross to the mainland. The winds battered them back and forth across the Minch until they eventually reached Loch Alsh. They occupied Eilean Donan Castle and, when another 1000 Highlanders, including Rob Roy and 50 MacGregors, joined them, they headed for Inverness.

General Wightman and a force of around 1,400 British regulars and Hanoverian clans caught them in Glenshiel and the Spanish dug themselves in. Wightman bombarded the Jacobite positions with mortars. There seem to be a number of attacks that the Highlanders and Spanish repulsed, but when it became obvious that they could not win, the Highlanders decided it was better to be elsewhere than to be blown up. The Spanish surrendered and were returned to Spain. Another Jacobite rising had failed.

The nearby Bernera Barracks were begun the following year to help overawe the local Jacobites.

Glentaisie, 2nd May 1565: near Ballycastle in Ulster, this was a victory of Shane O'Neill victory over Sorley Boy MacDonnell in the feud between the O'Neills and the MacDonnells. Clan Donald was trying to expand their territory in Ireland after losing much of their power in Scotland.

The MacDonnells and O'Neills had been allies in an earlier war when they had repelled English advances in Ireland. Shocked by the strength of Clan Donald, the English had sent Lord Deputy Thomas Radclyffe, Earl of Sussex to destroy them in 1558, but Clan Donald had defeated them. Instead the English made a separate truce with Clan Donald. When Clan Donald began to consolidate their territories Shane O'Neill realised he was in danger of losing his longstanding power in Ulster and a clan war began. Glentaisie was one result.

Shane gathered an army of an estimated 2000 men including gallowglass [heavy infantry] archers and Hebrideans. Clan Donald's reinforcements had not all come from the Hebrides so he was outnumbered. The O'Neills defeated his attempt at a holding action and attacked, pushing Clan Donald back in a decisive O'Neill victory with around 600 or 700 Clan Donald killed.

Glen Trool, 1307: Dumfries and Galloway. Glen Trool was a small but significant skirmish during the First War of Independence. After his defeats at Methven and Dalrigh, Robert I had withdrawn to the Hebrides, then returned to try and remove the occupying English from

Scotland. As he was sheltering in the Galloway hills, an English cavalry force led by John Mowbray penetrated Glen Trool. King Robert waited until they were strung out along a narrow track and rolled boulders upon them before sweeping down the hillsides and driving them off with heavy losses. The victory inspired others to join him and kept the resistance movement alive. A boulder now marks the site of the battle.

Gloom, Castle (or Castle Campbell), 1466; near Dollar, Central Walter Stewart of Lorn and his men destroyed the castle described then as: 'a certain manor with a tower of the place of Glowm situated in the territory of Dolar.'
The castle is still spectacular, with an interesting walk and wide views.

Gogar, 27 Aug 1650: outskirts of Edinburgh. This small skirmish was fought as Oliver Cromwell approached the town during his invasion of 1650. When David Leslie repelled his attack at the Flashes, Gogar, Cromwell withdrew toward the Braid Hills

Goir a' Bhlàir, Glen Suardal, on Beinn na Caillich, Skye. This is a legendary battle where the Clan Mackinnon defeated the Norse. The name means 'field of battle.'

Gylen Castle, 1647, Island of Kerrera, Strathclyde. This incident occurred during the wars of the mid seventeenth century. The MacDougall royalists in the castle held out against Major-general Leslie's Covenanting army. The Covenanters could take the castle by assault, but when the water ran out the defenders surrendered and were massacred. The castle was restored in 2006 and is open to the public.

H

Haddington, 1548/49: East Lothian. During the Rough Wooing, the Duke of Somerset fortified Haddington with an intricate *traice italienne*, the most modern type of defence known. He had hoped to base himself in Dunbar, but the Earl of Arran had ensured that it was impregnable and the English lost their chance of a base that could be supplied by sea.

In 1548 the French failed to take Haddington. French reinforcements arrived the following year, and closely besieged the English, so a combination of Scottish aggression, French stubbornness and the plague weakened the English. When the Earl of Angus defeated an English invasion at Drumlanrig, and Lord Hume retook Hume Castle, Haddington was the last remaining English stronghold in the south. The English abandoned the town and retreated.

Haddon Rigg, August 1542; near Kelso, Scottish Borders. While Henry VIII of England planned war with Scotland, the Borderers on both sides enjoyed a season of mutual reiving. Robert Bowes, the English East March Warden, led 3000 English Borderers into Scotland, concentrating on wasting Teviotdale. He left a section of his force at Hadden and sent out two smaller parties to scour the countryside. If the raiding parties should run into trouble, they were to retreat to Haddon, where the main body would ambush any pursuing Scots. The Earl of Angus and some Douglases accompanied the English.

George Gordon, Earl of Huntly, however, cut off the retreat of one of the raiding parties. The Earl of Angus reported that the English Borderers 'of Redesdale and Tynedale was the first that fled' but he hacked his way through to safety. Around 1000 of the English were killed or captured, as Huntly's men seem to have ridden the raiders into the ambush. Bowes was also captured.

Hailes Castle, 1401: near Haddington, East Lothian. This battle was fought during the English troubles of the late fourteenth and early fifteenth century. The Earl of Dunbar and Henry 'Hotspur' Percy raided into East Lothian. They burned Markle Castle and a village or two, and laid siege to Hailes Castle. The Hepburns held Hailes and refused to surrender, depending on its strong situation, with a moat on three sides and the River Tyne on the fourth to help them.

The English failed in two daylight assaults and pitched camp. However, Archibald, the 4th Earl of Douglas galloped from Edinburgh with a much smaller force and together with a sortie from the garrison, attacked the besiegers. The English fled as far as North Berwick.

There was another action at Hailes in 1446, when Archibald Dunbar attacked the castle by night, reputedly slaughtering the entire garrison. This massacre took place during the feud between the rival Black and Red branches of the Douglas family. The Dunbars supported the Red Douglases.

The castle is in the care of Historic Scotland and occupies a surprisingly peaceful site by the River Tyne.

Halidon Hill, 19th July 1333: near Berwick, Northumberland. This major battle was fought during the Second War of Independence. Supported by the English, Edward Balliol had proclaimed himself King of Scots, but the Scots had promptly driven him out. Now Edward III openly attacked Scotland. He brought an army north and laid siege to Berwick upon Tweed, while English parties raided and murdered deep into the Lothians.

The Earl of March held the castle of Berwick and Sir Alexander Seton the town, but the English had the ingenious Flemish engineer John Crabbe and a fleet of ships to help them. As it became obvious the besiegers were serious, the defenders agreed that the town would surrender if it were not relieved by the Eleventh of July.

When an attempt to divert Edward III by raiding in England failed, the Regent Archibald Douglas led an army toward Berwick. Sir William Keith took a small body of men through siege lines, but Edward refused to accept that the town had technically been relieved and hanged a hostage. The siege continued. When Douglas moved his army south to menace Bamburgh, the temporary residence of the English queen, Edward merely repeated his demand that Berwick surrender. The governor of Berwick agreed that unless the English army was defeated or 200 Scots entered the town by 19th July he should surrender.

The English positioned their men on Halidon Hill. Only five hundred feet hill, it was nevertheless a commanding height that gave them a strong defensive position. The Scots would have to advance over a marshy hollow and climb the hill, while the English archers fired upon them. Edward had placed his army in three divisions, each flanked by archers, who could catch the Scots in a continual crossfire.

Douglas led his men to attack the English. Climbing into a constant hail of arrows, the Scots army attacked in four schiltrons, which could neither avoid the arrows nor defend themselves against them. As the *Lanercrost Chronicle* said 'the Scots who marched in the front line were so wounded in the face and blinded by the multitude of English arrows that they... soon began to turn their faces away from the bows of the arrows and fall.'

It says much for the courage of the survivors that they continued to the English ranks, but were so depleted that they could do little. The Scots retreated, with only the Earl of Ross remaining on the field. His Highlanders fought to the death as the remainder ran. Archibald Douglas was wounded and captured. He died in English captivity. Five Scots earls died along with 70 barons, hundreds of knights and thousands of infantry.

In this example of lions led by donkeys, the Scots lost most of their national leadership, much of the fighting strength of the kingdom and also Berwick upon Tweed. Edward III showed Scotland the benefits of English civilisation by beheading his Scots prisoners. Edward Balliol became the token king of Scots and the following year Edward III annexed much of Southern Scotland to England. The Scots, however, had lost battles before. Resistance continued.

There is a small car park beside a small road between the A 6105 and the A1, from which the battle field can best be reached. There are also a number of interpretation panels.

Happrew, possibly February 1304: Peeblesshire, Scottish Borders. This skirmish occurred during the First War of Independence. Although defeated at Falkirk, William Wallace continued to organise resistance to the English. After a visit to France, where he had attempted to gather support, he returned to Scotland and teamed up with Sir Simon Fraser. Their combined force sheltered in the Ettrick Forest. Edward I, then in Dunfermline, sent a mounted force that defeated Wallace and Fraser at Happrew, near Peebles. The skirmish may have taken place at Sherrifmuir, a piece of flat land near the River Lyne.

Harlaw, 24 July 1411, Aberdeenshire, Grampian. This battle is also known as Bloody Harlaw and was seen as a major confrontation between Highlanders and Lowlanders, although Highlanders fought on both sides.

Donald, Lord of the Isles was attempting to realise his claim to the Earldom of Ross, through Margaret, his wife, who was the sister of the previous Earl. Donald called upon much of the strength of his Lordship, MacLeods of Lewis and Skye, MacDonalds, Camerons and the Chattan confederation. It was said he had 10,000 men, which was an army larger than that Bruce led at Bannockburn, and twice as large as the Bonnie Prince had at Culloden. More likely his army was much smaller.

Donald was a man of culture; he possessed Royal Stuart blood, spoke Gaelic, Scots and probably Latin and knew London as well as his Hebrides. He led his army across Scotland, defeated the Mackays at Dingwall and moved toward Aberdeen until reached Harlaw in the Garioch, less than twenty miles from Aberdeen.

Terrified by this army from the Gaelic west, the burgesses of Aberdeen grabbed their arms and marched to battle. They fought under Alexander Stewart, the Earl of Mar, who had obtained his earldom by abducting and marrying the Countess of Mar. He was a cousin of Donald's, the son of the Wolf of Badenoch and a one-time pirate. As well as Aberdonians, Mar had men from Mar and the Garioch, Angus, the Mearns and Buchan.

There seem to have been neither tactics nor manoeuvres when the two armies met, just a roaring charge by the Earl of Mar. The Gaelic version states that Red Hector MacLean routed Sir Alexander Ogilvy's left wing of Mar's army, while Donald's centre pushed Mar's main body back. The right wing of the Earl's army stood firm in a cattle fold and fought sword to sword with the Gaels. The casualties were horrific; an estimated 900 of Donald's men, 600 of Mar's and it was only nightfall that ended the battle. There were no winners, but Donald withdrew in the night and Mar's army claimed the field. Donald never did attain the Earldom of Ross.

There is a large monument on the supposed battle site, and cairns named as Drum's and Davidson's cairns, which may not have any genuine connection to the battle. One monument is supposed to mark the grave of women camp followers who were killed at the battle. However, the churchyard at Kinkell, near Inverurie, has a memorial to Sir Gilbert de Greenlaw, who was also a casualty.

Harpsdale, 1426, otherwise known as Harpsdale Hill, fought about eight miles south of Thurso, Caithness, Highland. This was a clan battle, part of the feud between the Gunns and the Keiths, although the Mackays under Angus Dhu Mackay also claim to have been involved. It seems to have been a bloody affair, but with no clear victor.

Harta Corrie, date uncertain but given as either 1395; near Sligathen, Skye. This battle was fought around the Bloody Stone in the Cuillins in Skye between the MacDonalds and MacLeods. One version of this battle claims that in 1395 the clans fought for a whole day in Harta Corrie. The MacDonalds won and piled the MacLeod corpses beside the boulder, hence the name. The tale that fairies made their bows from the ribs of the dead MacLeods is probably untrue, although there have been reports of ghostly warriors in the area. The name bloody stone is more likely to have come from the curious colouring of the rock, which is due to the presence of pyrites rather than the residue of some ancient encounter.

Helmsdale 1587: Sutherland. In a dispute over the superiority of the lands of Strathnaver, the Earls of Sutherland and Caithness feuded. The Earl of Caithness, backed by Mackay of Strathnaver and the earl of Orkney, advanced on Helmsdale. The Earl of Sutherland, with the Mackintoshes, Roderick Mackenzie of Redcastle, Hector Monroe of Contalich and Neil Hutcheonson and a body of men from Assynt, met him there. After some preliminary skirmishing, during which the Sutherland archers pushed back the Caithness men to Easter Helmsdale, the affair ended without serious bloodshed. The two rival earls agreed to meet in Elgin and hold a more civilised discussion.

High Bridge, rout of, 1745: near Spean Bridge, Highland. In this first engagement of the 1745 Jacobite rising, a party of Highlanders captured a body of Hanoverian troops. About a dozen Keppoch MacDonalds, under the command of MacDonald of Tirnradis, were at an inn beside the old bridge. A company of Hanoverian Royal Scots marched past on their way to reinforce the garrison at Fort William. The MacDonalds played their pipes and ran around the soldiers, yelling their slogans. There must have been an exchange of fire, because three or four of the soldiers were killed and their commander, Captain Scott, was wounded. Scott ordered a retreat, but Keppoch and another body of MacDonalds captured him and around eighty soldiers of the Royal Scots near Loch Oich. The Hanoverians were released on parole, and Captain Scott was one of the few Hanoverian prisoners who did not break his word not to serve against the Jacobites again. He later became a general.

In 1994 a cairn was raised to commemorate this Jacobite victory.

Hill of Clairdon, 1196: east of Thurso, Caithness, Highland. This battle was fought when Orkney was a Norse earldom and Caithness was also under Norse influence. Earl Harold the Elder led an army of Orcadians and Norse against a force from Caithness led by Harold the Younger and two nobles named Murt and Lifolf. The battle was to decide who should have the earldom.

Both sides attacked the other, and the smaller Caithness force pushed the Orcadians and Norse back to Murkle Bay, but when both Murt and Lifolf were killed, the tide of battle turned. The Norse chased the leaderless Caithness men from the field and Earl Harold the Elder took control of Caithness.

Homildon Hill, 14th September 1402: Humbledon Hill, west of Wooler, Northumberland. This battle was fought during the war with England that broke out in 1400. Archibald, the 4th Earl of Douglas, haplessly known as the *Tineman* because of his propensity to fight on the losing side, led an army into England. He raided as far as Durham but on his return Henry Percy and the traitor Earl of March met him at Humbledon Hill in Northumberland. The Douglas took up position on the hill and waited for the English to come onto his massed spearmen. Henry Percy suggested a quick advance, but the Earl of March advised using the English archers. Only after losing a great many of his men to the arrows did Douglas agree that the Scots should leave their position, although credit for the advance was given to the young Sir John Swinton, who died leading the first charge. Very few Scots followed and English archery had won another victory. They pursued the fleeing Scots with the usual butchery.

Archibald Douglas was captured with five arrows in him. He made a compact with Percy and Glendower and fought with them at Shrewsbury, and lost again. Two Scots barons died, with eighty knights and uncounted foot soldiers.

The nearby Battle or Bendor Stone is generally associated with the battle, but in reality the stone is many centuries older.

Hornshole Bridge, 1514: near Hawick, Scottish Borders. This skirmish occurred in the year following the Scottish defeat at Flodden, when English raiders were plundering and murdering in the Borders. One group of English camped on the banks of the Teviot at Hornshole, about two miles from Hawick. With most of the men killed at Flodden, only youths were left to defend the town. They gathered together and attacked the English, inflicted a defeat and captured the enemy standard.

The incident is commemorated in Hawick's annual Common Riding, while the statue of The Horse in Hawick High Street acts as a permanent reminder.

Hume (or Home) Castle, 1549 to 1650; Berwickshire, Scottish Borders. The Humes were the most significant family of the Merse, and their Hume Castle was an important stronghold in what is now Berwickshire. In 1547 the English besieged it. Lady Hume was in charge, as her husband was with the Scottish army. She resisted until the Earl of Somerset was about to hang her son in front of the walls, when she surrendered. Two years later the young Lord Hume retook his home, killing those English who resisted.

In 1569 the English arrived with a thousand horse, plus foot and used artillery to bombard the castle into submission. In 1650 Cromwell's army camped in front of it and Hume Castle came to the forefront of history. When Colonel Fenwick ordered the castle to surrender, Governor Cockburn replied:

Right Honourable, I have received a trumpeter of yours, as he tells me, without a pass, to surrender Home Castle to the Lord General Cromwell. Please you, I never saw your general. As for Home Castle, it stands upon a rock.

He was also reported to have made a second reply:

> *I Willie Wastle*
> *Stand firm in my castle*
> *And a' the dogs o' your town*
> *Will no pull Willie Wastle down*

Eloquence, however, is no defence against cannon fire and Hume soon after surrendered.

The Berwickshire Civic Society currently runs the castle, which was much altered in the late eighteenth century. It is open to the public during the summer.

Dance If Ye Can

I

Ill Raid, August 1513: Northumberland, England. After decades of peace, Scotland and England again slid into war when the English attacked France, Scotland's ally. The English kicked off the war with a raid over the Scottish border, and Alexander, 3rd Lord Hume retaliated with a counter raid of a reported 6000 men
As the Scots passed Milfield near Flodden on their return, the English under Sir William Bulmer ambushed them. The English archers caused heavy loss in this prelude to Flodden.

Inchbare, 16th April 1130, also called Stracathro, fought at Stracathro 4 miles north of Brechin, Angus. This battle was fought when descendants of Kenneth MacAlpin attempted to capture the throne from King David I. Many Scots did not recognise David as the true king, as his father, Malcolm III was illegitimate and had gained the throne by force. Probably more important was David's efforts to change the Gaelic culture of the country by importing Norman-English knights and importing the Roman Catholic faith to replace the native Celtic church. Feudal law also began to replace Celtic law as Scotland began to split between the Gaelic and Norman-English cultures.
Angus, Earl of Moray, a grandson of Malcolm III, but with Gaelic sympathies, raised rebellion with an army of around 10,000, and was joined by the Mormaer of Ross and Fergus of Galloway. They met in Moray and marched south to the Mearns and into the Stracathro area.
Edward de Morville, High Constable of Scotland, called up his Norman-Scots and their followers. They met at Forfar: de Morville, Cospatrick, Earl of Dunbar, and the Earl of Fife, so that the Constable had an army of around 8,500 men, many of them mounted. Scouts found the army of Angus at Inchbare on the River North Esk. The High Constable revealed about half his army and enticed Angus to attack on the level plain. However a premature charge by a few of the Norman-Scottish knights warned Angus of the hidden army and he formed his

men into what seems to have been a schiltron, or perhaps the shield wall of the Norse. The Constable's army made a number of cavalry charges, losing the Earls of Fife and Dunbar, but when a knight killed Angus, the rebels wavered. The arrival of mounted reinforcements for the Constable's army persuaded the rebels to withdraw. The Mormaer of Ross seems to have kept them together so there was no rout. The Constable claimed to have inflicted a major defeat, but his casualties would indicate that it was a close run thing.

To visit this unmarked battle site, drive north from Brechin on the B966 until Auchenreoch is reached, just before the Westwater Bridge. The battle was fought around Auchenreoch, which translates as Field of Great Sorrow.

Inchcolm, 1548/1549: Firth of Forth. During King Henry VIII's Rough Wooing, an English garrison was placed on Inchcolm. The idea would be to block trade with Leith and harass shipping but elements of the Scottish Navy caused the garrison much trouble, its attacks on Fife were repelled and it withdrew around 1549.

Inchgarvie, April 1651, Firth of Forth, During Cromwell's invasion, his warships attacked and knocked out the defences of this island

Inchkeith, 2nd June 1549: Firth of Forth. During the invasion of Henry VIII of England, an English garrison of around 800 men was left on the army. In 1549 a force of around 700 Scots and French under Chapelle de Biron assaulted the island and removed the English. There was further trouble in 1560, when the Auld Alliance had failed and the Protestant Scots were allies with the English. An English fleet under Admiral Winter blockaded the French garrison on the island, which surrendered.

Innerwick, 1298: East Lothian, scene of a reputed skirmish between William Wallace and Cospatrick, Earl of March. The encounter was said to have taken place at Corsekill Park.

Innerwick Castle, 1548: East Lothian. The Duke of Somerset captured and destroyed this castle of the Hamiltons during his invasion.

Inverdufatha, 877, possibly Inverdovat, near Crail in Fife, but it is also possible that this battle was fought in Atholl, Perthshire. In the 870s, Norse armies were rampant in Scotland. They captured Alcluith in 870 and defeated Constantine at Dollar in 875. Another Norse army, led by Halfdan, landed in Central Scotland in 877. This may have been the army that King Constantine fought, but very little is certain in early Scottish history. The Scots certainly lost the battle, which Skene in his *Celtic Scotland* placed in Inverdovat in north-eastern Fife.

Invergowrie around 1116; there are two different accounts of this event, where Walter Bower and Andrew Wyntoun both mention that King Alexander I was attacked at Invergowrie. Bower called the attackers 'ruffians from the Mearns and Moray.' He also said that Alexander subsequently called together an army and attacked his enemies. Wyntoun's version is similar, where the King pursues his attackers into Ross and defeats them. After his victory Alexander was known as Alexander the Fierce. There was undoubtedly animosity from Moray toward the Scottish crown.

Inverkeithing, 20 July 1651: also known as **Pitreavie**, Fife. After Cromwell murdered King Charles I, the Scots decided to withdraw support for his regime and recognised Charles II as king, once he had agreed to the Covenant. Cromwell promptly invaded Scotland. He sent General Lambert with 4500 men to threaten General Leslie's supply lines. Leslie sent Sir John Browne and a smaller Royalist army to stop it. The two forces met at Inverkeithing, south of Pitreavie House.

Lambert's generalship was better than that of Browne and he defeated the Royalists. Around 2000 were killed. It was said that eight of Hector MacLean's foster-brothers threw themselves in front of the Cromwellian pikes in an effort to defend their chief, each one crying 'Another for Hector' as they fell. Over 700 Macleans died, with the Cromwellians displaying their habitual savagery to Scottish prisoners.

Inverlochy 1431: Lochaber, Highlands. Although some Highland clans displaying intense loyalty to the later Stuart kings, the early Stuarts were rarely friends of the Highlanders. In 1428 King James I summoned many of the Highland chiefs to Inverness, hanged three and imprisoned the remainder. When he released them, Alexander, Lord of the Isles retaliated by burning Inverness. The King returned north, again snatched Alexander and threw him into jail.

Donald Balloch, Alexander's cousin, and Alastair Carrach, his uncle, raised an army in rebellion and the king sent Alexander Stewart, the Earl of Mar into Lochaber to quell them. Mar camped beside the river south west of Inverlochy Castle, deep in Cameron country, for Camerons were in his force. Carrach and 200 archers fired from the hills above him, as Donald Balloch came in a fleet of galleys from the south.

Caught between two forces, Mar's men were routed with a reported 1000 casualties, including the Earl of Caithness. Donald Balloch continued his campaign by ravaging the Cameron lands, but King James again marched an army north to restore approximate peace. Alexander remained in jail until the murder of King James in Perth, six years later.

Inverlochy, 2nd February 1645: near present day Fort William, Lochaber, Highland. This battle was fought during the Civil War of the mid seventeenth century. The Marquis of Montrose's Royalists defeated the Campbells and Covenanters.

James Graham, Marquis of Montrose was the King's Lieutenant General in Scotland while Alexander Leslie and Archibald Campbell, Earl of Argyll, led the Covenanters. Montrose, supported by Alasdair MacColla MacDonald commanded 1500 mixed Clan Donald Ulstermen, MacLeans of Mull and Atholl clans. He had already defeated two of the four Covenanting armies in Scotland and had sacked Aberdeen. In retaliation the Earl of Argyll with 2,500 Campbell and Lowland foot, and 1500 horse ravaged the royalist Gordon lands. Montrose crossed Scotland to hit the Campbell heartland, looting and destroying happily for a season until he tired and withdrew up the Great Glen.

Argyll whistled up his men and followed in his wake, digging in around Inverlochy Castle with an army larger than anything Montrose could command, despite the reinforcements that drifted to the royal banner. Trapped between Argyll at Inverlochy and the Mackenzie-Fraser garrison at Inverness, Montrose scaled the mountain massif of the Nevis range and swept down upon Argyll. While Argyll sat safe in a galley on Loch Linnhe, Montrose's swordsmen faced the Campbells, who were led by Duncan Campbell of Auchinbreck.

There were about 1000 Lowland infantry and maybe 2000 Campbells, with two artillery pieces and 50 musketeers in Inverlochy Castle. After a short prayer, Montrose's men fired a single volley and charged their flank. Montrose had Ulstermen on his flanks and men from Atholl, Glencoe MacDonalds, Appin Stuarts and Camerons in the centre. As the charge formed into wedges the Lowlanders broke and Montrose's Royalists closed with the Campbells. There was no quarter. Iain Lom, the MacDonald bard, put venom into his paean of victory: *Alastair, son of handsome Coll... you routed the sallow-skinned Lowlanders... at the time of unsheathing of slender swords, the claws of the Campbells lay on the ground with sinews severed.*

Old Inverlochy Castle may still be visited.

Invernahavon, 1370 or 1386: beneath Craigh Dubh at the confluence of Truim and Spey, Badenoch, Highlands. There are a number of versions of this clan battle, but they agree upon the main facts. Four hundred Camerons were raiding Macintosh land, when a combined Clan Chattan force of Macphersons, Mackintoshes and Davidsons opposed them. After that the traditions diverge.

One account says that when the Davidsons took the right of the Chattan line, the Macphersons, who normally fought there, withdrew from the field. Crossing the Spey, they stood on a small hill and watched the battle unfold. The Camerons won the fight, killing Macdaidh, the Davidson chief, and seven of his sons, as well as scores of the Mackintoshes.

Either Lachlan Mackintosh, chief of the clan, or the Camerons ordered his bard to compose a song pointing out the cowardice of the Macphersons. When they heard the song, the Macphersons chased after the Camerons and attacked them at Dalnach, possibly while they were in camp, and defeated them. It was said that a Cameron captain was killed at a corrie known as Coire Earlaich. The remaining Camerons retreated, with the MacPhersons skirmishing with them until they reached Loch Patag, where the rival chiefs apparently killed each other in an archery duel.

Inverness, 1196. When Earl Harold Maddason of Orkney hoped to annex Ross and Moray, he sent an army south under his son Thorfinn. King William I marched north and defeated the invasion near Inverness. William followed up by ravaging eastern Sutherland and Caithness and destroying Thurso. Harold surrendered.

Inverness Castle, 1307. During the First War of Independence, King Robert I captured and destroyed the castle of Inverness.
The present castle is a nineteenth century building used for a court house but with plans to convert it into a major visitor attraction.

Inverurie, probably 23rd May 1308, sometimes known as Barra, Hill, this battle was fought north of Inverurie Castle, near Old Meldrum, Aberdeenshire, Grampian. During the First War of Independence King Robert I gradually removed the Scottish opposition to his rule. In late 1307 and early 1308 he was in the northeast and met the forces of his main rival, John Comyn, Earl of Buchan.
Details of this battle are sketchy, but tradition claims that because Bruce was sick, Comyn thought he was helpless. When Bruce appeared on horseback, supported by a man on either side, the Comyns lost heart. King Robert routed Buchan's army, the survivors of which retreated to the castle at Fyvie, twelve miles to the north. Buchan fled to England, where he died later that year.
Irroisfoichnae, 727, possibly fought at Ross-Feochan, near Loch Awe in Argyll, Strathclyde. This battle was one of the many dynastic struggled between the various sects of Dalriada. In this legendary battle Selbach defeated Eochach, perhaps in a competition for the leadership of Lorne

Dance If Ye Can

Islay 1156: Somewhere off Islay, Inner Hebrides, Strathclyde. Although the Norse had controlled the Hebrides for centuries, it was not until 1098 that Magnus Barelegs of Norway formalised their ownership. Only fifty years later, the indigenous people were stirring. A warrior named Somerled, part Norse, part Gael, fought for his own hand against King Godred of Man.

It is possible that Somerled intended to conquer all the Hebrides, but Godred led a fleet to prevent this. The *Chronicles of Man* supplies some information:

In the year 1156 a naval battle was fought on the night of the Epiphany between Godred and Somerled and there was much slaughter on both sides.

Tradition asserts that Somerled had eighty galleys and after a full day's battle they rested at night. Somerled was victorious and the contestants divided the Hebrides between them. While Somerled obtained the islands south of Ardnamurchan, Godred retained those to the north. According to the *Chronicles of Man*, the matter did not rest there for:

In the year 1158 Somerled came to Man with fifty-three ships and joined battle with Godred and put him to flight. He ravaged the whole island and went away.

Clearly Somerled was a redoubtable naval warrior. He also sired sons who were the progenitors of the MacDonalds, MacDougalls and MacRuaridhs.

J

Jedburgh, 1332, Scottish Borders. When Edward Balliol announced himself King of Scots he invaded Scotland with a mixed army of English and Scots whom King Robert I had deprived of their lands, known as the Disinherited. Making his base in Galloway, he moved eastward. The patriots under the Guardian Murray and Archibald Douglas opposed him at Jedburgh, but were defeated in a small skirmish.

Jedburgh, 1409, Scottish Borders. This border town was attacked, burned or occupied no less than eleven times during the English wars. In 1409 the Scots retook the town and castle from an English occupation that had lasted since the Battle of Neville's Cross in 1346. The Scots destroyed the castle to prevent the English from using it against Scotland in future.

Jedburgh, 23rd September 1532; Scottish Borders. Surrey led the English in an attack on Scotland but met fierce resistance in Jedburgh:
I found the Scottis at this tyme the boldest men and the hottest that ever I sawe... the devyl was that nyght among them.
The English captured and destroyed the town, but the Scots raided that same night and stampeded 800 English horses.

Jedburgh, February 1572, Scottish Borders. When Jedburgh was at feud with the Kerrs of Ferniehurst, Sir Thomas Kerr led a mixed force of Kerrs and Scotts, a few English and a band of outlaws under Alexander Trotter to attack the town. He had 3000 men in total. To complicate matters, Scotland was torn between support for Queen Mary and the young King James VI. Jedburgh supported James VI and the Kerrs were Mary's men. When the Kerrs arrived, the town had six days supplies of food, and hoped for help from the main army of Kingsmen in Edinburgh.

Hearing that Lord Ruthven was coming to relieve Jedburgh with horse and musketeers, Kerr tried to stop him, but the townsmen sallied out and Kerr of Cessford, a rival branch of the family, supported the men of Jedburgh. Kerr of Ferniehurst was caught between both forces and dispersed.

Justice Mills, 13th September 1644, see **Aberdeen**

K

Keith's Muir, around 1370, near Durris, Aberdeenshire, Grampian. In the second half of the fourteenth century the Keiths and the Irvines of Drum were at feud. Tradition speaks of a battle at Keith's Muir, near the River Dee, where the Irvines were victorious and killed many Keiths. The pattern is familiar; the Keiths had raided Irvine land but were caught, laden with plunder and defeated.

Kells, December 1315: County Meath, Ireland. Edward Bruce, who was campaigning against the Anglo-Irish during the First War of Independence, fought this battle. After being crowned High King of Ireland, Edward Bruce faced Roger Mortimer of Wigmore and won a complete victory over Mortimer's 15,000 men. After his victory Edward Bruce devastated a great swathe of Ireland.

Kelso, 1545, Scottish Borders. The town and abbey of Kelso frequently suffered at the hands of the English. Probably the worst example was during the English invasion of 1545, when Hertford's army was intent on destroying everything that it could. Twelve monks and ninety citizens and laymen tried to hold Kelso Abbey against the English army. When the English artillery battered down the walls, Hertford sent in his Spanish mercenaries to take the building. The garrison withdrew to the tower, where they held out all night, with twelve men slithering down ropes to escape, but at dawn the English attacked again. It was said that the defenders were all murdered. To complete his work, Hertford stripped the lead from the roof and sent it into England.
Kelso Abbey is still a ruin, but is worth a visit, as does the remainder of this unique Border town.

Kentra, Ardnamurchan, Highland. In his splendid book *The West Highland Galley*, Denis Rixon speaks of two battles being fought in the sea off Gortenfern and Sgeir a Chaolais by Kentra. It is possible that the Norse or rival Hebrideans were involved, although finds on the beach of Cul na Croise include silver coins of Edward 1 of England as well as daggers, spears, clinch-nails and arrowheads. It is sites like this that make the destruction and theft of so many Scottish records, and in particular Gaelic records, so frustrating.

Kerrera, 1460: Inner Hebrides, Strathclyde. When James II died in 1460, Scotland reverted to a period of anarchy. Allan Ciar MacDougall, known as Allan of the Wood, hoped to gain the island of Kerrera, then owned by his older brother. Alan threw his brother into a dungeon in Kerrera and, it was said, intended to starve him to death.

Colin Campbell, Earl of Argyll, was distantly related to the imprisoned man and led a fleet of galleys in a surprise attack on Allan Ciar Macdougall. The Campbells defeated Allan's men and burned his galleys. Allan MacDougall fled across the bows of the Campbell galleys as they drove in Oban Bay.

Kessock Ferry, around 1384: near Inverness, Highland. This possibly apocryphal skirmish occurred when a body of Hebrideans camped outside Inverness in 1384. They told the Provost of Inverness that they would burn Kessock Ferry unless he paid them a large ransom. The provost pretended to agree and sent a keg of whisky to the Islesmen as sign of his good will. When the Islesmen were drunk, the Provost and men from Inverness massacred them.

Kildrummy Castle, 1306: Aberdeenshire, Grampian. During the First War of Independence, King Robert I sent his wife Elizabeth to Kildrummy for safety, but the pro-English faction captured the castle and King Robert's family was given to the English to be imprisoned. According to tradition, the English massacred the entire garrison, and rewarded a blacksmith who betrayed them by pouring molten gold down his throat.

The Castle was besieged again in 1335, during the Second War of Independence when Lady Christian Bruce, sister of the late King Robert 1 held Lord David of Atholl at bay until her husband came to her rescue. Christian was 62 years old, had been imprisoned by the English when they captured Kildrummy in 1306 and her first husband hanged.

Historic Scotland manages the castle, whose ruins are open to the public.

Killiecrankie, 27th July 1689: three miles north of Pitlochry, Perthshire, on the B8907. This battle was fought during the Jacobite Rising of 1689. When the Scottish Parliament accepted William of Orange as king rather than James VII, the supporters of James, mainly Catholic or Episcopalian Highlanders, rose in rebellion.

John Graham of Claverhouse, Viscount Dundee gathered a small army of around 2000 Highlanders and a few Irishmen and mounted Jacobite gentlemen. The veteran Hugh Mackay of Scourie was appointed Major-General and led an army to face Dundee. Among his regiments was William Cleland's newly raised Cameronians. In total he had around 4000 infantry, with 100 cavalry under Lords Belhaven and Armadale.

Mackay led his men through the Pass of Killiecrankie and selected a strong position on high ground on the northward side. Dundee waited until dusk and attacked with a swift advance that turned into one of the ferocious Highland charges that had worked so well for Montrose. A volley from Mackay's regulars killed hundreds but then the broadswords and Lochaber axes of the Highlanders were at work and the Williamites broke. It was a victory for the Jacobites, but in destroying Mackay's army they lost the irreplaceable Dundee. The Irishman Colonel Cannon took over the Jacobites and led them to defeat at Dunkeld.

The National Trust of Scotland operates a splendid interpretation centre, snack bar and bookshop a few hundred yards from the battle site. It is possible to walk from the centre to parts of the site, and to view places such as the Soldiers Leap, where a Hanoverian soldier is said to have leaped over the River Garry.

Kilsyth, 15 August 1645: north east of Glasgow, Strathclyde. This battle was the last major victory of Montrose. After defeating various Covenanting armies in the north, Montrose was based at Dunkeld in Perthshire.

General William Baillie was at Perth with around 6000 foot and 800 cavalry. His infantry was a mixture of veteran Covenanting regiments fresh from the English campaigns, recruits from the fishing villages of the East Neuk of Fife and the remnants of units that Montrose had already defeated, but his cavalry were regulars. There was also a smaller Covenanting force-marching to join with Baillie, so Montrose decided to defeat this army first.

He bypassed Bailie, reached the Kilsyth and prepared for battle. Bailie, who had followed, positioned himself on high ground nearby knowing that when the second Covenanting army appeared, Montrose would be trapped. However, the Committee of Estates, a mixed political and ecclesiastical body that really ran the Covenanting army, ordered Baillie to march past Montrose to meet the approaching force. Scottish armies in this period were cursed by interference from religious fanatics.

Montrose instructed his soldiers to throw away their plaids in the summer heat and knot the ends of their shirts between their legs so they had easier movement when they fought. He waited until Baillie's Covenanters were on the march in three groups and then he attacked. The Covenanters pushed back the initial assault, but their horse wilted before the assault of the Gordon cavalry. Montrose sent his MacLeans and MacDonalds forward as the Covenanters gave ground. A Highland and Ulster charge settled the issue. Around 3000 Covenanters died and it was said that in every haven of the East Neuk, fishing boats rotted on the beach due to the lack of men. General Baillie fled.

When the smaller Covenanting force dispersed, Montrose was left as master of Scotland, but in England, the royalist cause had fared badly. A combination of Cromwell and Scottish Covenanters had defeated his armies, so Montrose was the sole Stuart victor, and even his army dissipated in victory as the Highlanders returned to their glens and Alasdair MacColla MacDonald departed with most of his MacDonalds and Ulstermen. Montrose headed south, to the Borders and eventual defeat at Philliphaugh.

There is a small cairn as a memorial to this significant battle.

Kinclaven, 1297: ten miles north of Perth on the banks of the Tay, Perthshire. During the First War of Independence, a small English force was marching from Perth to reinforce the garrison at Kinclaven Castle. William Wallace ambushed them and pursued the fleeing English inside the castle. He captured the castle, killed the garrison and destroyed the place.
The castle is now in a very ruinous condition.

Kinghorn, 6th August 1332: Fife. When King Robert I and his chief captains were dead, the English again began to interfere in Scottish affairs. They sponsored Edward Balliol, gave him an army of English and Disinherited Scots and sent him to claim the kingdom of Scotland. Balliol landed at Kinghorn in Fife to be immediately faced with a small local force under Duncan, Earl of Fife, Alexander Seton and Robert Bruce, the illegitimate son of King Robert.
The English longbowmen won the brief skirmish, killing Seton and driving away the Scots so that Balliol could land in peace.

Kirkcudbright Fen, 1547: Kirkcudbright, Dumfries and Galloway. During the Rough Wooing, Sir Thomas Carleton led an English raid into southwest Scotland. He based himself in Dumfries and attempted a dawn attack on Kirkcudbright, but was repulsed, and retreated when McLellan of Bombie brought a Scottish force against him. The Kirkcudbright battle is notable for the incident when a Scotswoman from Kirkcudbright handed over her husband to one of the attackers to save his life. Presumably he was ransomed later.

Kirkton of Aberfoyle, 1671: Stirlingshire, Central. At a bridge outside the town the Grahams of Duchray skirmished with followers of his distant cousin, the Earl of Airth at a christening. More than a riot than a battle, there were few, if any, casualties.

Knockboy, 1565, Ulster, Shane O'Neill defeated an ambush laid by Clan Donald in the feud for control of the Glens of Ulster.

Knockbrecht Hill, 7/8th June 1689: Speyside, Highland. This incident occurred during the first Jacobite rising of 1689. During the manoeuvring before the battle of Killiecrankie, General Hugh Mackay was hunting for Dundee and his Jacobites. Sir Thomas Livingstone and 200 cavalry and dragoons were scouting in front. They came across a party of MacLeans and scattered them. Reassembling on Knockbrecht Hill, around a hundred MacLeans fended off the dragoons with musketry and a shower of boulders. Next morning, the 8th June, they charged downhill and sent Livingstone's horse running back.

Kringen, 1612, Norway; less of a battle than a massacre, Kringen is celebrated in the area of Norway where it was fought but is all but forgotten in Scotland. At that time footloose Scots frequently enlisted as mercenaries in foreign wars. Colonel Alexander Ramsay and Lord George Sinclair gathered three hundred men, mainly from Caithness, with the intention of fighting for Sweden in the Kalmar War, which had Sweden on one side and Norway-Denmark on the other.
Ramsay took his small force through enemy territory of Norway to get to Sweden but was ambushed en-route. It was a bad time to choose as three hundred Norwegian coscripts had recently been massacred by the Swedes.
Ramsay had intended to land at Romsdal but the pilot proved treacherous and left them at Klugness, away off route, which delayed them and allowed the Norwegians time to gather their forces. The Scots rested at Dovre on 24th August and feasted with the seemingly friendly locals before heading into the mountains.
As Ramsay's men threaded through the pass at Kringen a much larger force of Norwegians allowed the vanguard to pass and fell on the main body. It seems that a young woman rode bedside Ramsay's men and when she thought they were unprepared, blew a horn that was the signal for the ambush. Despite the surprise and the disparity of numbers, the Scots resisted for an hour and a half. Around a hundred and thirty were taken prisoner, only to be murdered by the Norwegians. Ramsay was captured and later returned to Scotland.

Dance If Ye Can

Kyle of Tongue, March 1746: Sutherland, Highland. This minor naval engagement may have had more significance than it seemed at the time. The Jacobites had captured a Royal navy sloop, *Hazard* in Montrose and renamed her *Prince Charles*. Laden with gold for the Jacobite cause, *Prince Charles* was intercepted off the north coast of Scotland by HMS *Sheerness* and chased into the Kyle of Tongue. The crew carried the gold ashore and headed for the main Jacobite army in Inverness, but the local Mackays were Hanoverian. They ambushed the Jacobites at Lochan Haken, and the gold was thrown into the loch. A strong Jacobite force was later sent to recover the gold, and perhaps these men could have proved influential at the final battle of Culloden.

L

Lagan a' chatha, around 1488: Glen Lyon, Perthshire. The name means Hollow of the Fight, and probably refers to this clan battle. In the fifteenth century the MacIvors owned most of Glen Lyon, but when their chief ordered the death of the brother of Stewart of Garth, the Stewarts decided on revenge. Tradition speaks of an attempted meeting between the rival chiefs on Craig Fhianniaidh, which ended when first one chief, and then the other, called upon hidden clansmen. The Stewarts won the ensuing battle, apparently chasing the MacIvors eight miles up the glen. In this affair, around 150 men were killed, and, according to legend, were buried at Camus Na Carn, the field of Cairns. The Stewarts moved into Glen Lyons. Tradition also tells of a sword and battle-axe being dug up on the spot in 1816.

Lagavraid, Ross, 1597. Another clan battle for which there is little information. It seems that the battle began with a dispute at a fair at Lagavraid, Ross-shire when the brother of the Laird of Raasay, John Macgillichallum argued with Alexander Bane, whose brother was Duncan Bane of Tulloch. As so often, other clans became involved, with the Munros backing the Banes and the Mackenzies the men from

Raasay. John Macgillichallum was killed, with some of the Mackenzies and a few Munros.

Lagebrad, 1480: near Conon Bridge, Easter Ross, Highland. The Lord of the Isles defeated a royal army. After King James III removed the Earldom of Ross from Angus Og of the Isles for treason, the MacDonalds rebelled to recover the title. The Earl of Atholl led a mixed army of Mackenzies, Rosses, Frasers, Rosses, Mackays and Brodies against the MacDonalds, but Angus Og defeated them soundly at Lagabraad or Lagebrad.

Lang Herdmanston, 14 February 1406; fought in East Lothian. In this skirmish, Sir James Douglas killed Sir David Fleming of Cumbernauld. The back story is more interesting. Young Prince James of Scots had been sent to France for safety but King Henry of England intercepted the ship and kept the prince prisoner in England in breach of all international conventions.

While young James was kept hostage in the Tower of London, the Duke of Albany was the de facto ruler of Scotland in defiance of feeble King Robert. In the meantime the Earl of Douglas, who also strove for power in Scotland, had hoped to control the prince. He sent his son, Sir James Douglas of Abercorn to attack the nobles who had accompanied the prince on the first leg of his journey. He killed Fleming and captured the remainder. In the meantime King Robert conveniently died and Albany took over a regent.

Lang Howe, 25 December 1307, upper Glen Esk, Angus, supposed site of a skirmish between King Robert I and the Earl of Buchan. There are persistent legends that King Robert was also at Tarfside and at the Hill of Rowan, nearby

Langside, 13 May 1568: south side of the River Clyde, Glasgow. This battle was fought between Mary, Queen of Scots and her half brother, James Stuart, the Earl of Moray. Queen Mary was viewed with suspicion because of her Catholicism, but when she also married James

Hepburn, the Earl of Bothwell, who was suspected of complicity in the murder of Mary's second husband, much of Scotland turned against her. Imprisoned in Loch Leven Castle, Mary escaped and soon raised an army of some 6000 men, headed by the Earl of Argyll and including many Hamiltons and Campbells. She marched toward Dumbarton Castle, where Lord Fleming remained loyal.

Mary's brother, the Earl of Moray led the Protestant Army of the Congregation of Christ. About 4000 strong, it was smaller than that of Mary, but much better led and in its ranks was Kirkcaldy of Grange, reputed to be the finest soldier in Europe. The armies met at the hamlet of Langside, near the moor of Govan.

When Mary's army advanced, Kirkcaldy met them with an ambush of hagbutters and cavalry, but the Hamiltons and Campbells pushed back the attack and rolled on. There was a spell of close fighting in Langside, but with Moray's cavalry looking fragile, Argyll fell from his horse. It may have been treachery, or an epileptic fit, but Kirkcaldy seized the moment and threw forward his Highlanders to win the day. Mary had lost perhaps a hundred men in around 45 minutes.

Langside was Mary's last battle, and soon after she left Scotland for her seventeen years of English captivity and eventual execution. The site of the battle is near Queen's Park, which name recalls the tragic queen, and those interested may like to visit the nearby Queen's Park, with its flagpole that marks the spot where Moray based his army.

Largs, 2nd October 2 1263: Ayrshire, Strathclyde. In this last ever battle between Scotland and Norway, King Alexander III defeated King Hakon. Norway had claimed the Hebrides ever since the campaign of Magnus Barelegs in 1098, although Norsemen had had *de facto* control long before. Somerled had won his independence in 1156, but Norway still had a version of feudal superiority, recognised or not.

Alexander II of Scots had attempted a recovery and had died at Kerrera in 1249; his son Alexander III hoped to continue his father's work. He opened his assault by diplomacy, offering to buy the Hebrides from King Hakon, who rebuffed the attempt. The Earl of Ross began the second stage by bringing his men over the narrow channel to the Island of Skye to pillage burn and destroy.

King Hakon retaliated by raising a huge fleet. *Hakons Saga* gives fascinating details, but all accounts agree that there were over 100 ships, and perhaps as many as 160. They sailed to Orkney and threaded through the Isles, gathering reinforcements from those Hebrideans who either recognised Hakon as their king or who hoped for Scottish plunder.

Hakon anchored the bulk of his fleet in Lamlash Bay in Arran and remained there while Alexander sent negotiators to stall for time. Some of the Islesmen began to plunder the upper Clyde and Loch Long as Hakon up- anchored for Cumbrae. When October gales thrust some of the Norse fleet ashore at Largs, the Scots attacked in a skirmish of arrows and shouting, and the Norse sent reinforcements.

Perhaps neither side wanted full scale battle, or perhaps decades of near peace had not brought forth many skilled warriors, for the fighting was half hearted and then the Norse retreated to their ships and sailed away. Hakon died in Kirkwall on the return journey, and King Alexander continued his campaign with bickering war and the diplomacy of silver coin. In 1266, Magnus, the new Norwegian king, agreed to sell the Hebrides to Scotland, although he retained Orkney and Shetland. The chiefs of the Hebrideans continued as before, probably uncaring which distant king claimed their allegiance.

There is an obelisk at Far Bowen Craigs, just south of Largs that commemorates the battle. There are also a number of standing stones that traditionally have associations, but are probably far older. The Holm, on the north east of Great Cumbrae Island, is reputed to be the burial place of certain of the Norse, which may or may not be genuine.

Leac-a-dotha c 1467: fought in Glenorchy on the slopes of Bendoran in Lochawe, Argyll, Strathclyde. After the death of the Stewart Lord of Lorn at his wedding day, his son Dougal Stewart raised war against the MacDougalls who had killed him. A siege of Dunstaffnage having failed, Stewart and his MacLaren allies fought the MacDougalls and

MacFarlanes at Leac-a-dotha. Allan Macdougall was the victor, with around 130 MacLarens among the dead. Not unusually in the area, Colin Campbell, Lord Argyll had been behind the scenes, manipulating one clan against the other for the ultimate gain of Clan Campbell.

Leckmelm, 1585: three miles south of Ullapool, Wester Ross, Highland. This battle was fought during one of the interminable clan feuds of the sixteenth century
The Earl of Sutherland took a dislike to Clan Gunn and sent two bodies of men to attack them. The first was defeated at Allt Camhna in Caithness. The second, under James MacRorie, John Gordon of Backies and Neil MacIan MacWlliam chased the Gunns across Scotland and caught them at Leckmelm on the shores of Loch Broom. Sutherland's men won the skirmish and thirty-two Gunns were said to be killed, and George Gunn, their captain, wounded and captured.
There is a field next to the farm of Leckmelm that is known as Blar Bog, which may mean battlefield or field of blood.

Leith, 1544: north of Edinburgh. During the Rough Wooing, Henry VIII of England sent a force to capture Edinburgh and Leith. There was little opposition to the landing, and the English took Leith with the usual orgy of looting and destruction. When at attempt to take Edinburgh Castle failed the Earl of Hertford took out his frustration on what remained of Leith, and knighted many of his men amidst the burning ruin of the town. The English returned after the battle of Pinkie, again burning and looting.

Leith, April 1560: north of Edinburgh. By this year Scotland had turned Protestant and was in armed dispute with the French, or Catholic, faction. Leith was the Court and headquarters of Marie, the Queen Regent and her French army in Scotland. The Scots army of the Lords of the Congregation laid siege to the fortifications with neither skill nor success, so appealed to the auld enemy of England to help against the auld ally of France.

Lord Gray came north with an army of some 7000 men and an English fleet entered the Firth of Forth. After a skirmish at Hawkhill, the French retired behind the walls of Leith. There were a number of sallies, with minor affrays taking place around Restalrig and Leith Links while the English raised siege batteries on Leith Links. In April Admiral Winter attacked but failed to overcome Leith's *trace Italienne* fortifications and around 1000 English were killed in a May assault. The French displayed the naked corpses of the dead from the battlements. The siege lasted two months and not until Mary of Guise died of stomach cancer on the 11th June was a peace treaty signed. The Treaty of Edinburgh saw both foreign armies leave Scotland, but not before the French had plundered Leith of everything that they could.

There are two grassy mounds in Leith Links which are said to be the site of English gun emplacements from that siege.

Leith, 1650: north of Edinburgh. When Scotland accepted Charles II as their covenanted king, Oliver Cromwell brought his army north. Fresh from their savage campaign in Ireland, Cromwell's veterans were possibly the most formidable force in Europe, but Scotland prepared to resist. Directed by General David Leslie and John Mylne, the King's Master Mason, the Scots repaired the fortifications of Leith. As well as a boom to prevent a seaborne assault, Leslie created a wall and trench along the line of the present Leith Walk.

Knowing the skill of Cromwell's veterans, Leslie remained behind his defences and repulsed every attack. General Lambert won a skirmish at Lochend while Cromwell began a bombardment of St Leonard's Hill. His subsequent attack was repelled, as was a seaborne attack on Leith. Leslie sent a force of cavalry on a raid that smashed through the Cromwellian camp on the Links before retiring with a host of Puritan horse on their heels. On the 24th July Cromwell made a major assault, which was beaten back, and his army began to suffer from disease. He retreated toward Dunbar, where Leslie trapped him before enduring the defeat of Dunbar.

Lesmahagow, March 1679: Lanarkshire, Strathclyde. During the reign of King Charles II, the authorities persecuted the Presbyterian Covenanters of southwest Scotland. Tradition tells of an incident near Lesmahagow in March 1679, when Lieutenant John Dalyell and twenty dragoons confronted an armed prayer meeting. Dalyell was killed in the ensuing skirmish.

Leven, Banks of, around 877: Fife. Legendary battle when the Danes invaded Fife. King Constantine defeated them on the banks of the River Leven before being killed in a second battle in the East Neuk.

Leven, Valley of, 704; possibly Dunbartonshire, Strathclyde; in this year the *Annals of Tigernach* mentioned a 'Slaughter of the men of Dalriada in the valley of Leven.' Possibly this refers to a battle between the Britons of Strathclyde and the Scots of Dalriada.

Leys or Leysmill, January 1446: about 3 miles North West of Arbroath, Angus. Tradition says that after battle of Arbroath the defeated Ogilvies made a stand at the Leys where Lord Ogilvy himself was slain. Carrying their fallen leader, his men retreated to the sanctuary of Kinnell church. Lord Ogilvy was interred in what was called the Ogilvy aisle.

Linan an Sicathan, reported as 1106, 1286 and in the sixteenth century: Balquhidder Stirlingshire, Central. This clan battle between the Buchanans of Leny and the MacLaurins of Auchleskin arose from a minor incident. During the fair of St Kessaig at Kilmahog, a Buchanan slapped a MacLaurin with a salmon. The two clans met again at the St George's fair in Balquhidder and began to fight. The Buchanans were winning when a young MacLaurin was killed. The MacLaurin's father shouted the clan's war cry 'Craig Tuirc' and the rest of the clan rallied and attacked the Buchanans with greater fury. Those Buchanans who were not killed by the sword were forced into a rapid section of the Balvaig burn, which gained the name 'Linan-an-Seicathan', the cascade of the dead bodies. There were said to be only two Buchanan survivors, both of whom were killed later.

Lindisfarne, c 590: Northumberland, England. In the sixth century, the various peoples of Britain were still settling into their places and carving out the territories that were to become Scotland, Wales and England. Around this time the British princes Urien of Rheged and Rhydderich of Strathclyde besieged the Anglian Hussa of Bernicia in his stronghold at Lindisfarne.

Morcant, an unidentified British leader, betrayed Urien, who was killed, possibly at the mouth of the river Low opposite Lindisfarne. The death of Urien marked the beginning of the downfall of the kingdom of Rheged, which had been centred on the Solway Firth. The story bears some similarity to the end of the legendary Arthur, betrayed by Mordred. It is possible that the Arthurian tale was based on the death of Urien.

Lindores, 621, Fife: supposed battle between rival branches of the Pictish royal line. As so often in Dark Age history, details are scanty.

Links, Battle of, spring 1549: fought at Montrose, Angus. When English ships landed 800 men to attack Montrose during Henry VIII attempts to subdue Scotland, the locals retaliated. The Provost gathered the men of the town and a body of French soldiers to ambush the advancing English. There must have been some warning, for the Scots had time to dig defensive trenches. It is said that less than 100 English returned to their ships. As the English rowed for safety, a local fisherman is said to have swum out to one of their boats and bored holes in it so it sank.

Linlithgow Bridge, September 1526: Linlithgow, Central. Following the death of James IV at Flodden, Scotland was left with an infant on the throne. A dozen years of trouble followed as regents led the kingdom and political factions attempted to increase their power by controlling young James V.

In 1526 Archibald Douglas, the 6th Earl of Angus, held the king and fought off attempts from Margaret, Angus's ex-wife and mother of James, to set him free. In the autumn of 1526 the Queen Mother enlisted the support of the Earls of Lennox and Glencairn, as well as Cardinal Beaton. They raised an army reputed to be 10,000 strong but probably less, and headed toward Edinburgh where the young king was held.

The Earl of Angus ordered the Earl of Arran to prevent Lennox from reaching Edinburgh. Arran took a small force of his Hamiltons to Linlithgow Bridge, hoped for reinforcement from Angus and the Earl of Moray and waited for Lennox.

When his scouts saw Arran waiting, Lennox crossed upstream to outflank him, but Arran rearranged his men in a strong defensive position protected by the River Avon, a patch of bogland and a hill. At first Lennox was successful, pressing Arran back by sheer numbers, but Angus arrived in time to scatter Lennox's army. The Earls of Glencairn and Lennox were both murdered.

There is a cairn that is said to mark the spot where the Earl of Lennox was killed.

Lintalee, 23 April 1317. This skirmish took place between the Jed and the Lintalee Burn around two miles south of Jedburgh, Scottish Borders. During the First War of Independence, the Earl of Arundel and around 10,000 men invaded Scotland. Sir James Douglas, now the Warden of Scotland, was at his manor at Lintalee and attacked the invaders with around 200 men. He ambushed their vanguard and killed a Yorkshire knight named Thomas Richmond. When an English party under a man named Ellis moved in Lintalee Manor, Douglas returned and wiped them out. Arundel withdrew.

Little Ferry 1746, fought at Loch Fleet, Sutherland, Highland during the Jacobite Rising of 1745/6. On his way south to join the Jacobite army of Charles Edward Stuart, the Earl of Cromarty arrived at Little Ferry on the north shore of Loch Fleet. The Hanoverian Earl of Sutherland was here and attacked the Jacobites. While the Earl of Cromarty and his officers fled toward Dunrobin Castle, his men ran toward the ferry. The boat was too small so many were left on shore. There was panic, with men hacking and stabbing at each other. The action prevented reinforcements reaching the main Jacobite army.

Loch a Naig, 1610: Wester Ross, Highland. This skirmish in Glen Torridon was part of a feud between the Mackenzies and the MacLeods. Alexander Mackenzie defeated a party of MacLeods and captured John Macallan Mhic after killing around sixteen of his men. The MacLeod survivors fled.

Loch Ossian, seventeenth century: Rannoch Moor, Perthshire. This skirmish relies wholly on a tradition that states that a party of Grants came from Strathspey to rob cattle from MacDonnell of Keppoch. The MacDonnells caught them and killed a few in a skirmish. The surviving Grants reached Loch Ossian and related their tale to a party of men that they met. Unfortunately this group was also composed of MacDonnells, who had been indulging in a raid of their own. 'It is a pity,' said the MacDonnells, 'you should not join your friends,' and massacred the rest.

Lochan a' Chath, or Achan a' Chath, 1645: north of Liachan, near Achandaul, by Fort William, Highland. The name means loch of the fight, or little field of the fight and is on the upper reaches of Allt Nan Dathaddariean. It was the final stand of a party of Campbells who had survived Montrose's victory at Inverlochy. There is also Tom Na Bratach, (Mound of the Banner) which is possibly where the Campbells planted their flag before fighting to the last.

Lochindorb Castle, 1335: six miles North West of Grantown on Spey, in the Dava Moor, Grampian. This siege took place during the Second War of Independence. The patriots were rapidly recovering Scotland from Edward Balliol's English party, but Lochindorb Castle held out. Andrew Moray conducted the unsuccessful siege. Lochindorb was held by Katherine de Beaumont, the widow of David Strathbogie, Earl of Atholl, who had died in the battle of Culblean. Moray withdrew when Edward III of England led a rescue mission.

The castle is now a ruin, and as it sits on a man-made island in the loch, access is difficult, but interesting. Edward Plantagenet of England had visited the castle, and a later owner was the Wolf of Badenoch, one of the more colourful bad men of Scotland. To remove the romance, view the water dungeon, where prisoners were incarcerated in a pit where the water was waist deep.

Loch Insch, date unknown, near Kingussie, Badenoch, Highlands. This loch is the traditional site of a battle where the defeated leader was one King Harald. He was said to have sat on the hill of An Suidh, above Kincraig to watch the fighting. He must have become involved at some stage, for he was supposedly buried on the side of Craig Righ Harailt in the hills behind Dunachton. An alternative, and possibly more accurate, theory claims that the Pictish King Nectan fought two battles on the shores of Loch Insch. In his first battle he defeated the Norse, but he was less successful in a later encounter with a rival Pictish force.

Loch Leven Castle, 1301: Perth and Kinross. During the First War of Independence, Scottish patriots, possibly led by William Wallace, captured the castle. The English laid siege to Loch Leven Castle in 1301, but John Comyn came to its relief. The English were back in 1335, when Alan de Cipont held them off.

Historic Scotland now manages Loch Leven Castle, which can be visited by boat. It is probably most famous for its associations with Mary, Queen of Scots.

Lochmaben Castle, nine miles north east of Dumfries, Dumfries and Galloway. This castle was one of many that endured a succession of sieges and assaults. Captured by Edward I of England on his return from the Battle of Falkirk, Robert I of Scotland recaptured it in 1306, only to lose it to the English and regain it after Bannockburn. In 1333 the English were again in control, but Archibald the Grim, Earl of Douglas recaptured it in 1384. James II removed the castle from the Douglases in 1455, but the new owners, the Maxwells, proved equally troublesome so James VI had to besiege Lochmaben. Since that date it has been quiet.

Not surprisingly, the castle is in ruins, but can be visited.

Lochmaben, 22nd July 1484: nine miles north east of Dumfries, Dumfries and Galloway. After the Douglases fell from royal favour, the Earl fled to England. The likewise exiled Duke of Albany, Alexander Stewart, who had handed Berwick to the English and tilted for the Scottish throne, soon joined him there. In July 1484 Richard III of England had given Douglas and Albany them his support and sent them northward with 500 men.

The Earls managed to reach the area of Lochmaben, where most of the population were at a fair. A rapid mustering of the Annandale men proved too weak to repel the raid, but when some royal troops appeared the invaders were gradually pushed across the Annan. When the local Maxwells joined in, Douglas and Albany were defeated. Robert and Edward Crichton, members of the Sanquhar branch of the family, were later granted charters for their part in the action. Alexander Kirkpatrick took the Earl prisoner and was rewarded with lands worth £100 a year 'to instigate others...to perform such services in future' Albany escaped to France and was later mortally wounded in a tournament. The nearby Merkland cross commemorates the death of Lord Maxwell.

Lochore Castle, Fife; situated on an island in a now drained loch. Local folklore claims that this was the site of a battle between Romans and Caledonians. The name has been changed from Inchgall, *island of the strangers*, and what remains of the castle is in Lochore Meadows Country Park

Loch Arklet, 711: Trossachs, Central. This was a legendary battle near Inversnaid, in which the Dalriadic Scots defeated the Britons. The *An-*

nals of Tigernach record this as the battle of Loireclat. This area seems to be thick with legendary encounters for which no real evidence exists, for instance the Spout of Blairessan at nearby Blairessan which was said to be the site of an encounter between Romans and Caledonians. There was yet a third legendary battle in 717 at Minvircc or Minuirc, which may refer to Clach-na-Breaton, the old boundary stone between Scottish Dalriada and British Strathclyde. As the Dalriads under Selbach again defeated the Strathclyde Britons, this may be another telling of the same battle.

Lochryan, c 841: Dumfries and Galloway. Legend speaks of a skirmish here when King Alpin of Dalriada led a raid into what would be Strathclyde or possibly Norse territory. It is possible that there was an ambush at a farm now named Little Laight, but originally termed Lacht Alpin, or Alpin's grave.

Loch Ryan, 10th February 1307: Dumfries and Galloway. This incident in the First War of Independence was more a massacre than a battle. Alexander and Thomas Bruce, brothers of the king, landed in Galloway with eighteen ships full of Hebrideans and Irishmen. The Bruces were supported by Sir Reginald Crawford and the Irish sub-king, Malcolm MacQuillan. They were attacked and defeated by the Macdoualls under their chief Dungal, allied with the MacCanns. The Bruce brothers were sent captive to Carlisle, where Edward Plantagenet ordered them executed along with Crawford and MacQuillan.

Loch Sallachie, 1516: Sutherland, Highland. With the Earl of Sutherland in Edinburgh, John Mackay of Strathnaver sent his brothers William and Donald to raid his lands in Sutherland. John Murray, acting on behalf of the earl, gathered a force and met the Mackays at Loch Sallachie. William and Donald Mackay were among the Mackay dead, but John Roy-Murray, brother of John Murray, was also killed.

Lon Harpasdal, 1426, Caithness, Highland. This battle occurred when Angus Dow Mackay raided into Caithness for plunder. The local men gathered at Harpasdal and there was a battle with many casualties. The King intervened and placed the son of Angus, Neil Mackay, into prison on the Bass Rock.

Lora, 573 AD, supposedly fought in Kintyre, Strathclyde, this extremely obscure battle was presumed to be a defeat for Duncan MacConail MacCongail

Loudon Hill, 1296: two and a half miles east of Darvel, Ayrshire, Strathclyde. This is a prominent, if small hill near the A71. During the early stages of the First War of Independence, William Wallace is reported to have defeated an English force in a skirmish at this site. Blind Harry's poem mentions picturesque details, but it appears that Wallace ambushed a supply column for Ayr near the pass known as the Winny Wizzen and killed the commander, a man named Fenwick.

Loudon Hill, 10 May 1307; near Darvel, Ayrshire, Strathclyde. This battle of the First War of Independence was significant as it showed that King Robert I could defeat an English army in the open field. Having returned to mainland Scotland from the Hebrides, King Robert won a skirmish at Glentrool and moved north to Ayrshire. His next step toward removing the English came at Loudon Hill. His opponent here was Amyer de Valence, Earl of Pembroke, the victor of Methven. King Robert positioned his army at the head of a narrow track, which had an area of bogland on either side. He added a number of ditches between the road and the bog to ensure that the English had to advance along a narrow front. Then he formed his men into a compact body and waited.
Valence had around 3000 men, eager to fight the Scots. As his outer horsemen hit the ditches, he was forced into tighter ranks, and King Robert had the Scots press forward, breaking the English organisation. The English at the rear began to run first, and then the remainder of Valence's force broke, with Valence fleeing to Bothwell Castle.

Dance If Ye Can

Loup Hill, May 1689: Kintyre, Strathclyde. This was a small skirmish in the first Jacobite war in which a Williamite force dispersed a small group of Jacobites. Casualties were minimal, yet the encounter was enough to push the Jacobites from the peninsula, which remained firmly in Williamite hands for the remainder of the campaign.

Lumphanan, 15 August 1057; Deeside, Mar, about 27 miles west of Aberdeen and three miles north west of Torphins. Returning from exile in England with an English army, Malcolm Canmore and King MacBeth fought first at Dunsinane and then, as Macbeth withdrew north, at Lumphanan. It seems to have been a minor affair, but MacBeth was mortally wounded and died soon after. Malcolm Canmore was now king and he began the long agony of removing the Gaelic culture from the mainstream of Scotland.

The village of Lumphanan has access to the battlefield, and other memorials are Macbeth's Well and the stone on which he was allegedly beheaded. There is also a cairn to mark where Macbeth died, ending a reign of seventeen years. Although Shakespeare's version is better known, it seems that Macbeth was a successful mediaeval king.

Luncarty, around 998: four miles north of Perth. Although some historians are doubtful that this battle ever took place, and no physical evidence has been found, tradition rates it highly and it seems to have been remembered more than others that may have more historical importance.

According to tradition, Kenneth III defeated the Danes, who were besieging Perth. As King Kenneth ruled from 997 to 1005, the battle would have occurred between those years, if the tradition was accurate. Most of the legend centres on the part played by a small band of men who attacked the right wing of the Danish army and turned almost certain defeat into victory. King Kenneth later rewarded the leader of that band with lands, and he founded the Hay family. That tale is almost certainly apocryphal.

More important was the part played by the future King Malcolm II, who commanded the right wing of the Scottish army. Whether or not the battle ever took place, or when, the legend does highlight the fact that Malcolm II was a warrior. Another tradition states that the Scots fought under the old royal standard of the wild boar, which indicates a date before the widespread use of the Saltire.

Lyne Water, 1308, Scottish Borders. In this skirmish of the First War of Independence, James Douglas defeated a party of Lothian men who were fighting for England. When the Lothian men were sheltering inside a building beside the Lyne Water, three miles from Peebles, Douglas ambushed them. He killed a few, but most escaped. In this encounter Douglas captured Alexander Stewart of Bunkle and Thomas Randolph, Bruce's nephew. Both later became prominent fighting for Robert I.

M

Mag Rath, c 637, also known as Moira: County Down, Ireland. This nearly forgotten battle was significant as it marks the withdrawal of Dalriada from Ireland. It seems that Domnall Brecc, King of Dalriada, supported Congall, King of Dal nAraide in this fight with Aed, the Ui Neill High King of Tara. It is possible that Dal nAraide were of the Cruithni people, which would make them kin to the Picts who lived in what is now Scotland, who were also known as Cruithni.

Mair, the, 1548: also called St Ninian's Mair, near St Monans, Fife. Mair was the local pronunciation of moor. This skirmish occurred during King Henry VIII's invasion of Scotland. Lord Clinton led English troops from their base at Inchkeith to land on the beach east of St Monans, probably intending to loot for supplies or, as Pitscottie said, capture Pittenweem and ravage further in Fife. Some accounts claim there were 1200 soldiers, others say as little as 1000 or as many as 5000. When the local laird sounded a horn to warn of the English landing, the seventeen-year-old Lord James Stewart with the Laird of Wemyss and the Prior of St Andrews raised a small force to defend the area. The Scots used straw-filled trenches to create a smokescreen to block the English archers while the local women sheltered behind a hill and made enough noise to convince the English of the imminent arrival of reinforcements. As the Scots attacked, the English retreated. The reported casualty list of some 600 English seems remarkably high.

Mam Garb, 31 July 1187: near Inverness, Highland, possibly Strath Garve, west of Strathpeffer. William I was not the best of Scotland's kings, despite being the first to bring the rampant lion onto the flag. He did not fare well in his expeditions into England, selling the independence of the realm to secure his own freedom, but he usually managed to quell any rebellion with adequate ruthlessness.
In the 1180s, Donald MacWilliam, a descendant of Malcolm Canmore through his first wife, rose in rebellion. The rebellion was centred in Moray and lasted a number of years before Roland of Galloway was sent north with an army of three thousand men to hunt Donald MacWilliam down. Roger of Howden related how Roland came across Donald at Mam Garb or Mamgarvia Moor and defeated him. Donald MacWilliam was killed in the battle, and his brother hanged at his side. Donald's head was given to the king as proof of death.

Man, 1158; The *Chronicles of Man* stated:
In the year 1158 Somerled came to Man with 53 ships and joined battle with Godred and put him to flight. He ravaged the whole island and went away.
Somerled seems to have been making sure of his claim to the southern Hebrides, or perhaps just making his mark.

Manau, 578: fought in an unknown location on the Isle of Man. Aedan Macgabhran of Dalriada won a battle, possibly against Baetan Mac Cairill of Dal Fiatach, another small Irish kingdom. It is also possible that this battle was the same as one fought in 582, which Aidan also won, after the death of Baetan. Despite the lack of detail these expeditions reveal the maritime power that Dalriada possessed.

Manau; Plain of, c 672: West Lothian or Central. As with so much in this period, details of this battle are scanty and facts remote. The available evidence suggests that the Northumbrian Angles held some sort of overlordship over the Picts, but in 672 the Picts rose in revolt. The Northumbrians defeated them on the Plain of Manau, which may be the area near Falkirk. One account said that two rivers were filled with the corpses of the Pictish dead, so this battle could be that recorded as the Battle of Two Rivers.

Manau, Plain of, 711. This battle was presumably fought in Central or West Lothian, which seems to have been a turbulent frontier area between the Picts and Northumbrians. Although the Picts had recently thrown out the Northumbrians at the battle of Dunnichen, this round went to Northumbria.

Mauchline Moor, around 787: Ayrshire, Strathclyde. Local legend mentions a battle here between a Pictish army and one from Strathclyde. The Strathclyde men apparently won.

Mauchline Moor, 12th June 1648: south of Mauchline, Ayrshire, Strathclyde. The 1640s were times of extreme turbulence in Scotland. In 1648 many men were unhappy that the Scottish authorities supported Charles II, and complained about this Engagement with Royalty. Around 2,000 of these anti-Engagers gathered on Mauchline Moor. The authorities sent Major General John Middleton to monitor events, or possibly to break up the gathering. Not surprisingly there was trouble, and Middleton won the day, with about 30 killed or wounded between the two armies. Another 65 anti-Engagers were taken to Ayr for trial.

There is a Covenanters flag hanging in the church at nearby Mauchline.

Megray Hill, 15th June 1639: north of Stonehaven, Grampian. In this minor skirmish at the very start of the First Bishop's War, the Covenanters defeated the Royalist Colonel William Gunn.

When King Charles attempted to introduce Episcopalian practises to the Church of Scotland, the Scots responded by drawing up the

Covenant and raising an army. The Royalist lairds and lords gathered their forces in Aberdeenshire. There were around 2,500 Royalists, mainly infantry, and when they met the more professional Covenanters of Aboyne at Megray Hill, a great many simply ran away. It was a skirmish with few casualties and the remains of the Royalist army retired to Aberdeen.

Melrose, 1322: Scottish Borders. During the latter stages of the First War of Independence, the Scots were in the ascendancy. Knowing that Edward II was planning an invasion, King Robert entered England, burned Preston and Lancaster, and returned to prepare Scotland for the English. Edward II marched as far as Edinburgh, to find that the ground had been cleared of crops and livestock so his army suffered from famine. On their retreat they attempted to sack Melrose Abbey, but Douglas ambushed them and killed many of their light horsemen. King Robert followed their retreat with a strong raid to Rievaulx and Byland.

Melrose, 1378: Scottish Borders. When an English force raided into Scotland, Archibald the Grim, Earl of Douglas, and the Earl of March defeated them near Melrose. They ransomed their captives, which caused the English to complain that "the Earl of March and Douglas, and the latter's cousin Sir Archibald...are harassing the English Borderers by imprisonment, ransoms, and otherwise."

Merchiston, 1571: Edinburgh. During the Long Siege of Edinburgh Castle, William Kirkcaldy of Grange, fighting for Queen Mary, bombarded Merchiston Castle with its Kingsman garrison. Merchiston guarded the southern approach to the city.

Merchiston, 5th May 1572: Edinburgh. Kingsmen from Leith supporting the Protestant King James VI, repulsed an assault by Kirkcaldy's Queensmen, who supported the Catholic Queen Mary. They repeated their success five days later. However, it was not all bad news for the queen, for there was yet another skirmish at Merchiston on the 31st May when the Queensmen were victorious.

Methven, 19th June 1306: eight miles east of Perth, Perthshire. This battle was fought during the First War of Independence. Soon after the coronation of King Robert I at Scone, he gathered his army and sought to challenge the occupying English. De Valence, Earl of Pembroke had taken Perth. Barbour says that Bruce requested that de Valence should leave the walls of Perth and fight a chivalrous battle in the open, but the Englishman declined, claiming that he did not fight on a Sunday. King Robert took de Valence at his word and retired to his camp at Methven, where the English attacked. These details may be true, or merely an attempt to excuse a Scottish defeat caused by failure to post pickets.

Barrow is probably more accurate when he suggests that King Robert's army was scattered, with some men foraging and others in bed when de Valence attacked. The English won well, killing many and capturing a number of high ranked men including Thomas Randolph and Alexander Fraser. Bruce managed to escape with about 500 men, only to fall victim to the MacDougalls at Dalrigh. Professor Barrow suggests that these two battles may have saved Scotland by turning Bruce from an orthodox commander to the superb guerrilla leader that he became.

Mingary Castle: Ardnamurchan, Highland. This castle on the most westerly promontory of the Scottish mainland has witnessed some stirring events. In 1515 Sir Donald MacDonald of Lochalsh laid siege to MacIain of Ardnamurchan in Mingary, but was repelled, to return and capture the castle in 1517. Again in 1588, during a MacLean-MacDonald feud Sir Lachlan MacLean besieged Mingary. A hundred Spanish soldiers helped him, part of the crew from a ship that survived the scattering of the Armada ship, and sheltered in Tobermory Bay. A force of MacDonalds and their allies chased the besiegers away. The Campbells of Cawdor successfully attacked Mingary in 1612, and repelled a MacDonald counter in 1622. However, Alastair MacColla

MacDonald captured Mingary in 1644, only for General David Leslie to retake it in 1647.

Now a picturesque ruin, the castle can be visited.

Moiry Pass, 25th May 1315. This battle of Edward Bruce was fought in Armagh, Ireland during the War of Independence. When the O'Neills of Ulster asked for aid against English, the Scots saw the opportunity to open a second front, using the Irish discontent against their English and Anglo-Norman overlords. Edward Bruce and Thomas Randolph of Moray landed with an expeditionary force at Larne and soon after won the battle of Moiry Pass.

Monacrib, c727. This battle was part of a civil war between various claimants for the throne of the Picts. Hungus, Oengus or Ungus of the Picts defeated Elpin, also of the Picts. One traditional battle site was at Moncrieff in Strathearn.

Monadh-Carno; or Mornith Carno c 729: possibly near Loch Insch, Badenoch, Highland, where the Pictish King Nechtan traditionally fought at least one battle. One version states that Oengus defeated Nechtan and the tribute collectors of Nechtan were killed. Another version claims that the battle was fought in the Carse of Gowrie, at Moncur or Moncur Castle near the Sidlaw Hills, and says that Hungus defeated his rival Nechtan.

Mondynes, 12 November 1094: about twenty miles south of Aberdeen. After King Malcolm III died at Alnwick, his brother Donald took the throne. Duncan, Malcolm's son by his first wife, had lived in the English court as a hostage, and now returned with Anglo-Norman help to depose Donald. It seems that Duncan was not popular in Scotland, possibly because of his English connections, and an army led by the local mormaer, Duncan's half-brother Edmund, backed by Donald, faced him at Mondynes. It is unclear how much Anglo-Norman help Duncan had at this battle, but he was clearly defeated.

There is a standing stone in a field at Mill of Mondynes, and local legend says that Duncan was buried underneath. The same legend claims that the stone must be kept whitewashed.

Mons Graupius: 84. The location of this battle is uncertain but was presumably in eastern Scotland north of Dundee. It was fought between the invading Romans under Agricola and an army of Caledonians under a man known only as Calgacus, the Swordsman.
In 78 AD the Romans were already firmly in control of much of southern Britain. The governor of Britannia, Julius Agricola, began a series of campaigns that were intended to complete the conquest of the British mainland. By the end of 83 the Romans seem to have been in the Mearns and had constructed a line of forts along the southern edge of the Highlands, centred on the legionary fortress of Inchtuthill south of Dunkeld. In 84 the Romans again pushed north, supported by their fleet.
The Caledonians conducted a guerrilla war, hitting isolated portions of the Roman army but not yet facing the professional soldiers in a major battle. One Caledonian attack penetrated the encampment of the 9th Legion in Strathearn, and inflicted some casualties before being repulsed.
Calgacus eventually faced Agricola at Mons Graupius. The Caledonians sent their wives and children to a place of safety and massed to stop the invader. The battle was fought between the hills and the sea, with dense woodland behind the Caledonians. Tacitus, Agricola's son in law and perhaps not the most unbiased of chroniclers, says that Calgacus had 30,000 warriors. Agricola had about 8000 soldiers and stationed his 3000 horse in the wings and the iron-clad legions in the centre. The bulk of the Caledonians were on rising ground behind their charioteers, who were on the plain. By this period, chariots were an anachronism in battle, but it seems that the Caledonians were skilled in their use. The infantry waited, armed with spears or long swords and small shields.

The Romans began with a volley of missiles that the Caledonians avoided, and replied with a shower of spears of their own. It is possible that the presence of the chariots obstructed the movements of the Caledonian infantry as they descended slowly from the hill, and then charged. There is no doubting the bravery of the Caledonians, but the Roman legionnaires were professionals in an army that had made its name defeating undisciplined peoples. The Caledonian's long swords were unwieldy before the tall shields and stabbing swords of the legions and they were forced to retreat. They 'fled to the woods' but retained their spirit, ambushing any Romans that followed.

According to Tacitus, around two thirds of the Caledonians escaped, probably including Calgacus. After the battle Agricola may have returned to his base in central Scotland.

Montrose, April 1644. Angus. During the civil wars of the mid seventeenth century, a royalist force under Irvine of Drum and Nathaniel Gordon stormed and captured the town.

Montrose, 1745: Angus. During the Jacobite Rising of 1745, Montrose tended to favour the Stuart, or Jacobite, cause. The Royal Navy sent HMS *Hazard* to bombard the town, but the Jacobites, with French help managed to capture her. In a later encounter HMS *Milford* sank the French vessel *Le Fine* in the North Esk River at Montrose.

Monzievaird, 25 March 1005; possibly fought north of Crieff in Strathearn, Perthshire. This battle seems to have been a straightforward dynastic struggle between Malcolm II and Kenneth III. Malcolm killed Kenneth and his son Giric at Monzievaird. He ensured that his own dynasty would continue by also eliminating Kenneth's grandson, and probably just about anybody else who could possibly have a claim to the throne. Malcolm seems to have been a ruthless, but highly successful king who expanded and consolidated the borders of Scotland against opposition from Norse and English.

Mortlach, 1010: possibly Mortlich 4 miles west of Dufftown, Moray. This was one of Malcolm II's victories over the Danes. A Danish force had invaded Moray and captured the castles of Elgin, Nairn and Forres. Malcolm marched through Glenfiddich to meet them at Conval. On seeing the Scots, the Danes retreated toward Balvenie Castle, with Malcolm in pursuit. Traditional accounts state that the armies met beside the Dullan Water, near an outcrop of rock known as the Giant's Chair. The Danes seem to have repelled the initial Scottish attack, killing two of the Scottish leaders, but a second attack was more successful and Malcolm is said to have thrown a Danish leader from his horse and personally strangled him. Tradition also claims that the Scots dug pits into which the Danish bodies were thrown, which sounds suspiciously like a repeat of the Battle of Bloody Pits

Mount Blair, Angus, this hill was the traditional site of a battle between the Picts and the Vikings in the ninth century, but unfortunately there seems no historical evidence to back the claim.

Moy, Rout of, 16th February 1746: Invernesshire. This incident occurred during the last few weeks of the 1745 Jacobite Rising. Hearing that Prince Charles was at Moy House, Lord Loudon, at Inverness with government troops, marched to capture him. The Hanoverians were mainly MacLeods, with a piper, Donald Ban MacCrimmon in the van. Lady Macintosh, who was a Farquharson of Invercauld by birth, ran through Moy House in her petticoats and ordered her retainers to watch for the attack. A blacksmith, Donald Fraser and five men fired at the advancing Hanoverians and killed the piper. When Loudon's men heard the defenders call on imaginary clans to help, they believed that they were outnumbered and withdrew.

Mugdock, 750: Stirlingshire, Central. There is a tradition of a battle here, with various versions and indeed names. In one, Tuedebar of Strathclyde defeated Oengus MacFergus, King of the Picts. In another the Scots defeated the Picts at Mygedawg, which is supposed to be Mugdock and in a third King Tuedebar defeated Talorgan of the Picts. It seems that Tuedebar of Strathclyde did defeat the famous Angus MacFergus of the Picts, who in 756 allied himself with Eadberrht of Northumbria and again attacked Dumbarton, only to be defeated again.

Mulroy, 4th August 1688: Inverness-shire. The MacDonnells of Keppoch and some Camerons defeated the Macintoshes in what may have been the last clan battle. The battle was fought on a small height above Roy Bridge. The Mackintoshes and MacDonnells of Keppoch were at feud, and Macintosh, with some government troops under Captain Mackenzie of Suddie marched to Brae Lochaber to drive the MacDonnells out of district. The Macintoshes were winning until one man turned the tide and the MacDonnells gained heart. The Macintoshes fled, leaving their chief a prisoner. There is a cairn with a plaque to commemorate this encounter.

Muness Castle, 1608: four miles from the pier at Belmont, Unst, Shetland. This most northerly castle in Scotland was built for Laurence Bruce, Sheriff of Shetland at the end of the sixteenth century, but he fell out with his half brother, Earl Patrick Stewart. The Earl invaded Unst with 36 men and cannon, intending to capture the castle, but he inexplicably changed his mind and withdrew. In 1627 the French arrived in Unst and burned down the castle.
Historic Scotland manages this most interesting castle.

Myton, 20th September 1319, also known as the Chapter of Myton: Myton-on-Swale, North Yorkshire, England. During the First War of Independence, the English under King Edward II and Earl Thomas of Lancaster were besieging Berwick. King Robert I sent Sir James Douglas and the Earl of Moray to raid deep into England as a diversion. The Scots drove down nearly as far as York, where Edward II's Queen Isabella was residing. Fearing capture, she fled to Nottingham. The Archbishop of York gathered a force of townsfolk, priests and monks and challenged the Scots at Myton on Swale.
The English fought under the archbishop's silver crucifix, but the contest was uneven. Douglas set fire to damp hayricks and let the smoke blow in English faces and waited in a schiltron for the English to advance. When the Scots yelled their battle cry the English fled, the Scots

pursued and cut off English retreat at a bridge over Swale. William Ayreminne, Edward's Keeper of the Rolls was captured and the Mayor of York was killed. When news of the rout reached the English camp at Berwick, there were serious disputes. The Earl of Lancaster and a large part of the army left to defend northern England and King Edward had to abandon the siege.

N

Neidpath Castle, 1650: about two miles west of Peebles, Peeblesshire, Scottish Borders. During the civil wars of the mid seventeenth century, Hay of Neidpath, Earl of Tweeddale, commanded a regiment for King Charles. After the battle of Dunbar, Cromwell's army attacked Neidpath Castle, which surrendered after a brief bombardment.
There is a car park at this castle, which is open to the public.
Nesbit Muir, August 1355: Berwickshire, Scottish Borders. After a brief truce, the Second War of Independence resumed in August 1335 with raids and counter raids across the border. William Ramsay of Dalhousie commanded the first Scottish probe, which was so successful it even fought off an ambush and captured Sir Thomas Gray, Warden of Norham Castle and future historian. William, Lord of Douglas defeated the English counter raid in a neat little battle at Nesbit Muir in Berwickshire.

Nesbit Muir, 22nd June 1402. Berwickshire, Scottish Borders. The fifteenth century began with warfare between Scotland and England. After the dispossessed Earl of March had led an English raid into Lothian, Sir Patrick Hepburn of Hailes took a retaliatory force south. He was badly defeated at Nesbit, where the English captured many knights and gentlemen.
Neville's Cross, 17th October 1346, near Durham, England. Although this battle of the Second War of Independence is largely forgotten in Scotland, it was a major defeat that saw the capture of the Scottish

king. In early 1346 the English had been virtually expelled from Scotland and the country was enjoying a period of peace and optimism. There was a truce with England, but when the English invaded France with a huge army, King Philip implored King David of Scots to 'remember the bonds of blood and friendship between us.' Not for the last time, the Scots prepared to sacrifice their men for the sake of an ally. After a couple of successful raids, King David II invaded England with 12,000 men. Right from the start there was trouble as rival factions bickered, but David drove south, looting and destroying. By the middle of October the Scots were near Durham, and the English had gathered their own forces to oppose him. Henry Percy and Ralph Neville commanded the English, supported by William de la Zouche, Archbishop of York. King David was so poor a commander that he neglected to post scouts and only learned of the English presence when their rearguard badly mauled a foraging force under William Douglas of Liddesdale.

Once informed, however, David formed the Scots into three battalions of spearmen, but he placed them on rough land where advance was difficult. The English were also in three, albeit much smaller, battalions and for a while both armies merely watched each other. When the English moved forward and began the nearly inevitable arrow storm the Scots began a slow advance, hampered by the terrain. As soon as the arrows and ground broke the tight schiltrons, the Scots were vulnerable to the English men at arms. The Steward and Patrick of Dunbar were among the first to flee, but David fought as long as he could, ignoring the arrows that lodged in his body, but when he fled he was surrounded and captured, fighting furiously. In courage at least he was his father's son, but he paid for his lack of military skill with eleven years of English captivity.

Scotland had paid a heavier price, with a host of the leading lords killed as well as an unknown number of men with lesser rank. In addition the English captured the Black Rood of St Margaret. There is a waymarked battlefield trail and interpretation panels on the field.

Newburn, 28th August 1640, also known as Stella Haughs: Tyneside, England. This skirmish was the only action of note during the Second Bishop's War, when King Charles I attempted to impose an Episcopalian system of religion on Scotland. Expecting compliance, instead he got the Covenanters, as much of the country signed a covenant pledging to defend the Presbyterian faith.

When King Charles continued to force the issue, Alexander Leslie led a Covenanter army of some 20,000 over the border toward Newcastle. Charles had a small royal force of perhaps 15,000 men in the area and a few thousand defended the fords near Newburn. The Covenanters, blue ribbons tied in their bonnets above their left ears, marched on, with James Graham, Earl of Montrose in the van. Leslie positioned his musketeers around the village of Newburn and his artillery to cover the ford over the Tyne. Lord Conway, in command of the royal troops, had explicit orders to fight. When Leslie sent a herald to ask Conway for permission to cross peaceably, Conway refused, and his English soldiers jeered as the herald rode back.

As a lone Covenanting officer rode into the ford, one of the defenders killed him. Leslie ordered a small body of his horse to cross but Royalist cannon repelled them. The Scottish cannon opened up and in a three hour barrage the Covenanters badly damaged the English positions. Many English deserted and Leslie sent in another body of horse, which the English countered with a charge of cavalry. The Scots withdrew and continued with the artillery barrage and then a general advance. An English cavalry charge on the Scottish Life Guards was repelled and the English foot ran. Their attempt at an ambush was defeated and the Scottish Covenanters had won the day.

In sharp contrast to the later behaviour by English armies, Leslie ordered that the prisoners should be well treated and then released, and the fleeing English were allowed to escape. The Covenanters captured Newcastle and dictated terms to King Charles.

Much of the site can still be visited.

Norham, 28th August 1513: Northumberland. In this minor prelude to the debacle of Flodden, James IV captured Norham Castle, the ruins of which still stand beside the Tweed. English Heritage manages the castle, which can be visited.

North Inch, 1396: Perth. In a battle more famous in literature than history, this encounter seems to have been an attempt by the king to settle a feud by a chivalric contest. Two clans, reputed to be Chattan and Kay, or Mackay and Chattan, each picked 30 warriors to fight to the death in North Inch; a flat meadow by the Tay at Perth.

Accounts given of this battle vary. Wyntoun says it was between clan Qwhewyl and clan Ha, and that the opposing sides fought within barriers and fifty or more of the combatants were slain, but he did not say who won. Bower, who wrote around 1455, says the Clan Kay and Clan Quhele agreed to settle their quarrel before the King at Perth by a combat between thirty chosen men on either side, armed only with their bows and arrows, swords and without their plaids. Of the sixty, all but one of Clan Kay was slain, but eleven of Clan Quhele survived. Maurice Buchanan in 1461 in the *Book of Pluscarden* says the fight was between the captain of the rival clans and their most valiant friends, with swords and bows, each having no more than three arrows. He says five on one side and two on the other lived.

It is even possible that the clans were Mackintoshes and Macphersons. There is a tradition that the *feadan dubh*, the black chanter of the Macphersons, was played to encourage the clan. The fact that these clans agreed to the contest says something about the barbarity of the age. The fact that King Robert III and his court watched this gladiatorial contest says more; late mediaeval Scotland was not a quiet place in which to live. The North Inch is now a public park, with open access to the battle site.

O

Old Cockpool, April 1570: Dumfries and Galloway. With Queen Mary in England, there were various attempts in Scotland to gain her return.

In order to keep the pro-Marian nobles quiet, Queen Elizabeth of England sent Lord Scrope over the border to waste their lands.

Scrope entered Scotland on 18th April and camped at Ecclefechan. On 20th April he sent Simon Musgrave to despoil the country. Musgrave burned his way through the South West until he reached Old Cockpool, where he had the best of a skirmish with Lord Maxwell and had taken 100 Scottish prisoners before the Maxwells rallied and drove him back. At another encounter near Cumertrees Musgrave claimed to have captured several lairds.

Orra, April 1583, also known as Aura: Ulster, Sorley Boy MacDonnell and Clan Donald defeat O'Neill and the McQuillans. It was fought at Slieve-an-Aura (Sieveanorra), the Hill of Battle.

Turlough O'Neill had hired a number of MacDonnell men for a separate war, so the MacQuillans attacked Clan Donald in Ulster. Sir Hugh O'Niall of Edenduffcarraig joined the MacQuillans, who were also helped by two English companies under Captain Thomas Chatterton. Sorley Boy MacDonnell had only a small force of lightly armed men, presumably because his Gallowglass, heavy infantry, were fighting for O'Neill. He tricked the MacQuillans into charging across a bog where their heavy Gallowglass and English cavalry floundered. The light MacDonnell infantry cut them up. Hugh O'Niall and Chatterton turned tail and ran, but the MacDonnells caught and killed both. Rory MacQuillan was also killed in the pursuit.

Otterburn, 15th August 1388: also known as Chevy Chase; this battle was fought a mile north west of Otterburn in Northern England and was less an international encounter than another episode in the cross border feud between the English Percies and the Scottish Douglases. On this occasion the Douglases won.

James Earl of Douglas had taken an army into the Percy lands of Northumberland, burning what he could not steal. It was a successful raid that netted much plunder and more prestige, and Douglas also gained the standard of Henry Percy, better known as Hotspur.

The Percies were as valiant as the Douglases. Hotspur whistled up his followers and followed the Scots until the two armies clashed in the wild moorland at Otterburn, not far from the Roman Wall. Neither side had thought of peace, nor, it seems, of tactics, for they fought at close quarters by moonlight. As so often in a close fight, the Scots won, but they paid a high price. Legend says that Douglas and Percy fought hand to hand, and Douglas was wounded three times. He died on the battlefield, but had his men call 'Douglas!' to keep up their spirits and eventually the Percies were defeated. Henry Percy surrendered to the bush that hid the dead body of his adversary and the Douglases returned to Scotland with their booty. Perhaps the *Ballad of Otterburn* is too kind in its remembrance of chivalry, but it does not shirk from the bloodshed and slaughter that stained the old border.

There is a car park off the A696, a mile north west of Otterburn. There is also the Percy's Cross Memorial.

P

Palm Sunday, 1429: location unknown. This clan battle was fought between the Mackintoshes and Camerons. Like so many clan battles, this one is confusing. It seems that members of Clan Cameron were assembled in a church and some of the Mackintoshes attacked and set fire to the building. Another account points to a battle fought on this day, in which the Mackintosh were victorious, but also took casualties

Perth, 7/8th January 1313: King Robert I captured the town. During the First War of Independence the English had fortified Perth with some care, adding stone walls and towers to its moat and river. Perth was in an obviously strategic situation, as the lowest bridging point of the River Tay. Augmenting the strength of the town was the calibre of its governor. Sir William Oliphant had earned his fame when he defended Stirling Castle against King Edward I on behalf of King John Balliol. Released after four years in an English dungeon, he now held Perth for Edward II.

When King Robert arrived the siege was a few weeks old and he gave orders for the men to withdraw. The defenders, Scots and English scoffed, his own men would have complained, but Robert merely marched them a few miles away and returned on a dark night a short time later. Leading from the front, King Robert waded the winter Tay, clambered over the walls and killed those of the garrison who did not surrender.

Taking Oliphant prisoner, he ordered that the walls should be thrown down.

Perth, 1339. During the Second War of Independence, Sir Thomas Ughtred held Perth for the English-Balliol faction. In April of 1339 the Steward began to besiege Perth, with a French flotilla ensuring no supplies could come by sea. The Earl of March and a body of French soldiers helped Stewart. The Scots starved out the defenders, drained the moat and began digging mines beneath the walls. Still Ughtred held out, until all the surrounding country was wasted and there were rumours of cannibalism. It was not until August that he surrendered, and his English soldiers were permitted to return home.

Philliphaugh, 13th September 1645: near Selkirk, Scottish Borders. This battle was the last of Montrose's campaign of 1644 and 1645. He had beaten army after Covenanting army until his Ulstermen and Highlanders were sated with loot. After the victory at Kilsyth many returned home, the Gordons withdrew to Aberdeenshire and Alasdair MacColla MacDonald took many of his Ulstermen to the west.

With around 500 Ulster MacDonalds commanded by Magnus O'Cahan, and perhaps 100 Scottish cavalry, Montrose headed south, toward the Border. He reached Philliphaugh, near Selkirk, and encamped. It was there that David Leslie found him, the Covenanting scouts locating the royalists despite the mist that slithered down from the border hills. Leslie had an army of 6000, many of them veteran of the English campaigns.

Montrose fought. His cavalry charged, to be swallowed by the Covenanting horse so that half were killed or unhorsed. Then Leslie

Dance If Ye Can

thrust on over the Highland and Irish foot. Around 450 of the royalists were killed fighting, the remainder after they surrendered, on the orders of the ministers that accompanied Leslie's army. Around 300 women and children, camp followers, wives, sons and daughters, shared the fate of their men. Montrose tried to fight to the end but he was pushed on to a horse and led away as his army died where it stood. There is a cairn to commemorate the Covenanter victors at Philliphaugh, which stands beside Harehead Wood

Pinkie, 10th September 1547: fought beside Musselburgh, East Lothian. When Henry VIII decided that his baby son should marry the infant Mary, Queen of Scots, he would accept no refusal. He sent his armies north to convince the Scots of the sense of the match. In September 1547 the Earl of Somerset invaded with 18,000 men, partly to break French influence in Scotland, partly to break Scotland's will. The English army marched up the East March with a fleet guarding the right flank, wiping out anything that stood in its path.
The Earl of Arran collected an army of about 30,000 and faced Somerset at Pinkie. Somerset refused a request by the Earl of Huntly for a personal duel, and when Hume's border riders sallied out, they were beaten off in a smart little skirmish. The Earl of Angus forsook his advantageous position with secure flanks ad launched an attack. While the English ships battered the Scottish left with their cannon, the Scots broke the English horse but fell before superior artillery and gunfire. Once again the long-range tactics of the English proved superior, and when the spearmen were thinned the English horse returned to carve up the survivors.
More died in the retreat than in the battle, for the English gave no quarter and an estimated 10,000 Scots died, with another 1500 captured. During the battle the local people of Tranent hid in the mine workings, but the English lit fires at the entrances and suffocated them. They showed more clemency toward Edinburgh, but the Scots had been beaten in a battle, not in a war, and refused to hand their queen

to the mercy of an English king who clearly had no concept of the meaning of the word.

It was the Earl of Huntly, a participant in the battle, who made the sardonic quip: 'I like not this wooing' and gave this period in Scottish-English relations its name of the Rough Wooing. Pinkie was the last major battle between Scotland and England. The English won the battle but, as usual, ultimately lost the war.

This battle was seminal in Britain, as the English had a renaissance army that combined horse, foot and artillery, while the Scots continued to fight with mediaeval tactics. There is a memorial stone in Crookstone Road in Musselburgh.

Piperdean, 15 September 1436: near Cockburnspath, Berwickshire, Scottish Borders. Scots under William, Second Earl of Angus defeated English under Percy and Sir Robert Ogle. Sir Richard Percy was killed and Ogle was captured, together with most of the English who survived. This battle could either be seen as a classic Scottish –English conflict or a cross-border family feud, but Henry, the Second Earl of Northumberland brought an army of around 4000 men to invade Scotland. William Douglas, Earl of Angus met him at Piperdean and there was a bloody conflict. Among the Scots was Sir Adam Hepburn, Constable of Dunbar, who may have been guarding his lands. Child suggests that this battle, rather than Otterburn, was the original of the ballad *Chevy Chase*.

Pitgaveny, 1040: fought near Elgin, Moray. This is the traditional site of a battle where Macbeth defeated Duncan I. There are various versions of the story, but one claims that Duncan had led an army to besiege Durham in England but was repulsed. He gathered another force and headed into Moray, where MacBeth killed him at Bothnagowan, now known as Pitgaveny. Either he died in action or was wounded and died later in Elgin Castle.

Pressen, 1338: near Wark on Tweed, Northumberland. During the Second War of Independence, the Earls of Salisbury and Arundel were besieging Dunbar Castle. From his base in Midlothian, Alexander Ramsay of Dalhousie engaged in a guerrilla campaign against the English supply columns. He defeated an English force in a skirmish at Pressen and captured the English leader, Robert de Manners. At this time the Scots guerrillas were known as 'grey wolves.'

Preston, 17th-19th August 1648: fought on Robbleton Moor, Lancashire, England, during the Engagement when Scotland supported King Charles against Cromwell. Although he was a prisoner of Cromwell, King Charles I still managed to negotiate with Scottish Royalists. The king agreed to persuade his people to accept the Covenant if the Scots helped him regain his throne. Scotland sent the English parliamentarians a demand to release the king, disband his army and accept the Covenant. The Parliamentarians would not contemplate the first two, and, although they had already agreed the third, they had no intention of keeping their word.
Scotland raised yet another army and sent it under the Duke of Hamilton to invade England. The plan called for Royalist uprisings in England and Wales, but when they came they were feeble and easily suppressed. A few thousand English joined Hamilton's force of 15,000, but these were not the same Scots who had fought at Newburn and Marston Moor. Ministers of the Kirk had weeded out many of the best men, and three thousand of the best were left behind, so it was a pale shadow of a Scottish army that reached Preston.
The Cromwellian General Lambert drew Hamilton on, and Cromwell attacked in a day long skirmish that culminated in hedge of pikes. The English royalists broke first, then the Scots. Around a thousand were killed, double that number captured to be sent to the English colonies as slaves. Hamilton surrendered and, with his usual lack of humanity, Cromwell had him publicly murdered with a beheading axe.

Preston, 1715: Lancashire, England. This battle was fought during the 1715 Jacobite Rising. While the Earl of Mar gathered the Jacobites in Scotland, there was also some support for a Stuart monarch in England. The Earl of Derwentwater raised a number of English Catholics, joined with some Borderers and hoped for Scottish support. Mar sent him Mackintosh of Borlum and two thousand men.

Mackintosh crossed the Forth in a fleet of small boats and marched south. After a period of disagreement and countermarching, the combined force entered England, where the MP for Northumberland, Thomas Forster joined them. It was Forster who suggested a march on Liverpool, but rather than gain recruits, the Jacobites lost men from desertion and the Hanoverians marched two small armies toward them. The Jacobites ducked into Preston and threw up quick fortifications. They repelled the first assault by the Scottish Cameronians, but more Hanoverian soldiers arrived, and Forster lost his courage. Mackintosh and Derwentwater planned a break out, but Forster tamely surrendered.

Prestonpans, 21st September 1745: East Lothian. In this first major battle of the 1745 Jacobite Rising, the Highlanders showed that they had lost none of their old verve. After landing in Scotland, Charles Edward Stuart gathered a small army of Highlanders and a few Irish and Lowlanders. He marched south on General Wade's new roads, evading the Hanoverian army sent to trap him.

After a quick skirmish, Charles Stuart's army occupied Edinburgh but failed to take the castle. While the Jacobites glared at the old grey walls, the Hanoverian General John Cope was in East Lothian with 3000 redcoats.

Charles led less than 2000 Jacobites out of Edinburgh to do battle, but Cope's army was waiting. They were in a secure position, with their flanks covered by impassable bogland. However, a Jacobite sympathiser, young Anderson of Whitburgh guided Charles through the bog and around the flank of Cope's red-coated army.

Cope's army waited at the saltpans of Preston, facing the wrong way as the Jacobites advanced in two lines, fifty yards apart. They moved in silence, but when they were seen, they raised their slogans and charged. The redcoats broke in a five-minute battle and those who did not fall beneath the broadswords surrendered. The Hanoverians had fought badly, with Cope in the van of those who retreated. The only redcoat success was Colonel Gardiner of Bankton, who stood his ground until the Jacobites cut him down. In contrast to the later actions of Hanoverian commanders, the Jacobite leaders insisted that the prisoners were humanely treated.

There are two monuments for this battle; one is on the southern side of the battlefield, and another to the south west commemorates Colonel Gardiner, who is said to have been killed in the garden of his own house.

Puddocky Ford, 1544: beside Edinburgh. This skirmish occurred during the Rough Wooing. The Earl of Hertford's English army landed at Granton, which was then known as Grantaine Cragge, and marched across Wardie Muir. Although Cardinal Beaton had placed artillery at the ford at Puddocky to halt them, the English stated that the artillery had 'small effect and less resolution' and did nothing to stall the English advance. The English marched over the top of the defenders to plunder and loot in Leith.

R

Raith, 596: near Kirkcaldy, Fife. Local tradition speaks of a battle that was fought here between a combination of Dalriadic Scots, Britons and Picts against an invading force of Angles. There is a slight possibility that the legend is a corruption of the more historically accepted battle of Cattraeth. It is also possible that it is a shadow of a genuine raid along this coast.

Raploch Moss, 1307: three miles west of New Galloway, Dumfries and Galloway. During the First War of Independence, King Robert I defeated an English party in a skirmish here. A stone, known as Bruce's Stone, near Clatteringshaws Loch commemorates the action.

Rath Castle, 1205: Ulster. In 1177 the Anglo-Norman John de Courcy invaded Ulster and built Dundrum Castle, then known as Rath Castle, above Dundrum Bay. In 1199 Hugh de Lacy, another Anglo-Norman, was authorised by King John of England to remove de Courcy and take over Ulster. De Lacy strengthened Rath, but de Courcy turned to Reginald, Regent of Man and the Nodreys for help. Reginald gathered a fleet of around 100 galleys from Man and the Western Isles, landed in Strangford and laid siege to Rath. Walter de Lacy raised an army of Gallowglasses, possibly from the southern Hebrides, and, attacking Reginald in the rear, defeated him.

Ratho, 596 Midlothian. Legend credits this battle to King Aidan of Dalriada, who was victorious. Unfortunately, legend does not give many details.

Ravoabjorg, 1046: perhaps off The Berry, island of Hoy, Orkney. This sea battle was fought between two rival Earls of Orkney, Thorfinn and his nephew Rognvald. Rognvald had thirty large vessels from Norway, Shetland and the Hebrides while Thorfinn's sixty smaller vessels came from Caithness, Scotland and the Hebrides. The boats were lashed together as a floating platform for fighting and a poet, Arnor, who was an eyewitness, spoke of the blood oozing from the hulls of the ships during the battle.

The larger ships proved better. When he was clearly losing, Thorfinn cut the grappling ropes to disengage from the battle. Retreating to disembark the dead and wounded, he persuaded the watching Kalf Arnason, a Norwegian with six large ships, to join him. Kalf agreed and attacked the smaller of Rognvald ships; when the Norwegians of Rognvald saw their side begin to lose, they fled and Thorfinn won. It was a short-lived victory, however, for shortly later Rognvald returned with a single ship and burned Thorfinn out of his house.

Red Ford, (Ath Dearg), 1294, Lorne, Pass of Lorne between Loch Avich and Loch Scammadale. This battle may also be known as Loch Avich. This was the supposed site of a skirmish between MacDougalls and Campbells, which the MacDougalls won. If this battle took place, it may be significant in creating enmity between the Campbells and MacDougalls, a feud that decided who would support Robert Bruce and who Comyn in the later Wars of Independence. At that time the MacDougalls were the Lords of Lorne while the Campbells had not yet started their rise to power. The MacDougalls, traditionally led by John MacDougall the Lame, son of Alexander killed the Campbell chief Colin Mor.

There is a cairn, Carn Cailean, to mark where the Campbell chief died, and the Piper's Knowe is said to be where the Campbell piper played throughout the battle.

Redhall Castle, siege of, 1650: near Colinton, Lothian. During Cromwell's invasion of Scotland, Sir James Hamilton, the Laird of Redhall, with a reported sixty men, repulsed a number of Cromwellian assaults. Cromwell ordered an artillery bombardment, and besieged the house until Hamilton's powder was finished, whereupon he blew open the doors and attacked again. After a furious resistance Redhall was captured and looted, but Cromwell reputedly released Hamilton as he had given such a brave defence. If so then that was a rare moment of humanity in Cromwell's dealings with Scotland.

Reidswire, Raid of the, 7 July 1575: near Carter Bar, Scottish Borders. This skirmish has the distinction of being the last in which Scotsmen fought Englishmen as official national enemies. The old border had its own laws, with Days of Truce in which both sides met in peace to discuss disputes and seek redress for injuries. These times were intended to be sacrosanct, with no violence on either side.

During the Day of Truce in July 1575, an argument arose between the English and Scottish officials over one Harry Robson, a noted freebooter, strangely referred to as Farnstein. The Scottish Warden, Sir John Carmichael, Keeper of Liddesdale, nearly came to blows with Sir John Forster, the English Middle March Warden. It appears that the Tynedale men started the fighting, but the Scots were quick to respond, particularly when the Jedburgh contingent arrived, reputedly crying

'Jethart's here!' The English retreated with casualties, the Scots captured Forster and a handful of other prisoners, and the whole affair blew over.

Renfrew, 1164: also known as Bloody Knock: Strathclyde. Somerled is one of the great figures in mediaeval Scotland. His name is said to mean 'Summer sailor' and possibly refers to a man who raided in summer and remained at home in winter. After he had reclaimed Argyll and the Southern Isles from the Norse, Somerled had an uneasy relationship with the King of Scots, sometimes friendly, sometimes hostile. As a lord with lands in Scotland and the nominally Norse-owned Hebrides, Somerled was in an uncomfortable position, made all the worse by the islesmen's notorious independence.

By 1164 his relationships with Scotland had deteriorated into open warfare. He collected a fleet of 160 ships, filled them with warriors from the Hebrides, Argyll, Kintyre, Dublin and perhaps Galloway and thrust at Scotland. Contemporary accounts tell of a battle in which Somerled, his son and most of his army perished. Apparently Somerled landed at Renfrew and positioned his men on a hill called the Knock, between Renfrew and Paisley. His numbers are not known, but one figure of 15,000 seems high. Walter Fitz Alan, the Steward of Scotland, led Scotto-Norman knights and local levies to attack the Islesmen. Not until the seventeenth century did a tradition start that Somerled was assassinated, but the Argyll Stones at Renfrew commemorate his death.

Restalrig, 6th November 1559: Edinburgh. During the religious troubles of the sixteenth century, the French, under Marie, Queen-Regent of Scotland, occupied Leith. The forces of the Protestant Lords of the Congregation, with English help, strove to drive them out. In this skirmish at Restalrig, the French were successful and the Scots were 'driven through the myre at Restalrig.'

Restenneth, around 830: Angus. Hector Boece mentioned that there was a battle at Restenneth. King Alpin of Dalriada was besieging a fort at Forfar, when Feredich, King of the Picts marched against him with an army. The two fought at Restenneth, and Alpin won, killing Feredich.

Rhunahaorine Point, 24th May 1647: near Tayinloan, Kintyre, Strathclyde. During the civil wars of the mid seventeenth century, Alastair MacColla MacDonald commanded a small Royalist army of Ulstermen and Highlanders. At this time he was retreating down the Kintyre peninsula, closely pursued by David Leslie's larger force of Covenanters. The forces met at Kilcalmonell, an encounter known as the battle of Rhunahaoirine Point. Leslie, who was a more than competent commander, defeated MacDonald, who lost around 80 men.

Roag, Skye: near Roag and Loch Caroy, Skye. Around here was fought what is sometimes claimed to be the last battle between Macdonalds and MacLeods on Skye. According to tradition, the clans fought in the mist and their blood dyed the heather a deep purple. Tradition also claims that two piles of stone mark the event, but these are Neolithic chambered cairns. There are alternative claims for the last Skye battle.

Romanno Bridge, 1st October 1677, Scottish Borders. Unusually, two gypsy clans clashed here in what might be the only battle of its type in Scotland. Both families had been travelling from the fair in Haddington, and some disagreement arose. The Faas were a well-known Scottish gypsy clan, with a cottage in Yetholm as their palace. The Laird of Romanno arrested those who survived, and Robert Shaw and his three sons were hanged in Edinburgh's Grassmarket.

Roscobie, 1097: Fife. Edgar was one of Scotland's strangest kings. It was said that he defeated King Donald Bane in battle at Roscobie to win the kingship, but if so it was an action well out of character. For the remainder of his life Edgar shunned conflict, so he was known as Edgar the Peaceable. He was so pacific that he allowed King Magnus of Norway to formally annex the Hebrides and Kintyre. Edgar also seemed to avoid women, for he died unmarried and childless, an enigmatic figure in an age of warriors and lust.

Roslin, 23rd February 1303: Midlothian. This battle of the First War of Independence has been termed the bloodiest of the entire war, which it was not, and it has been claimed that the Knights Templar were heavily involved. The real story has enough interest not to need any embellishments.

Edward Plantagenet of England ordered Sir John Segrave to thrust at the Scottish patriots who held out west of Edinburgh. Segrave advanced in three divisions. It is unlikely the English host numbered anything like the 30,000 mentioned in popular song, but they would still be formidable.

The Scots gathered to meet them. At a time when William Wallace was reduced to little more than a leader of guerrillas, and Robert Bruce had not yet ascended the stage of leadership, it was John Comyn and Sir Simon Fraser who commanded the Scottish force that advanced from Biggar. They attacked Seagrave's leading division at Roslin. The Scots were successful, killing many of the English including Ralph Manton, cofferer of the wardrobe, and capturing the wounded Seagrave and other knights. The second English division came into action, rescuing Seagrave and a few others, but the Scots had shown that, even without Wallace, the lion still had claws. This battle poses an interesting question: if a Comyn had been king, rather than Bruce, would the ultimate fortunes of war still have gone Scotland's way?

There are many place names in the area that suggest the battle was particularly bloody. For instance there is the Killburn, Shinbanes Field and the Hewin. There is also a small monument near Dryden Farm, part of the Roslin Institute where Dolly the Sheep was cloned.

Rothesay Castle, 1228: Island of Bute, Strathclyde. The original castle on this site was reputedly built on the orders of Magnus Barelegs after he secured the Hebrides for Norway. In those days the castle was on the coast, but much land has been reclaimed since. The castle entered recorded history in 1228 when Olave the Black led a Norwegian attack to take the castle from the Steward of Scotland. The Scots defended themselves with arrows and by pouring down burning pitch, but according to the *Anecdotes of Olave the Black*, the Norse hewed into the walls with their axes and the defences collapsed. The Norse gained the castle.

In 1263 the Norse were back when King Hakon led his fleet south, but that was their last invasion. The English captured Rothesay next, but in 1306 Robert Boyd of Cunningham recaptured in by amphibious assault. The English returned in 1334, until the Scots again threw them out. The Earl of Ross was next in 1462, and then the Master of Ruthven besieged the stone walls in 1527 and the Earl of Lennox in 1544, fighting for his English masters. Cromwell took it in the early 1650s, and finally the Earl of Argyll in 1685.

Historic Scotland now manages the ruins of much fought-over Rothesay Castle, which is open to the public.

Roxburgh, Scottish Borders: about a mile west of Kelso on the River Teviot. Once there was a proud castle and a bustling town. Now there are a few walls, the ripple of the Teviot and a farmer's fields. Where one of Scotland's most prominent mediaeval communities stood, sheep graze. The location was too close to the border and the castle too handy for English occupation to survive. Some of Roxburgh's actions are below.

Roxburgh Castle: February 19/20th 1314. Scottish Borders. During the First War of Independence, the English recognised the importance of Roxburgh. They captured it as soon as they could and held tight. At that time Roxburgh was colloquially known as *le Marche Mont* and until 1314 appeared impregnable to Scottish attacks. On a February night Sir James Douglas led his men in a steady crawl toward the walls, with black cloaks camouflaging their armour. Using rope ladders built by a man known as Sim of the Ledows, the Scots climbed the walls and fell on the garrison. Those who showed fight were killed. The captain, a Gascon named Guillemin de Fennes, surrendered the next day. Chivalrously, Douglas allowed his prisoners to return to England.

Roxburgh Castle: 1322. Scottish Borders. During a skirmish outside the castle walls, Edward Balliol and the Disinherited captured Andrew Murray, the Guardian of Scotland, and the Flemish engineer John Crabbe.

Roxburgh Castle, 30th March 1342: Scottish Borders; Sir Alexander Ramsay captured the castle from English in a surprise assault. It was his last action before being kidnapped and starved to death by his rival, Sir William Douglas, the Dark knight of Liddesdale. The English took back the castle in 1346, after the Scottish defeat of Neville's Cross.

Roxburgh Castle (near) 1356. With the English again in control of Roxburgh, the Scots ambushed their supply columns. On this occasion in 1356 the castle governor was riding with an escort through the Ettrick Forest and William, Earl of Douglas ambushed him, killing many of his men.

Roxburgh Castle, August 1460. The Scots again had to retake the castle from an English garrison. With Roxburgh the only remaining pocket of Scotland held by the English, King James II took an army south. He demolished the English dominated town of Roxburgh and laid siege to the castle. However on the 3rd August, one of the siege cannons known as the Lion burst, with the explosion tearing off the king's leg. He died shortly after and two days later the castle surrendered. There appear to have been no prisoners taken. Roxburgh remained a ruin, although the English used the site for a fortress during the invasion of 1547.

Ruiag – Shansaid, 1437: Caithness, Highland. This battle was also known as the Chase of Sandside or Upper Dounreay. Neil Wasse Mackay had been imprisoned on the Bass Rock for his involvement in an earlier invasion in Caithness. As soon as he was released he gathered the Mackays and again plundered Caithness, leaving a body of men at Drum Hollistan as a rearguard.

The local men – possibly Gunns - gathered at Dounreay but the Mackays defeated them and they retreated to the Forss Water, where reinforcements came along and it was the Mackays turn to withdraw. The rearguard joined them at Sandside, where the Mackays trapped them and there was some ugly killing near an ancient fort known as Cnog Stangar. The Caithness men fled with the Mackays in pursuit.

Rullion Green, 28 November 1666: Pentland Hills, near Penicuik, Lothian. In the 1660s Charles II restored bishops and other elements of the Anglican Church to the Kirk of Scotland. There was much resistance, particularly in the southwest, and the king responded with a series of acts dedicated to suppressing Presbyterianism.

In a largely spontaneous rising, around 3000 poorly armed Covenanters led by Colonel Wallace marched from the west to Edinburgh. Unsure of the correct procedure, but trusting their king, they intended to present their case of persecution to Charles or his representative. When the Edinburgh authorities slammed shut the gates and manned the walls against them, the Covenanters withdrew. After a long march in appalling weather, desertions had sapped their numbers to about 1000, and then General Tam Dalyell marched the regular army to face then on the slopes of the Pentland Hills.

The Covenanters took a position in Turnhouse Hill and waited, singing psalms as the red-coated army formed line. Despite their complete lack of military knowledge, they withstood three cavalry charges before they broke. About fifty Covenanters were killed, and those who were captured faced the noose or transportation.

There is a small railed memorial near the site of the battle.

Ruthven Castle, September 1594: Badenoch, Highland. During the religious wars that burned through north-eastern Scotland in the 1590s, the Earl of Argyll and his protestant force besieged the Catholic Earl Huntly's castle of Ruthven. Clan MacPherson under their chief Andrew held Ruthven and forced away Argyll.

Ruthven Barracks, 1745: Badenoch, Highland. Ruthven Castle changed hands a few times during the civil wars of the seventeenth century, and was also converted to a military barracks. In 1745 it contained a company of the 6th Foot, a regular Hanoverian regiment. When the Jacobite Rising broke out, the majority of the company marched with General Cope, leaving Sergeant Molloy and fourteen men as garrison.

Two hundred Jacobites attempted to take the barracks that year, but Molloy and his men fended them off. However in 1746 Gordon of Glenbucket brought 300 Jacobites. Still Molloy resisted for three days, beating off a determined attack before surrendering. As usual the Jacobites treated their prisoners well, and on his release the sergeant was promoted to lieutenant.

Situated one mile north of Kingussie, the ruins of the barracks are open to the public. Historic Scotland manages the site.

S

Saint Andrews Castle, Fife. Prominently situated on top of a cliff, St Andrews Castle was further protected by a deep ditch in the rock on its landward side. The original castle was built in the late twelfth century, but was much altered in the fourteenth. In English hands for much of the First War of Independence, the Scots retook it in 1314, only to lose it again in the 1330s. Andrew Murray recaptured and destroyed it. Much later in the century Bishop Walter Trail rebuilt the castle and it was used as the palace for the Archbishop of St Andrews.

By the 1540s, the new ideas of Protestantism had come to Scotland. After Cardinal David Beaton ordered the Protestant George Wishart burned at the stake in 1546, a group of Protestants captured the castle, murdered the Cardinal and hung his body from the walls. The Regent Arran promptly besieged the castle. After a period of mining and counter-mining, a fleet of French ships under Leo Strozzi appeared in St Andrews Bay. The French cannon battered the castle into submission within a week. The defenders, including John Knox, were sent to France as galley slaves.

Historic Scotland own what remain of the castle, which has a museum, shop and splendid views out to sea.

St Tayre, Chapel of, 1464 or 1478. Ackergill, Caithness, Highland; this battle is also known as Tears or Tyer or Allt Nan Gamhna and was fought between the Keiths and Gunns. The clans had decided to settle their long-standing feud with fair combat of twelve men a side. George Gunn, the clan chief, brought twelve horsemen, but George Keith of Ackergill put two men on each horse and attacked the Gunns when they were at prayer. Not surprisingly, the Keiths won.

An alternative site for battle is a burn named Altnagown. At least seven Gunns were killed including George the Crowner. The surviving Gunns hid in Strathnaver and planned revenge. Nothing now remains of St Tayres.

St Bride, 1010, Douglasdale, Lanarkshire, Strathclyde. In this probably apocryphal battle, Malcolm II is said to have defeated a Danish invasion.

Sark, or Lochmabenstane, 23rd October 1448: fought just south of Gretna, Dumfries and Galloway. When Scotland and France renewed the Auld Alliance, an English force under the Percy Earl of Northumberland invaded Scotland.

Hugh Douglas, Earl of Ormonde and brother of the 8th Earl of Douglas, commanded the Scottish force that was mustered to give battle. Douglas's army of 4000 seemed to be composed of men from the Borders and West, with Maxwells and Lord Johnstone, the Sheriff of Ayr and Sir John Wallace. Percy had around 6000, including a contingent of Welsh, who enjoyed the reputation of being the fiercest fighters on the English side. The Scots won, with estimated 1500 English killed or captured, and some hundreds drowned in the River Sark.

The Lochmaben stone was an ancient standing stone, part of a stone circle. It fell down in 1982. It may still be seen. There are various legends that connect this stone to druids, Merlin or the stone from which King Arthur pulled Excalibur.

Sauchieburn, 11th June 1488: fought south of Stirling, Central. James III possessed the Stuart charm but insufficient iron for his nation. He gained Orkney and Shetland for Scotland as a dowry and dissuaded Edward IV from supporting Clan Donald before he launched the royal forces against the Isles, but he was a prince of the Renaissance before its time and preferred artists to warriors. His pursuit of wealth irritated the nobles, his use of favourites angered them and they plotted for power.

In 1488 the nobles rose in rebellion and Scotland split in two. Using the fifteen-year-old Prince James as a figurehead, the nobles gathered an army drawn mainly from the southern counties of Scotland. King James III rode to meet them with the sword of King Robert I at his waist and a polyglot army of townsmen and Highlanders behind him. When the fighting started at the Saughie Burn the rebels pushed the royal army back to the Tor Wood. Prince James distinguished himself in a charge across Stirling Bridge, but a counter attack by Ross of Montgrenan taught him that the impetuosity of youth was no match for a yard of Highland steel and he retired in haste.

In the midst of the chaos, King James fell from his horse near Beaton's Mill. He found sanctuary in a cottage and asked the gude-wife for a priest, but the man she brought was an assassin who stabbed the king to death. Young Prince James never forgave himself for his part in his father's demise and wore an iron chain all his life. He was probably still wearing it on Flodden Field.

Queen Victoria erected a monument over the grave of James III at Cambuskenneth Abbey.

Saughs, Raid of, possibly late seventeenth century. This skirmish was fought near head of Water of Saughs, Angus. A party of thirteen caterans – Highland robbers- raided the area around Fern, escaping with cattle and horses. A local farmer named Macintosh led the eighteen men who pursued them. When Macintosh caught them, there was a brief fight and very few of the caterans survived to flee.

Scaithmuir, or Skaithmuir, 1316: near Coldstream, Scottish Borders. At this period of the First War of Independence, the English held Berwick upon Tweed. They used mercenaries from various parts of

Europe, and in this case Raymond Cailhau led a party of eighty Gascons to raid for supplies in Scotland. Sir James Douglas and around forty of his men came across them at Scaithmuir by Coldstream. Cailhau sent some of his force to Berwick with his loot and formed a defensive schiltron. Douglas withdrew to a ford, displayed his banner and waited. Seeing the disparity of numbers, Cailhau attacked, and for a while it seemed as though he would be successful. However, when Douglas killed Cailhau, the Gascons lost heart. The loot was recovered and most of the Gascons were killed.

Sclatterford, November 1513: Roxburghshire, Scottish Borders. After the battle of Flodden the Scottish Borders were ripe for English raids. In one, Lord Dacre led a strong force to Sclatterford, where the Scots defeated it.

Scone, c904: near Perth, Perthshire. Constantine II was one of Scotland's longest surviving Dark Age rulers, being king from 900 until 943. He began his reign with a victory over the Norse at Scone in 904.

Sherrifhallmuir, 1573: Dalkeith, Midlothian. At a time when Scotland was split between Kingsmen, who supported the Protestant King James VI and Queensmen, who followed Mary, Queen of Scots, the Regent Morton based himself for a time at Dalkeith. A body of Queensmen attempted to capture him but was defeated. Because rain had dampened the gunpowder, there were few casualties on either side.

Sherrifmuir, 13th November 1715: near Dunblane, Central. After George the First ascended the throne in 1714 the Jacobites intensified their attempts to return the Stuarts to the throne. The Jacobite Rising of 1715 had a good chance to succeed. Much of Scotland was disillusioned with the Union and would accept a Jacobite monarch, thousands of Highlanders had come out and the French were interested in becoming involved. Unfortunately the Jacobites chose a poor military commander.

Bobbing John Erskine, the Earl of Mar held a supposed hunting party at Braemar and gathered support for the Jacobites. With around 8000 men behind him, he captured Perth and headed for Stirling and the Forth. The Earl of Argyll, 'Red John of the Battles', with around 3000 Hanoverians opposed him, but Argyll was a soldier and Mar only a politician.

The armies met on the muir above Dunblane and fought a drawn battle. The right wing of each army was victorious with Mar's MacDonalds pushing back the Hanoverian foot, but his left falling before the cavalry. When the smoke cleared, Argyll had nearly 700 casualties to Mar's 232 but Mar had not crossed the Forth. Instead he retreated to Perth, leaving the south in Hanoverian hands. The rising was over in all but name.

This battlefield has a 1915 memorial to Clan Macrae, and there is a rock known as the Gathering Stone which traditionally has associations with the battle. It is possible that the clans did raise their standards on this spot, but the stone is much older. In 2002 the 1745 Association also erected a neat cairn to commemorate the battle.

Skerries, February 1316: fought in County Kildare in Ireland. After the battle of Bannockburn, some Irish chiefs invited the Scots to help remove the Anglo-Normans from their country. Edward Bruce led a small force over and won a number of victories, so that he was crowned High King of Ireland. Unfortunately famine hit the country and his Scotto-Irish army plundered what food remained. Edward Bruce defeated the English and Anglo-Normans in the north and in early 1316 John de Hotham, Chancellor of Ireland gathered a much larger army and encountered Edward Bruce at Skerries, near Ardskull. All the odds were with the English and Anglo-Irish but Edward Bruce defeated them. News of the victory encouraged further Irish uprisings against English rule.

Skibo, c 1477: Sutherland, Highland. MacDonald of the Isles, then an ally of Edward IV of England brought an army of around five hundred men into Sutherland and set up camp beside Skibo Castle. It is possible that he came by sea, and if so then this is one of the rare occasions that West Highland galleys sailed to this coast. The Earl of Sutherland sent Neil Murray with a force to remove the MacDonalds. When MacDonald began to plunder the countryside, Murray attacked them, killed Donald Dhu MacDonald and around fifty others. The remainder retreated.

Skida Moor, around 980, Caithness, Highland. There seem to have been two battles on this moor, now better known as the Moss of Wester, near Watten. In the first, around 980, Liotr defeated Magbiodr in what appears to have been a purely local encounter. The second may have been in the very early eleventh century between the Norse and the Scots, in which the Norse were victorious over a Scottish force commanded by one Magbiod, which name is sometimes given as MacBeth. Sigurd, Earl of Orkney was connected with this latter encounter.

Skirmish Hill, see **Darnick**

Slains, c 1012: near Peterhead, Aberdeenshire, Grampian. There seem to have been a number of encounters between the Danes and Scots in this area. One was fought around 960, when a party of Vikings were defeated at Aldie Hill near Cruden. Around 1010 Malcolm II is supposed to have defeated a Danish army, and the name Cruden conveniently comes from the name Croch Dane, 'slaughter of the Danes.' A persistent legend says that the Danish pay chest was buried here and never recovered. A further battle or perhaps the same one retold, occurred around 1012 around a mile west of Slains Castle, and again saw a Scottish victory, this time over Canute or Knut of Denmark. The present golf course apparently is where the heaviest fighting took place. Incidentally the present Slains is a replacement for the original castle, which was further south. King James destroyed the first version after Huntly's revolt in the early 1590s. Also intriguingly, the present castle is said to have been the inspiration for Bram Stoker's Dracula. It is a ruin, but worth a visit for the historical and literary associations, as well as the wide views.

Sligathan, see Harta Corrie

Sollas, 1849: North Uist, Outer Hebrides. One of the most notorious instances of the Clearances, when the landlord of Sollas threatened the tenants with forced emigration unless they accepted eviction. The resulting riot reached the newspapers, as Lord Cockburn gave the culprits short sentences.

Solway Moss: 24th November 1542, south of Lochmaben on the Solway Firth. James V was never popular with his nobles. He preferred the company of artists and intellectuals to that of soldiers, and excluded his great lords from his councils. When the English invaded and were defeated at Haddon Rigg, James raised first one army, which refused to cross the border, then a second, which he led toward the border. He turned aside at Lochmaben but sent the army south.

The Scots were around 10,000 strong, led by Lord Maxwell. The English defensive force numbered around 3000, with Sir Thomas Wharton, West March Warden in command, and what occurred was the strangest battle in Scottish history.

When the first English were seen at the Solway Moss, Maxwell sent his Border horse to skirmish, and then Oliver Sinclair, King James V's favourite, announced that the king had made him commander of the army. The army had not been happy to fight for James, and morale had probably slumped when the king had left them, but now there seemed no point in fighting at all. Nobody wanted to fight for Sinclair. The very concept of the war seemed strange; at a time of religious turmoil, many were unsure if they were fighting for Catholic France or for an unpopular king.

Wharton's light horsemen from the English border rode at the Scots, and few retaliated. There was no real fighting; merely a movement back toward Scotland or a mass surrender. There were as estimated seven to twenty Scots killed in the battle but around 1200 surrendered, mainly to spite the king and his favourite. The English lost seven en in this least bloody of all battles. King James retired to Falkland and died within a fortnight.

There is an interpretation panel near Arthret Church, but no monument.

Soor Plums of Gala, 1337: also known as Raid Stane. Galashiels, Scottish Borders. This skirmish occurred during the Second War of Independence. A party of English were foraging near Galashiels and the youths of the town found them gathering plums at what is now Englishman's Syke. The Galashiels youths attacked and wiped out the English. The incident is commemorated in the town's coat of arms and in the annual Common Riding. The Raid Stane, and a plum tree, can be seen beside a car park at the Netherdale stadium of Gala Fairydean football club.

Sreith, 752, possibly fought in the Mearns, Angus or Grampian. Early accounts claim that two rival Pictish forces fought this battle, but details are very scanty.

Stalc, 1468: near Castle Stalker, Appin, Strathclyde. When the Stewarts and MacDougalls were disputing the lands of Appin and the Lordship of Lorn, other clans were dragged in. In this incident, a battle was fought on the hills above Castle Stalker. The Stewarts and MacLarens fought against the MacDougalls and MacFarlanes. The Stewarts were victorious and Allan MacDougall, also known as Alan MacCoul, chief enemy of the Stewarts, was killed. The battle was said to be a bloody affair with hundreds of men involved, particularly from the MacFarlanes.

There is a monument at the site.

Standard, the, 22nd August 1138: also known as Northallerton; fought at Cowton Moor, near Northallerton, England. King David I of Scotland had invaded England to support his kinswoman Matilda against Stephen in the English civil war. The Scottish army was a combination of Scotto-Norman knights, spearmen from Lothian and warriors from Galloway. If English chronicles are trustworthy and were not written as propaganda, the Scots army behaved badly, raping, pillaging and murdering on their march south.

Thurstan, Archbishop of York led the English, who composed a solid mass of dismounted Norman knights, with a line of archers in front and English militia on the flanks. The battle was named after the Banner of the Sacred Host that flew from a ship's mast in the English positions.

The apparently naked Galloway men started the battle with a brave but reckless charge but were slaughtered by archers. The few that broke through the archers exchanged blows with the armoured knights. The Scots-Norman knights under David's son Henry followed, smashing through the English flanks and may have won the battle had they turned against the English centre. However an Englishman held up a severed head, claiming it was King David's, and the impetus of the attack wavered.

Believing that their king was dead, the surviving Galloway men retreated, and the Lothian men joined them. King David, who had done little to order the fighting, had lost his battle. His army retreated in bad order.

There is a small stone monument to this English victory.

Steeplegate Hill, around 1590: south east of Huntly, Grampian. At this time the northeast was in ferment with a group of clans and families allied against the Earl of Huntly. Skirmishes and looting was common. Clan Chattan had come into Huntly's land to waste and spoil, and Huntly caught them near a hill named Steeplegate, where he defeated them with around 60 Chattan casualties.

Stirling, August 1571: Central. In the early 1570s, Scotland was split by a civil war between the usually Catholic supporters of Mary, Queen of Scots and the Protestant followers of King James VI. Taught by the harsh genius of Buchanan, James spent much of his childhood at Stirling. In 1571 the Earl of Lennox was acting as regent and guardian of the infant King James VI when the Earl of Huntly and Lord Claud Hamilton led a force of 400 men to the town and kidnapped the king. As the attackers stopped to loot, the burgesses rescued the king, but Lennox was killed in the skirmish.

Stirling, 12th September 1648: Central. This skirmish occurred during the later Civil wars. After Hamilton had led a Scots royalist army to destruction at Preston, the Earl of Lanark tried to defend Scotland for the king against the Covenanting Earl of Argyll, at that time an ally of Cromwell. As Argyll advanced a rather makeshift army of 1,300 men against Stirling, Sir George Monro, one of Lanark's commanders, marched against him. Argyll fled, but some of his men fought before the rest broke. About 400 were taken prisoner and perhaps 200 killed.

Stirling Bridge, 1297: Central. Without doubt one of the most significant battles in Scottish history, Stirling Bridge was fought during the early period of the First War of Independence. The English under Edward I had overrun Scotland the previous year, and thought that there was no more to be done, but William Wallace led a resistance movement in the south of the country and Andrew Murray in the north. They combined to lead an army with few feudal lords but patriotism amazing for the age.

Edward Plantagenet retaliated by sending a conventional army under the Earl of Surrey and Hugh de Cressingham. There should have been no contest, for the English were expert at war and had excellent professional soldiers, while the Scots were not. The English had Anglo-Norman knights with Gascon mercenaries, Welsh archers and English men at arms. The Scots had spears and whatever weapons they could find.

Wallace and Murray took up position on the slopes of Abbey Craig, about a mile north of the strategic Stirling Bridge. When the English sent two Dominican friars with a request for the Scots to yield, Wallace is said to have replied:

tell your commander that we are not here to make peace but to do battle to defend ourselves and liberate our Kingdom. Let them come on and we shall prove this in their very beards.

Too arrogant to use a nearby ford, the English advanced toward the wooden Bridge of Stirling, the lowest bridging point of the Forth. The Scots waited until the English were partly across the bridge, and then chopped it down, nicely dividing the English army. As the English van struggled in an area of bogland, Wallace and Murray led their spearmen forward. There was an hour of ugly fighting as the spears hacked at the English cavalry. Surrey turned tail and fled with the remainder of the English army.

Over 100 English knights died, and they had heavy infantry losses especially among the Welsh archers. Stewart and Lennox, Scots on the English side, changed sides and attacked the baggage train, killing many of fleeing English, but Andrew Murray was severely wounded and died in November. Wallace became Guardian of Scotland.

The Wallace Monument on Abbey Craig marks the spot where William Wallace traditionally stood to watch over the battle. It is a monument worth visiting for its own sake, with impressive views and various fascinating displays and artefacts.

Stirling Castle is one of the icons of Scotland. Situated at the waist of Scotland, it seems to connect east and west, north and south. Much of Scotland's history occurred in and around this castle, with an estimated sixteen sieges or attacks. Historic Scotland manages this castle, which is open to the public and has an impressive array of attractions. Only a few of the battles, sieges and skirmishes are set below:

Stirling Castle, 1297. In 1297 Stirling faced a Scottish siege. Wallace took the castle from William Fitz Warin, William de Ros and Marmaduke Tweng. The English surrendered when their food ran out. The English recovered the castle after Falkirk, and the Scots had to recapture it late in 1299, when John Sampson surrendered

Stirling Castle, 1304. In one of its most famous sieges, Sir William Oliphant and thirty men held the castle for the Scots during the First war of Independence. When Edward I demanded Oliphant's surrender, the Scottish knight requested permission to speak to his feudal superior, Sir John Soules, on the subject. King Edward refused and spent three months in the siege. Oliphant no longer held the castle for the absent King John Balliol, but 'for the lion' the lion rampant of Scotland.

It was unusual in that period to fight for an abstraction, but Edward Plantagenet did not appreciate the distinction and experimented with a bombardment of lead balls, stone balls, Greek fire and possibly gunpowder, before he used a new siege engine called Warwolf. He finally accepted Oliphant's surrender on the 20th July.

Stirling Castle, 1337. In 1314 the castle surrendered to the Scots after Bannockburn, but the English regained control under the puppet king Edward Balliol, rebuilding the ruins that the Scots had left. A Scottish siege in 1337 failed, but in 1342 starvation once again compelled the English garrison to surrender.

Stirling Castle, 1571. At a time when Scotland was split into factions supporting Mary, Queen of Scots or the young King James, the castle held for the king. It repelled an attack by Queensmen in this year.

Stirling Castle, 1584. A group of rebellious nobles captured the castle, but when King James approached in May, they handed it quietly back, to retake it in 1585, and again return it.

Stirling Castle, 1651. In August General Monck and his Cromwellian army laid siege to the castle. The castle's artillery replied, but Monck was an experienced soldier. With the walls crumbling under modern artillery and mortar shells falling within the castle, the garrison surrendered after an eleven-day bombardment.

Stirling Castle, January 1746. During the Jacobite Rising, the Jacobites placed artillery on Gowan Hill, but the garrison's gunnery destroyed them.

Stonehaven, Raid of, 15 June 1639. During the early stages of the civil wars of 1639, Montrose, later to be prominent for the king, fought for the Covenant. On this occasion he was with Aboyne when Covenanting cannon fire dispersed a force of Gordons and Highlanders.

Stornoway, Island of Lewis, Outer Hebrides. The name Stornoway means Steering Bay, which points to the nautical nature of this Hebridean town with its safe harbour. The Nicolsons were reputed to have built the first castle here around 1100, but it was soon lost to ancestors of the MacLeods. Surprisingly for Scotland, Stornoway Castle did not feature much in history until 1506, when the expansionist Earl of Huntly reduced the castle on behalf of King James IV. The Earl of Argyll was here in 1554, but left with no success. However it was not until the closing years of the century that Stornoway leaped to the front page of national events.

James VI had the idea of planting Lowlanders in the Gaelic lands to erode the Gaelic culture and 'civilise' them. He granted Lewis to a group of Lowlanders known as the Fife Adventurers. These men took a body of 500 soldiers and mercenaries to the islands and attempted to 'root out the barbarous inhabitants' or wrest control from the native MacLeods. It was an early form of genocide. Some of the results follow:

Stornoway, 1599. Neil MacLeod with '200 barbarous, bludie, and wiket hielandmen' armed with bows, darlochs – quivers – two handed swords, hackbutts, pistols and other weapons attacked the Fife Adventurers and killed around twenty-two.

Stornoway, 1601. Tormod MacLeod attacked the Lowland settlement in Lewis; the Lowlanders fought well but surrendered.

Stornoway, 1607. Neil MacLeod and 300 men attacked the Fife Adventurers settlement in Lewis. The Lowlanders abandoned the attempt the following year and the Mackenzies gain the island of Lewis instead.

Stornoway Castle, 1653. Lewis, Outer Hebrides. Cromwell's forces bombarded, captured and destroyed the castle. The following year a force of Mackenzies ambushed and defeated a body of the garrison.

Strathardle, 903, Perthshire. At the beginning of the tenth century the Danes were running riot in Scotland. One body came from the eastern coast of Scotland and marched into Strathardle. A Scottish force met them at Tulloch in Glenfernate, pushing the Norse back to Enochdhu, where the leader of the Scots was reportedly killed.

Strathaven, June 1679: Strathclyde. During the religious troubles of the late seventeenth century, the Covenanters won a victory at Drumclog. One account states that after the battle Graham of Claverhouse withdrew through Strathaven and some of the citizens tried to block his passage. The dragoons cut down a few on their charge through. The local museum in Strathaven has some Covenanting objects.

Strathcarron, 642, near Larbert, Strathclyde. The Britons of Strathclyde under Owen or Eugein defeated the Dalriadans and killed their king, Domnall Brecc, who seemed to have a knack of losing battles. A British poet celebrated the victory by writing that 'ravens gnawed the head of Domnall Brecc'. This battle saw a swing in the balance of power in western Scotland, with Strathclyde eclipsing Dalriada for a time.

Strathearn, 903: Perthshire. After two years campaigning and plundering in Scotland, the Norse were finally defeated in Strathearn. The Scots fought behind the crosier of Saint Columba. It is interesting to speculate whether this battle may be the same as that fought between the same adversaries in the same year, and with the same result, in Strathardle.

Strathfleet, Sands of, c 1477: Sutherland, Highland. Shortly after the defeat of the MacDonalds at Skibo, another party of MacDonalds arrived in Sutherland and began to ravage Strathfleet. Robert Sutherland, brother of the earl, gathered an army and attacked the MacDonalds at the Sands of Strathfleet. The Sutherland men were successful, killing many of the MacDonalds and sending the remainder back.

Strome Castle, 1602: between Fort William and Gairloch, Loch Carron, Wester Ross, Highland. Situated between the Mackenzie lands of Kintail and the MacDonalds at Lochalsh, Strome Castle was an obvious trouble spot. James V granted it to the Glengarry MacDonalds in 1539 and from the 1590s until 1602, the rival clans fought for control.

The siege of 1602 was one event in a feud between the Mackenzies of Kintail and the Glengarry MacDonalds. After the Mackenzies had killed some MacDonalds, Kenneth Mackenzie of Kintail arranged for a meeting before the court in Edinburgh. Glengarry preferred a more direct attack on Mackenzie lands, but Kintail obtained a commission against the MacDonalds and invaded Morar.

The Mackenzies were besieging Strome, which held out until, according to tradition, some 'silly women' from the castle poured water into the gunpowder casks. A Mackenzie prisoner escaped with the information and the Mackenzies captured the castle from the MacDonalds, and then blew it up. Another version claims that the captain of the fort betrayed his trust. However, there is no dispute that the Mackenzies obtained the castle and blew it up.

There are only fragmentary ruins, but the views are worth the visit.

Strone Nevis, 1654: Lochaber, Highland. After Cromwell invaded Scotland in 1651, he eventually defeated all organised resistance. The Scots resorted to guerrilla warfare, with the Camerons of Lochaber under their chief Ewan refusing to accept the garrison that was placed in their country. In this skirmish Ewan Cameron led a small force that defeated a much larger Cromwellian force from Inverlochy, now Fort William, who were ravaging his lands. Most of the Cromwellian troops were killed. Next day the governor of the fort ventured out with most of his garrison, and Ewan Cameron tried to lure him into a trap, but the Cromwellians retreated to their base.

Sumburgh, Plains of, date unknown but possibly sixteenth century: Mainland, Shetland. After raiding Foula, a party of men from Lewis sailed from Foula to Sumburgh Head, at the extreme south of Mainland. According to Dr Samuel Hibbert, one of the Sinclairs of Brow gathered the men of Dunrossness on the Plains of Sumburgh and attacked the invaders, who were badly defeated. This was said to be the last of many battles between Shetlanders and Lewismen.

Dance If Ye Can

Summerdale, 1529: four miles north east of Stromness, Orkney Mainland. After Orkney was transferred from Norwegian to Scottish control in 1468, the former property of the Earldom was rented out to tacksmen who collected the rents. Not all were honourable men. When William Sinclair, tacksman and Justice Depute of Orkney, was guilty of abusing his power, a body of Orcadians seized Kirkwall castle from him. James and Edward Sinclair, William's cousins, led the revolt.
William Sinclair appealed to John Sinclair, Earl of Caithness and another kinsman for help. Together they raised an army of some 500 men and invaded Orkney. James and Edward Sinclair gathered the Orkneymen together. The two armies fought in the moors at Stenness at Summerdale, by Kirbister loch. It seems that the Orkneymen were armed mainly with agricultural implements and stones, but a desperate charge settled the issue.
Around 30 of the invaders were killed in the fighting, and hundreds drowned when they fled to Scapa Flow. It is good to know that James Sinclair was later knighted and Edward officially pardoned and no more battles were fought on Orcadian soil.

Swinton, 1558, Berwickshire, Scottish Borders. At a time when Marie, the Queen Regent ruled Scotland, and Scots, French and English were bickering along the border, Henry Percy led around 3,000 Northumbrians into Scotland. They burned Duns, reived a host of cattle and were caught by a small Scottish army near Swinton. The English won the fight, scattering the Scots, and Percy brought his loot safely into England.

T

Talla Moss, 1488: near Stirling, Central. After the battle of Sauchieburn, the Earl of Lennox led a minor insurrection along with Lord Lyle against those who had killed the king. He was defeated at Talla Moss.

Tankerness, 1136: sea battle off the Mull Head of Deerness, Orkney. At that time Orkney and Shetland were under Norwegian ownership. The King of Norway granted Rognvald the earldom, but his cousin Paul, who had *de facto* control, was not inclined to give way.

Rognvald planned a double attack, with one fleet of ships from Norway attacking Shetland, and a second fleet from the Hebrides attacking Orkney. The Shetland fleet was captured without a struggle but the Hebridean fleet gave more trouble.

Olvir Rosta, Roaring Oliver, commanded the Hebrideans. His ships were smaller, but he had twelve to Paul's five. Olvir's ships attacked Earl Paul east of Mull Head, but Paul, backed by doughty fighters such as Olaf Rolfsson of Gairsay and Sweyn Breastrope, fought hard. Olaf's larger vessel defeated three of the smaller Hebrideans, while Sweyn knocked Olvir overboard. Paul chased the Hebrideans east of Mainland, past Ronaldsay and into the Pentland Firth; five of Olvir's ships were taken and the rest fled.

Tannach Moor, 1438 (disputed) also known as Blar Tannie, near Wick in Caithness, Highland. In this, the first recorded large battle between the Keiths and the Gunns, the Mackays also seem to have been involved. The two clans had been feuding inconclusively for a while but in 1438 the Gunns planned a major incursion on Keith land with as many allies as they could muster. Keith of Ackergill asked the Mackays for help and Neill Bass Mackay obliged with a sizeable force. The combined Keith-Mackay army met the Gunns on the moor of Tannach, three miles from Wick and the Keiths were victorious.

Tantallon Castle, 1491 – 1651: near North Berwick, East Lothian. Tantallon Castle is one of the most impressive sights of East Lothian, a red walled stronghold built on a promontory overlooking the North Sea and the Bass Rock. It was built by William, the First Earl of Douglas around 1358.

'Ding doon Tantallon,' says an old Scottish rhyme, 'build a brig to the Bass.' Both events were reckoned impossible, and a glance at the twelve-foot thick walls and deep defensive ditches will show why.

However in 1491 the Douglas Fifth Earl of Angus turned traitor and James IV marched an army to Tantallon to try his luck. He was not greatly successful, but his son, James V was back in 1528. During the Rough Wooing the Douglases took the English side. Based in Tantallon, the English ambassador wrote that the castle was 'of such strength as I neded not feare the malice of myne enymeys.'

When Cromwell invaded in 1650, a band of around 100 guerrilla fighters based themselves on Tantallon and played havoc with the invader's supply chain. Cromwell had to divert 3000 men and most of his artillery to finally reduce the castle, which speaks volumes for its residual strength.

Historic Scotland manages the massive ruins of Tantallon, and there is a car park, shop and toilets.

Tarbetness, or Torfness or Standistone: 14th August 1040, possibly fought in the south of the Moray Firth, with traditions pointing to Burgness. Earl Thorfinn of Orkney defeated King Duncan of Scots. At that time the Norse Earldom of Orkney controlled much of Scotland north of Inverness.

According to the *Orkneyinga Saga*, Duncan, named as King Karl Hundasson raised a large army to fight Earl Thorfinn 'and they met at Tarbatness in the south of the Moray Firth.' Thorfinn was victorious. There is a possibility that the battle was fought at Standing Stone in the parish of Duffus. Some authorities believe that this was a naval battle, but the *Orkneyings Saga* makes no mention of ships. The saga's naming of Duncan as Karl may be a calculated insult, with Karl possibly meaning peasant, and Hundasson, son of a dog.

Gaelic sources claim that Duncan was later murdered after hiding in a smith's house.

Tay, 24 August 1332: Firth of Tay, Angus. This battle was fought during the Second War of Independence. After the battle of Dupplin, the English and Disinherited occupied Perth. The Scots patriots began to blockade the town. As the English gained supplies by ships sailing up the Tay, the ubiquitous Flemish engineer John Crabbe led a Scottish flotilla from Berwick to attack the English fleet and complete the blockade. Although the English ships outnumbered the Scots by eight to one, the Scots captured the English flagship *Beaumondscogge* and killed the crew. However, that was their sole success. Using their numerical superiority, the English crushed the Scottish attack and the Scottish survivors withdrew.

Thornton Castle, 1548: East Lothian. The Duke of Somerset captured and destroyed this castle of Lord Home during the Rough Wooing.

Threave Castle, 1455: about a mile west of castle Douglas, Dumfries and Galloway. When the Douglas family became too friendly with the English, King James II murdered the 8th Earl. The King besieged Threave for two months. Despite his use of the heavy artillery piece known as Mons Meg, the castle only surrendered when James resorted to bribery. There was another siege in 1640 when the Covenanters took the castle after a thirteen week siege.

Historic Scotland manages for this castle, which is situated on an island in the River Dee. The ruins may be visited by boat.

Thurso, 1040: Caithness, Highland. At a time when the Norse Earls of Orkney controlled much of northern Scotland, King Duncan sent up an army to attempt to wrest Caithness from their power, or at least force the earl to pay tribute for it. According to the *Orkneyinga Saga*, Moddan, nephew of Duncan, had been appointed the Mormaer of Caithness. He commanded the Scottish army. Thorkell Fostri and an army from Caithness and Orkney surprised and defeated Modden near Thurso. Thorkell then led his army south to join Thorfinn, Earl of Orkney in his victory over Duncan at Tarbatness

Thurso, 1196: Caithness, Highland. This battle was fought about a mile and a half east of Thurso. The local ruler was Harald Maddason, who was renowned for his cruelty. In 1196 Harald grabbed the lands of another Harald, named the Young, who had a claim to the Earldom. Both men raised armies and fought it out near Thurso. Harald Maddason killed young Harald and defeated his army, before continuing his terror. In the eighteenth century, Sir John Sinclair built a tower on the site of young Harald's death.

Thurso, 1612: Caithness, Highland. When a Thurso man named Arthur Smith was accused of the capital crime of forgery, King James VI ordered Donald Mackay of Farr, John Gordon of Gospeter and John Gordon the son of Gordon of Backies to arrest him. The lords brought thirty-six men to the town. John Sinclair of Skirkag, nephew of the Earl of Caithness gathered the townspeople to resist the arrest and there was a skirmish in the streets. John Sinclair of Skirkag and Arthur Smith were killed and many were injured on both sides.

Thurso, 1649: Caithness, Highland. The Mackays of Strathnaver had planned to raid Thurso on a Sunday when the good people were in church. The local men learned of the Mackays intention and devised retaliation. They filed into Old St Peter's Church, sang the first psalm and secretly left to wait in ambush. When the Mackays came, the Thurso men attacked them, sent the survivors back, and returned to church for the remainder of the service.

Tillyangus, 1571: Clatt, about 33 miles North West of Aberdeen, Aberdeenshire, Grampian. In the 1570s Scotland was split between the mainly Catholic followers of Mary, Queen of Scots, and the mainly Protestant supporters of King James VI. The Gordons were Queen Mary's mainstay in Aberdeenshire and they clashed with the Forbeses. In this encounter Adam Gordon led a smaller force against Black Arthur Forbes, who was positioned in a series of entrenchments on the hillside of Tillyangus. The Gordon attack was successful and the Forbes force broke and fled. The Gordons chased them to Druminner Castle.

Tioram Castle, near Acharacle, Loch Miodart, Highland. This area was said to have been the scene of a battle in the twelfth century, when Somerled defeated the Norseman Torquil at a ford across the River Shiel. Somerled was victorious. That same century Castle Tioram was built and became the home of Clan Ranald MacDonald. The castle was attacked during a clan feud in 1554, and Cromwell's men captured it in 1651, then in 1715 Alan MacDonald of Clanranald burned it to prevent the Hanoverians from using the castle as a garrison.

The ruins of this castle are closed to the public but may be viewed from nearby.

Tippermuir or Tibbermore, 1st September 1644: three miles west of Perth, Perthshire. This battle of the Civil War was the first victory of the Marquis of Montrose over the Covenanters. Promised 10,000 men by the Earl of Antrim, he received 1,600, and they were badly equipped and armed. However they were experienced in the Irish wars and were led by the fierce veteran Alasdair MacColla MacDonald. Most were Ulster or Hebridean MacDonalds with a grudge. When Montrose found them, they were about to do battle with the local Atholl clans, but Montrose persuaded both forces to combine under his leadership, and led the entire 3000 against the armies of the Covenant. Bereft of artillery and with one round for each of his few muskets, Montrose ordered his men to gather rocks as missiles.

His immediate opponent was Lord Elcho with 6,000 foot and around 800 cavalry led by Lord Drummond. The cavalry were splendidly armed with four pistols each, as well as a carbine and lance. There was also David Grant's Perth militia and a number of cannon. A body of Perth burghers came to watch the battle as the armies formed up on the level plain of Tippermuir, beneath Methven Hill.

The Covenanters cried 'Jesus and no Quarter!' and captured the Master of Maddertie that Montrose had sent as a herald. Elcho began the action by sending forward his cavalry. Alasdair MacColla countered with his MacDonalds, pushing back Drummond's men. When Montrose followed with a full Highland charge the artillerymen fled. The Highlanders then broke the Covenanting musketeers as the Ulster MacDonalds smashed into the Covenanter's centre. They fired their single volley as they closed, supported by those Highlanders who had only stones and raw courage.

When the Covenanters fled Montrose led his men to occupy Perth. Only Sir James Scott of Rossie attempted to form a rearguard, but the Atholl Highlanders thrust them aside. The Covenanters lost 2,000 dead, mostly in the pursuit, but Montrose also took 1,000 prisoners for the loss of one man killed in action and another who died of his wounds.

Torbhean Ridge, 1187: also known as Tomhahurich, near Inverness, Highland. Tradition speaks of a battle here between Donald Bane 'a Hebridean chief' and Duncan Mackintosh, son of the Governor of Inverness Castle. The story claims that Mackintosh sallied out with part of the garrison of Inverness Castle to combat Donald Bane. Both leaders and many of the followers are said to have died. This may be a confused account of the battle of Man Garbh in which Roland of Galloway killed Donald MacWilliam. Donald Bane may have been the same person as Donald MacWilliam; grandson of that Donald Bane, brother of King Malcolm who lost his claim to the crown to Malcolm's son Duncan.

Tobanarael, 1543: Trossachs, Stirlingshire, Central. In 1543 the Earl of Menteith held his wedding feast on Inchnahome in the Lake of Menteith. However his timing was unfortunate as a party of caterans passed by, led by the Tutor of Appin, known as Donald of the Hammer. The caterans were returning from a raid into Stirlingshire, but the temptation was too much and they stopped to loot the feast.

William Graham, Earl of Menteith raised a small force and followed the caterans to Tobanareal, on a ridge between Menteith and Strathgartney. Other accounts say that they met at Craigvad. The Earl attacked the caterans, and in the battle, he and all his men were killed, while only Donald of the Hammer and one man of the caterans escaped alive. A slightly different version of this tale claims that the Earl of Menteith was a guest at the wedding and the battle was fought at Tyepers Well in the Trossachs.

Torran-Dubh, 1517: near Rogart, Sutherland, Highland. This battle is also known as Torran Dobhach. This clan battle was fought between Alexander Sutherland and John Mackay.

In 1514 John, the 9th Earl of Sutherland died and his sister Elizabeth became 10th Countess of Sutherland. She hoped to marry into the Gordon clan, giving the Gordons the Earldom of Sutherland as well as of Huntly. John Mackay, chief of the clan, did not wish the Gordons to have such power.

In 1517 the Earl of Sutherland travelled to Edinburgh, leaving his brother- in- law, Alexander Sutherland to govern his lands. John Mackay of Strathnaver took the opportunity to gather all his manpower and anyone else who would follow him and ravage Sutherland. Alexander Sutherland, together with John Murray and William Mackames collected all the men that they could and faced the Mackays at Torran Dubh near Rogart. Sutherland first pushed the Mackay vanguard back, and then selected a number of men to attack the Mackays, with his brother Donald Sutherland in charge of the main body. The Mackays fought hard, but the Sutherland men at last won. John Mackay survived but he lost over 200 of his men in the battle, including Neil MacIan Angus of Assynt, and more were killed in the pursuit. Alexander Sutherland lost a reported 38 killed, which seems very low compared to the Mackay losses.

Toubacanti, February 15 1700: Darien, Central America. In the late seventeenth century, Scotland suffered from a series of bad harvests. The country also had difficulties with trade, partly owing to the 1603 Union of the Crowns, which hampered relations with some of Scotland's old trading partners. The Scots attempted to form a trade entrepot in Central America, but found themselves at odds with Spain, who claimed the area.

When the Spanish attacked the Scottish colony, Campbell of Fonab led a Scottish force, helped by local tribesmen, into the jungle to repel attack. The Scots and Darien men defeated the Spaniards in what was Scotland's last victory as in independent nation. This was a preemptive strike on a superior Spanish force in a strong defensive position, but the Scots eventually had to leave Darien. The loss of money and confidence helped drive Scotland toward the 1707 Union with England.

Towie Barclay Castle, May 1639: near Fyvie, Aberdeenshire, Grampian. This minor skirmish occurred when the Royalists attacked the castle but were repelled. David Pratt had the unwanted distinction of becoming the first man killed in a Civil War that would last years and eventually involve all the nations of the British Isles.

Traigh Gruinart, 5th August 1598, Isle of Islay, Strathclyde. At the end of the sixteenth century, the Macleans of Duart were at feud with the MacDonalds of Islay. Sir Lauchlan Maclean attempted to claim Islay for himself, as Angus MacDonald was an old man and his son, Sir James too young to resist. The Macleans invaded Islay in force, and Sir James MacDonald offered to present the case to the king for arbitration, or to share the island between them. Maclean refused and prepared for battle.

Although the Macleans far outnumbered the MacDonalds, many of the latter had experience in the Irish wars against the English. The two forces met at the head of Loch Gruinart at a place known as Traigh Gruinart. Sir James MacDonald wheeled his vanguard until the sun was at his back, shining in the eyes of the Macleans, and drove their vanguard back into their main body. After a fierce fight Sir Laughlin Maclean and eighty of his captains and around 200 others of his clan were killed. MacLean's son Lauchlan Barrach was wounded and retreated to his galleys with the remainder of his army. Sir James MacDonald was also wounded, shot with an arrow, and there were around thirty MacDonald dead and sixty wounded.

When King James heard about the battle, he granted Islay to the Campbells and placed James MacDonald in Edinburgh Castle. Carnnan Oighre on Beinn Bhan is said to be the burial place of a warrior from the Island of Arran who fell in the battle, while Clach Mhic ilean, MacLean's Stone, a short distance away, is traditionally where the dead MacLean chief lay for a while. There is also a legend that Dubh

Sith – the Black Fairy came across from neighbouring Jura and volunteered to help the Macleans, but the chief rebuffed him with insults. The fairy quickly changed sides and joined the MacDonalds. Allegedly it was his arrow that killed the chief of the MacLeans.

Tranent, 1797: East Lothian. At the end of the eighteenth century, Britain was at war with the French republic. The government passed a Militia Act, which called up men to serve in the militia. Many Scots disagreed with the Act for two reasons; firstly although it was ostensibly directed against the French, the militia could also be used against the Scottish people, and secondly because the main burden fell on the working classes.

The United Scotsmen, a radical group who campaigned for an independent Scottish republic along French lines, helped organise resistance to the Act. There were riots in various parts of the country and at Tranent the organisation sent a message to those empowered to enforce the act promising no co-operation. The United Scotsmen made a list of prominent Unionists and planned to burn their houses.

In East Lothian the miners gathered behind a drum, crying 'No Militia'. The reaction was predictable as the Cinque Ports Dragoons charged them, killing eleven and wounding twelve, before looting and raping in the collier's villages. The protests did not succeed, and Scotland continued to pour her men into the war with Republican France.

Tullich, Pass, 1652: near Braemar, Grampian. This skirmish between General Lilburn of the Cromwellian army and the Camerons occurred during the Cromwellian occupation of Scotland. Ewan Cameron, the young chief of the clan, was prominent in resisting the invaders. The Camerons were part of Glencairn's Royalist army and were ordered to hold the Tullich Pass to delay or prevent Lilburn from attacking the Royalist forces. There are two versions of this action, but it seems that Lilburn did eventually come through the pass, but too late to damage Glencairn's men.

Trot of Turriff, 14th May 1639: Aberdeenshire, Grampian. In this early action of the civil war, the Royalists led by Colonel William Johnson, Sir George Ogilvy and Sir John Gordon forced the Covenanters out of town. Around 2,000 Covenanters had formed up at Turriff, but the Gordons assembled about 800 men and some artillery. They reached Turriff at dawn on the 14th May and immediately sounded trumpets and drums and opened up with the cannon. After a very brief defence, the Covenanters withdrew.
There had been an even briefer encounter at Turriff on the 14th February, when a Royalist force under Huntly met a number of Covenanters, but there was no firing and no bloodshed on that occasion.

Trumpan, various dates given from the fifteenth century to 1578: Isle of Skye, Highland. This clan battle was one of a series between the MacDonalds and MacLeods. Tradition claims that eight MacDonald galleys crossed from Uist to Skye and landed at Ardmore. The MacDonalds moved inland and burned the church, with the worshippers still inside. Either the MacLeods in Dunvegan saw the smoke, or a young girl escaped from the church with the news, for the MacLeods gathered and attacked the MacDonalds. As the MacLeods were winning, the MacDonalds ran for their galleys, but the ebbing tide had left them stranded. The MacLeods killed the entire MacDonald force, lined them beneath a dyke and pulled it on top of them. That incident gave battle its alternative name, Blar Milleadh Garaidh; battle of the spoiling of the dyke. Trumpan Churchyard still exists.

Trumpan, Skye: Highland. A few years after the Spoiling of the Dyke the MacDonalds again raided. Again the MacLeods caught and defeated them at Trumpan. The MacLeod blacksmith was weakening through loss of life when his wife cried 'turn to me', but when he did so a MacDonald killed him. An apparent third battle in the same area was going badly for the MacLeods until they unfurled the Fairy Flag and their numbers seemed to double so they won the fight.

Tuach Hill, near Kintore, Aberdeenshire. This legendary battle was fought between King Kenneth II and the Danes. According to the story Kenneth was having a hard time with the Danes when the local residents drove a herd of cattle covered with oak leaves at the Danes. The cattle broke the Danish lines and the Scots won.

Tuacks, Bloody, around 1529: Westray, Orkney. Lewismen had raided Orkney, but the men of Westray defeated them. There were no Lewis survivors. It is quite possible that this an alternative to the Battle of Summerdale, fought between the same opponents in the same year, with the same result.

Tullimoss, Perthshire, 1489. See Talla Moss

Tuitean Tarbhach, c1400: south west Sutherland, Highland. The name is said to mean the field of great slaughter, and the battle was fought between the MacLeods and Mackays. However, there are at least two versions of the story.
In one, the Tutor of Mackay, Hugh Dubh Murray, mistreated the sister of Malcolm Macleod of Lewis. MacLeod's sister was the wife of Angus Mackay of Strathnaver. The MacLeods naturally raided Strathnaver, but on their return the Mackays led by Hugh Mackay and Alexander Murray of Cubin attacked them. The Mackays won the battle, with the usual tale of a single MacLeod survivor.
A second version said that MacLeod's daughter was married to Iain Caol and MacLeod raided to avenge an insult to her, with the same result.

Two Rivers, 671: site not known. Ecgfrith of Northumbria defeated the Picts who were rebelling against Northumbrian rule. After the battle there was peace for a decade.

U

Dance If Ye Can

Urquhart Castle, Drumnadrochit, Highland. Situated on a promontory on Loch Ness since the thirteenth century, Urquhart has seen many sieges. The forces of Edward Plantagenet of England were first to capture it, but the Scots regained it within a couple of years, only for the English to regain it in 1303. The Scots took it back when Robert I defeated the Comyns. In 1644 the Covenanters looted Urquhart, and it saw its last siege in 1690, when Grants, fighting for the Hanoverians, defeated a Jacobite siege.

Today Historic Scotland manages this picturesque ruin with facilities for tourists and information boards, although it is often better known as a site from where to watch for the Loch Ness Monster. There is also an exhibition room and an audio visual display of the history of the castle.

V

Verneuil, 17 August 1424: Normandy, France. Scotland and France were often allied against English aggression, with one nation or the other lending support to repel an invasion. In this instance the Scots were helping France during the Hundred Years War. The Franco-Scottish army contained French, Scots and Italians, while the Earl of Bedford led the English. The Franco-Scots outnumbered the English, who dismounted and placed their fearsome archers on the flanks.

Archibald Douglas led the allies. He was known as Tineman for his habit of being on the losing side in all his battles. The English advanced first, but a French cavalry charge and swept away the English archers. However, rather than hitting the flanks of the English centre, they then attacked the baggage, where around a thousand English archers cut scores of then down. The English advanced on the allies and drove the French centre from the field. As at Cravant the Scots stood their ground, despite being deserted by both French and Italians. Refusing to surrender, the Scots fought to the end. Most of the 6000 died, including fifty knights, with only a few wounded being captured.

W

Weardale, 1326/1327: Durham, England. During the First War of Independence, Sir James Douglas had led a raid deep into England. An English army, including the future King Edward III had attempted to lure the smaller Scottish force into battle, but Douglas outmanoeuvred them in a series of skirmishes. On one occasion Douglas led the Scots in a night attack on the English camp, killing an estimated 300 men. During this attack the Scots yelled 'A Douglas, A Douglas, you will all die Lords of England!' Douglas proved that he was a master of guerrilla warfare, and ran the English ragged without bringing them to a full-scale battle. This campaign was the final nail in the coffin of Edward II attempts to defeat Scotland and the next year saw the Treaty of Edinburgh that recognised Scotland's continuing independence.

Worcester, 3rd September 1651: Worcestershire, England. After Cromwell's victory at Dunbar and his army's advance northward, King Charles II led yet another Scottish Royalist army into England. There were 14,000 men, with David Leslie as military commander, but despite the king's hopes, few English rallied to the Royal standard. English parliamentary propaganda turned the English and Welsh people against the Scots, despite any latent Royalist sentiment. Once again, the Scots were alone.

On the 22nd August Charles halted at Worcester. Cromwell had been gathering his forces. No doubt aware that David Leslie had proved his tactical master around Edinburgh, Cromwell gathered an army of 28,000 regular troops, nearly twice the Scottish strength. He also had a further 3,000 militia.

The Royalists fortified Worcester and hoped for reinforcements. Cromwell planned to attack on both sides of the River Severn. Lieutenant General Middleton launched a counter attack, but an English traitor had betrayed the plan and Middleton was driven back.

On the 3rd September Cromwell's men advanced up the west bank of the river. There was harsh fighting along the Teame, with the Cromwellian Lambert throwing an assault team across, only to meet a force of Highlanders that forced them back. Cromwell advanced with three brigades on the Highlander's flank and the Scots retreated.

Charles and the Duke of Hamilton led a counter attack that pushed back Cromwell's right wing, but Cromwell called back his three brigades and stabilised the position. The Royalists withdrew into Worcester and a street fight followed as the massive Cromwellian army flooded over. King Charles escaped with the Duke of Buckingham and Lord Wilmot, as most of the Scots commanders fought on until they were killed or captured. As usual there was little mercy for the Scottish prisoners. Many were sent as slaves to the West Indies. Yet there was still jubilation in Scotland when Charles II returned as king after Cromwell died.

Worcester has many memories of the battle, from the scars left by cannon at Powick Church to the remains of the Royalist artillery fortification at Fort Royal. It would be an idea to visit the Civil War Visitor Centre at the Commandery in the centre of the city.

Y

Yester Castle, 1547: near Gifford, East Lothian, during the Rough Wooing of Henry VIII, the English attacked Yester Castle. The 4th Baron Yester repelled the first English attack, and the English withdrew, but returned in 1548 and captured the castle. Historic Scotland now manages the ruins, which are said to be haunted.

Part Three
A Scottish Timeline

AD 80: Julius Agricola, Roman Governor of Britannia, invaded what is now Scotland
AD 84: Battle of Mons Graupius. Romans defeat Caledonians
AD 90: Romans withdraw south of the Forth
AD 121-129: c Hadrian's Wall built
AD 139: c Antonine's Wall built
AD 209: Campaign of Severus
AD 297: First mention of the Picts
AD 360: First mention of the Scots
AD 367: Major raids by Scots and Picts on Roman Britain
AD 397: St Ninian recorded as bringing Christianity to Galloway
AD 408: c Romans leave Britain
AD 490: If King Arthur existed, it was around this time
AD 503: Around this time Fergus Mor MacErc is alleged to have established Dalriada
AD 563: St Columbus settled on Iona
AD 600: Around this time the Britons ride to defeat at Cattraeth
AD 603: Battle of Degsastan, Angles defeat Aedan of Dalriada
AD 638: Angles of Bernicia capture Dun Eidyn, Edinburgh
AD 685: Picts defeat Northumbrians at the Battle of Dunnichen/Nechtansmere

AD 697: Law of the Innocents to protect women and non combatants
AD 732: Oengus MacFergus victor in Pictish civil war
AD 795: First recorded Viking raid on Iona
AD 843: c. Kenneth MacAlpin becomes first king of united Scots and Picts
AD 850: Around this time the capital of Scotland is at Scone, and the religious capital is at Dunkeld
AD 870: Norse captured Alcluid/Dumbarton after siege
AD 875 – 878: widespread Norse attacks in Scotland
AD 903: Norse defeated in Strathearn
AD 937: Athelstan of England defeats Scots and allied army at Brunanburh
AD 971: Around this time, Lothian was added to Scotland
AD 973: Battle of Luncarty, King Kenneth II defeats Norse
AD 1005: Battle of Monzievaird, Malcolm II becomes king
AD 1006: Malcolm II defeated at Durham
AD 1018: Battle of Carham, Malcolm II defeats English, confirms Tweed as Scotland's southern border: Strathclyde annexed
AD 1040: Battle of Pitgaveny, King Duncan killed
AD 1057: Battle of Lumphanan, the future Malcolm III defeats MacBeth
AD 1072: Malcolm III marries Margaret; Norman-English influences begin
AD 1093: Malcolm III killed at Alnwick
AD 1138: Battle of the Standard, English defeat David I of Scots
AD 1156: Somerled wins the southern Isles in a sea battle of Islay. He was the progenitor of Clan Dougall, Clan Donald and the MacRuaridhs
AD 1157: Scottish southern border is now at Tweed and Solway
AD 1164: Somerled defeated at Renfrew
AD 1165: William I king; his red lion rampant standard will become the Scottish Royal standard
AD 1174: After being captured at Alnwick, William I agreed to allow England feudal superiority over Scotland
AD 1189: Quitclaim of Canterbury, Scotland buys freedom back from Richard the Lionheart of England

AD 1192: Scottish Church becomes a 'special daughter' of Rome.

AD 1230: Norse attack and capture Rothesay Castle in an attempt to regain control over the Hebrides

AD 1249: Alexander II dies while attempting to wrest the Hebrides from Norway

AD 1263: Battle of Largs: Alexander III defeats Norse

AD 1266: Scotland gains the Hebrides in the Treaty of Perth

AD 1286: Alexander III dies in an accident. Scotland is left without a king as the Golden Age ends

AD 1286: Alexander's granddaughter, Margaret, the Maid of Norway is queen. She is three years old.

AD 1290: Margaret, the Maid of Norway, dies en-route to Scotland

AD 1291/2: Scots ask Edward Plantagenet of England to help select a new monarch. He chooses John Balliol and demands to be 'Overlord' of Scotland

AD 1295: Scotland signs Treaty of Paris with France, Auld Alliance begins.

AD 1296: Edward I invades Scotland, sacks Berwick and defeats Scots at Dunbar; John Baliol abdicates and hands his kingdom to Edward Plantagenet. Edward demands that Scots nobility sign loyalty to him. Most agree. England steals the Scottish Records, the Black Rood of St Margaret and the Stone of Destiny.

AD 1297: William Wallace and Andrew Murray lead the Scottish resistance. They defeat the English at Stirling Bridge.

AD 1298: Wallace becomes Guardian of Scotland; Battle of Falkirk. Edward I and his Welsh archers defeat Wallace

AD 1303: Scots maul English at Roslin

AD 1304: Edward Plantagenet captures Stirling Castle

AD 1305: Wallace is betrayed to the English, who murder him after public torture

AD 1306: Robert Bruce murders John Balliol and is later crowned King of Scots

AD 1307: English murder two of King Robert's brothers; Robert wins battles at Glen Trool and Loudon Hill

Dance If Ye Can

AD 1314: King Robert defeats the English at Bannockburn
AD 1315: Edward Bruce crowned King of Ireland
AD 1318: Scots recapture Berwick
AD 1320: Declaration of Arbroath, the first of its kind in the world
AD 1326: Scottish parliament met; about this time serfdom dies out of Scotland
AD 1328: Treaty of Edinburgh ends the First War of Independence. This Treaty was later ratified at Northampton
AD 1329: King Robert dies. His five-year-old son David II is king
AD 1332: Edward III of England sends an army under Edward Balliol; Scots defeated at Dupplin. Edward Balliol crowned king, under English control
AD 1332: Second War of Independence begins; Edward Balliol chased out of country.
AD 1333: Edward III defeats Scots at Halidon Hill and captures Berwick. David II sent to France
AD 1335: Battle of Culblean, Scots defeat Balliol's forces
AD 1338: Black Agnes defies English at Dunbar
AD 1346: King David II defeated at Neville's Cross
AD 1349: The Black Death, the 'Foul Death of the English' kills about a fifth of the Scottish population
AD 1356: Edward Balliol sells his claim to the Scottish throne to Edward III
AD 1371: Robert II, the first Stewart monarch
AD 1388: Battle of Otterburn, Douglas defeats Percy
AD 1390: Alexander Stewart, the Wolf of Badenoch, destroys Elgin Cathedral
AD 1396: Battle of the Clans at Perth
AD 1402: Battle of Homildon, a bad Scottish defeat
AD 1406: Young Prince James sent to France for safety but English pirates capture him. English hold him until 1422
AD 1411: Battle of Harlaw as Donald of the Isles fights the Earl of Mar
AD 1412: St Andrews University founded
AD 1422: Battle of Bauge, fought in France, Scots defeat English

AD 1424: King James I crowned
AD 1427: King James begins an anti-Gaelic movement
AD 1429: Lord of the Isles rebels and burns Inverness
AD 1437: James I murdered in Perth
AD 1440: Earl of Douglas murdered in Edinburgh
AD 1451: Glasgow University founded
AD 1452: James II murders the new Earl of Douglas in Stirling; Douglases revolt
AD 1455: James II quells the Black Douglas rebellion
AD 1457: James II bans football and golf. Scotland ignores him
AD 1460: James II killed by an exploding cannon at the siege of Roxburgh
AD 1469: When James III marries the Norwegian Princess Margaret. Orkney and Shetland are pledged to Scotland as her dowry.
AD 1472: Orkney and Shetland become part of Scotland
AD 1482: English invade. They capture Berwick, which will remain English for an indefinite period
AD 1488: Battle of Sauchieburn, nobles defeat King James III
AD 1493: King James IV removes the Lordship of the Isles from Clan Donald
AD 1494: Aberdeen University founded
AD 1495: Whisky distilling first mentioned
AD 1496: Education Act
AD 1502: A Treaty of Perpetual Peace signed with England. King James Marries Princess Margaret of England
AD 1507: Printing introduced to Scotland
AD 1511: *Michael* launched at Newhaven, possibly the largest ship in Europe
AD 1512: New treaty with France, dual nationality between both nations
AD 1513: When England attacks France, James IV invades England; he is badly defeated and killed at Flodden
AD 1528: Patrick Hamilton burned at St Andrews for being a Protestant. James V escapes from Douglases

Dance If Ye Can

AD 1532: College of Justice established

AD 1538: King James V marries the Frenchwoman Marie de Guise

AD 1540: King James V sails around the isles to overawe the Hebridean chiefs

AD 1542: Battle of Solway Moss, English defeat the Scots; Mary, Queen of Scots was born. Battle of Haddon Rigg

AD 1543: Treaty of Greenwich: Mary is to marry the son of Henry VIII, their heir is to rule both countries. When English fail to ratify the Treaty, the Scots Parliament backs off.

AD 1544: Henry VIII sends armies into Scotland to persuade the Scots to marry Mary to his son. This episode was known as the Rough Wooing.

AD 1545: Battle of Ancrum Moor: Scots defeat English

AD 1546: Cardinal Beaton burns the Protestant George Wishart at St Andrews. Protestants take the castle, execute Beaton and hold out under siege

AD 1547: French ships and artillery capture St Andrews Castle; Battle of Pinkie, English defeat Scots

AD 1548: English invade again. French send army to help the Scots on agreement that Queen Mary would marry Francois, son of King Henry II of France

AD 1551: After bitter fighting the English retreat from Scotland

AD 1552: Society of St Andrews formed to play golf.

AD 1557: The first Covenant as Scots begin to turn to Protestantism owing to abuses in Roman Catholic Church

AD 1558: Mary marries Francoise. Any children are to both Scotland and France. If there are no children, France will own Scotland

AD 1559: John Knox preaches his first sermon, in Perth

AD 1559: Mary becomes Queen of France, along with her husband, King Françoise

AD 1560: Treaty of Edinburgh: English and French forces leave Scotland; Scottish Parliament begins Protestant Reformation. When King Françoise dies; Mary loses her power in France

AD 1561: Catholic Mary becomes Queen of Protestant Scotland

AD 1562: Battle of Corrichie, Queen Mary defeats the Earl of Huntly
AD 1563: Queen Mary's witchcraft act – witches to be burned as heretics
AD 1565: Mary Marries Lord Darnley in a Catholic ceremony. King James VI born
AD 1567: Darnley murdered near Edinburgh; when Mary marries the Earl of Bothwell, one of the suspects, she loses support. Mary sends him into exile. She is imprisoned and later abdicates.
AD 1568: Mary defeated at the Battle of Langside; she flees to England and imprisonment
AD 1570: civil war that will last for three years
AD 1572: John Knox died
AD 1573: Edinburgh Castle surrenders, Mary's supporters have lost
AD 1578: Twelve-year-old James VI takes control of country
AD 1579: Bible first printed in Scotland
AD 1582: University of Edinburgh founded
AD 1587: Act passed to quiet the Borders, Highlands and Islands
AD 1589: King James marries Anne of Denmark.
AD 1591: King James begins an anti-witch campaign in Scotland
AD 1593: Marischal College, Aberdeen founded
AD 1596: Alliance with England as James VI is named next in line for the English throne
AD 1597: Fife Adventurers attempt to colonise Lewis
AD 1603: James VI inherits crown of England on death of Elizabeth. Battle of Glen Fruin as MacGregors defeat Colquhouns.
AD 1609: Statutes of Iona: James continues his assault on the Gaelic culture; he also sends Scots to Ulster to keep the Catholics quiet
AD 1610: Bishops restored to Scottish church
AD 1611: James VI has the King James version of the Bible published
AD 1611: John Napier invents logarithms
AD 1616: Church of Scotland attempts to open a school in every parish in the country, with the idea to read and write in English.

AD 1617: James VI attempts to introduce Anglican practises to the Church of Scotland. He lectures Scots on the superiority of English culture.
AD 1633: King Charles crowned at Scone
AD 1637: Riots in Edinburgh over attempts to anglify the Kirk
AD 1638: Thousands sign the National Covenant, which declares the Kirk was independent from outside control
AD 1639: First Bishop War ends without much fighting; Pacification of Berwick
AD 1640: Second Bishop's War; Scots successful at Newburn
AD 1642: After a Catholic revolt in Ulster, a Covenanting army crosses to defend Scots settlers
AD 1643: Scots offer to help English parliament if they promise to accept the Solemn League and Covenant. English agree
AD 1644: Covenanter army of 20,000 supports English parliament; helps defeat Royalists at Marston Moor. Marquis of Montrose begins his Scottish campaign for the king
AD 1645: Battles of Inverlochy, Auldearn, Alford, Kilsyth and Philliphaugh; Scotland becomes a theocracy; plague follows in wake of war
AD 1646: King Charles surrenders to Scots
AD 1647: Scots hand king to English parliament
AD 1648: moderate Covenanters decide to support King, invade England and lose at Preston
AD 1649: English execute King Charles I: Scots proclaim Charles II as king
AD 1650: Montrose's last campaign ends in defeat at Carbisdale; Charles II Comes to Scotland and signs the Covenant. Cromwell invades, wins Battle of Dunbar
AD 1651: Charles II crowned; battles of Inverkeithing and Worcester; Monck ravages Dundee
AD 1652: Cromwellian occupation and forced union
AD 1653: Glencairn's rising in Highlands; Camerons resist invasion
AD 1660: Restoration of Charles II

AD 1661: Episcopal government imposed on Scotland; Covenanters remain in Southwest
AD 1666: Pentland Rising
AD 1672: Court of Justiciary founded
AD 1679: Battles of Drumclog and Bothwell Bridge
AD 1680: Birth of radical Cameronians: Battle of Airds Moss
AD 1682: Advocates Library founded
AD 1684: Anti-Presbyterian Killing Times begin
AD 1685: Charles II died; his later years had been spent persecuting the Covenanters. James VII, a Catholic, succeeds. Earl of Argyll fails in a Presbyterian Rising
AD 1687: James VII Indulgence allows complete religious toleration
AD 1688: Government execute Presbyterian James Renwick in Edinburgh; Prince James Francis Edward, the Old Pretender, born; James VII Chased to France for being Catholic
AD 1689: William and Mary chosen as joint monarchs: Presbyterian Church of Scotland guaranteed, Scottish Parliament granted new powers, Scots soldiers to fight in William's wars: Jacobite Rising: Battles of Killiecrankie and Dunkeld
AD 1690: Skirmish at Cromdale, end of Jacobite rising. Presbyterian religion formally established
AD 1691: William seeks amnesty with Highland chiefs
AD 1692: Massacre of Glencoe
AD 1695: Company of Scotland founded; Bank of Scotland founded
AD 1696: Education Act; King William's Ill Years
AD 1698: First fleet sails for Darien
AD 1699: King William bans English and English colonies from trading with Darien. Society for Propagating Christian Knowledge begins anti-Gaelic campaign
AD 1700: Battle of Toubacanti, Darien abandoned; famine in Scotland
AD 1701: Trouble between Scots and English parliament over succession question. When James VII dies, French recognise his son as King James VIII of Scotland and III of England
AD 1702: King William dies, Anne Stewart becomes queen

AD 1703: Act of Security passed; Scots say they do not have to have same monarch as England; Act Anent Peace and War;
AD 1704: Scots parliament threatens to bring back soldiers from France unless Anne accepts the Act of Security.
AD 1705: English Aliens Act threatens Scottish trade; use of economic threats to force Scotland to Union negotiations
AD 1706: Union negotiations amidst threats by England and anti-Union riots in Scotland
AD 1707: Treaty of Union; Scotland unites with England as Great Britain; riots in Scotland, possible bribes for the Commissioners and promise of more trade to bring some prosperity to Scotland; Scotland had 45 MPs, England had 513
AD 1708: threat of Jacobite Rising, French fleet in the Forth
AD 1712: Government attacks Presbyterian Church with Toleration Act and patronage
AD 1713: Bill to repeal Union defeated by only four votes in House of Lords
AD 1715: With King George on the throne, high taxes, poor trade, Scots soldiers fighting in Europe, Scots Mint closed and Scots Law subordinate to the House of Lords, many Scots unhappy. Jacobite Rising, Battle of Sherrifmuir
AD 1719: small Jacobite rising, Battle of Glenshiel
AD 1723: Society of Improvers created to modernise farming
AD 1725: Riots against the Malt Tax in Glasgow; Disarming Acts intended to Pacify Highlands; road building campaign in highlands, Black Watch formed
AD 1727: Royal Bank of Scotland founded
AD 1728: Edinburgh Medical School founded
AD 1730: Emigration from highlands to North America begins
AD 1736: Porteous Riots in Edinburgh
AD 1743: Potato introduced into highlands
AD 1744: Company of Edinburgh Golfers founded
AD 1745: Jacobite Rising, Battle of Prestonpans, Jacobites reach Derby

AD 1746: Battle of Falkirk and Culloden; Jacobite Rising collapses; Duke of Cumberland murders wounded and savages Highlands
AD 1747: Act of Proscription attacks Gaelic culture
AD 1754: St Andrews Society of Golfers founded
AD 1759: Carron ironworks established as Industrial Revolution speeds up: Scottish regiments heavily involved in British wars
AD 1767: The classical New Town of Edinburgh started; New Testament printed in Gaelic
AD 1770: Glasgow Tobacco Lords making huge profits from American colonies; beginning of deepening of Clyde
AD 1775: Glenturret Distillery, oldest in Scotland, founded
AD 1771: Final volume of the Encyclopaedia Britannica published in Edinburgh
AD 1773: Emigrants leave Loch Broom for Nova Scotia: first wave of Clearances at full swing
AD 1782: Proscription Act repealed
AD 1786: Burns publishes *Poems Chiefly in the Scottish Dialect* at Kilmarnock: cotton industry vastly important in west central Scotland
AD 1787: Lighthouse built at Kinnaird Head
AD 1790: Forth and Clyde Canal opened
AD 1793: Friends of the People active; War with France
AD 1797: United Scotsmen; Militia riots
AD 1801: Gaelic version of the Bible published
AD 1802: The steam powered *Charlotte Dundas* operates on Forth and Clyde Canal
AD 1807: Beginning of the notorious Sutherland Clearances
AD 1815: Battle of Waterloo, French wars end
AD 1818: Honours of Scotland rediscovered in Edinburgh Castle
AD 1820: Scottish Republican Rising, Radical War
AD 1822: Caledonian Canal opens
AD 1831: First Scottish passenger railway
AD 1832: First Reform Act
AD 1833: Factories Act
AD 1838: Victoria Queen

AD 1843: The Disruption; Free Kirk of Scotland founded
AD 1846: Potato famine in highlands: Corn Law repealed
AD 1869: *Cutty Sark* launched on Clyde: Scotland a major shipbuilding, Engineering and industrial nation
AD 1872: World's first international football match held in Edinburgh
AD 1879: Tay Bridge Disaster
AD 1881: Eyemouth disaster; University College Dundee founded
AD 1882: Battle of the Braes in Skye
AD 1885: Scottish Office founded
AD 1886: Crofters Holding Act
AD 1887: Wallace Monument opened
AD 1888: Scottish Liberals agree that Scotland should have Home Rule: Keir Hardy founds the Scottish Labour Party
AD 1890: Forth Rail Bridge opens
AD 1914: First World War begins
AD 1915: Glasgow rent strike
AD 1916: Battle of the Somme
AD 1918: First World War ends; between 125,000 and 150,000 Scots killed
AD 1919: Glasgow riots: government send in the army; German fleet scuttled in Scapa Floe
AD 1919: First transatlantic airship flight leaves from Drem
AD 1928: Women achieve franchise equality with men; National Party of Scotland founded
AD 1930: population of St Kilda removed; massive unemployment in Scotland, and massive emigration
AD 1934: Scottish National Party founded; *Queen Mary* launched on Clyde
AD 1938: *Queen Elizabeth* launched
AD 1939: Second World War starts: Battle of the Forth
AD 1941: Clydeside Blitz
AD 1945: Second World War ends: around 59,000 Scots killed; SNP wins By-election at Motherwell and Wishaw
AD 1947: Edinburgh Festival starts

AD 1949: National Covenant for Home Rule
AD 1950: Four Nationalists recover the Stone of Destiny from London, return It the following year
AD 1952: Scots unhappy that Queen Elizabeth should carry the title 'the Second' as she is the first Queen Elizabeth in Scotland
AD 1964: Forth Road Bridge opens
AD 1965: opening of the Cruachan Hydro-Electric station
AD 1966: Tay Road Bridge opens
AD 1967: *Queen Elizabeth II* launched
AD 1972: Scotland annexes Rockall
AD 1974: SNP have 30% of vote but only 11 seats
AD 1975: Labour proposes a Scottish Assembly; North Sea oil comes ashore
AD 1978: Scotland Act passed, but 40% of electorate must agree devolution AD 1979: Scotland votes yes for Devolution, but falls 0.8% behind the 40% level; Margaret Thatcher becomes Prime Minister, she is no friend to Scotland
AD 1988: Piper Alpha disaster: Lockerbie Disaster
AD 1989: Scottish Constitutional Convention meets; Thatcher uses Scotland as a Guinea pig for the Poll Tax (against the Articles of Union)
AD 1995: Skye Bridge opens
AD 1996: closure of Ravenscraig; Scotland no longer making steel; Stone of Destiny returned to Scotland, 700 years after it was stolen
AD 1997: Labour back in power. No Conservative seats in Scotland
AD 1999: New Scottish Parliament opens with domestic power in Scotland but overall control remains at Westminster
AD 2004: New Scottish Parliament Building opens
AD 2014: Referendum: 45% in favour of independence, 55% against
AD 2015: SNP gain 56 of Scotland's 59 seat

Select Bibliography

Hundreds of publications were checked to write this book, and some are mentioned in the text. The list below contains only a sample of the works consulted.

Primary Sources

Anderson, A. O: *Early Sources of Scottish History*, volumes 1&2 (Stamford 1990)

Anglo-Scottish Relations, 1174 – 1328. Selected Documents, edited by E. L. G. Stones, 1965

Bannerman, J: *Studies in the History of Dalriada*, (Edinburgh 1974)

Barbour, John, *The Bruce*, translated by A.A.H. Douglas, 1964

Bede: *A History of the English Church and People*, translated Leo Sherley-Price: (Harmondsworth, 1955)

Boece, Hector, *The Chronicles of Scotland*, edited by E. Batho and W. Husbands, 1941

Bower, Walter, *Scotichronicon*, edited by D. E. R. Watt, 1887 - 1993

Calendar of Border Papers, vols 1 and 2 (1560-1603)

Dickinson, W. Croft, Donaldson, Gordon & Milne, Isabel: *A Source Book of Scottish History, Volume Two from 1424 to 1567* (Edinburgh 1953)

Fordun, John: *Chronicle of the Scottish Nation*, (edited by William Skene, published Edinburgh 1872)
Egil's Saga, translated by C. Fell and J. Lucas, (London 1975)
Froissart, Jean, *Chronicles:* translated Berners, (London 1963)
Laxdoela Saga: translated M. Press, (London 1965)
Njals Saga: translated Magnus Magnusson & Hermann Palsson, (Harmondswirth 1974)
Orkneyinga Saga: The History of the Earls of Orkney: translated by Hermann Palsson & Paul Edwards (London 1978)
The Annals of Tigernach, edited by Whitley Stokes, volumes 11 and 12
The Annals of Ulster, edited by W. M. Hennesy and MacCarthy (Dublin 1893-1901)
The Anglo-Saxon Chronicle: editors D. Whitelock, D.C.Douglas and S. I. Tucker, (London 1961)
Spalding, J. *The history of the troubles and memorable transactions in Scotland, from
the year 1624 to 1645*, printed for T. Evans, London
The Chevalier De Johnstone: *Memoirs of the Rebellion in 1745* (London 1746)
The Regimental Records of the Royal Scots (Dublin 1915)

Secondary Sources

Adams, Frank: *The Clans, Septs and Regiments of the Scottish Highlands* (London 1928)
Anderson, M. O: *Kings and Kingship in Early Scotland* (Edinburgh 1973)
Archibald, Malcolm: *Scottish Battles* (Edinburgh 1990)
Armstrong, R. B. *The History of Liddesdale* (Edinburgh 1883)
Barrow, G. W. S: *Robert Bruce and the Community of the Realm of Scotland* (Edinburgh, 1976)
Black, C. Stewart Scottish Battles (Glasgow, 1936)
Brander, Michael: *The Making of the Highlands*, (London, 1980)

Buchan, John: *Montrose* (London 1928)
Campbell, Alastair, *The battle of Brunanburgh* (1938)
Chadwick, N.K: *Celtic Britain* (London 1963)
Chadwick, H. M: *Early Scotland: The Picts, The Scots and the Welsh of Southern Scotland*, (Cambridge 1949)
Christianson, Philip, *Bannockburn: a Soldier's appreciation of the battle* (Edinburgh, 1966)
Christianson, Philip, *Bannockburn, the story of the battle* (Edinburgh, 1960)
Crawford, B: *Scandinavian Scotland*, (Leicester 1987)
Davidson, James: *Scots and the Sea*, (Edinburgh 2003)
Dent, John, Rory McDonald, and Council Scottish Borders, *Warfare and fortifications in the Borders*, (Melrose, 2000)
DeVries, Kelly, *Infantry Warfare in the 14th Century*, (Woodbridge, 1996)
Dillon, Myles & Chadwick, Nora: *The Celtic Realms* (London 1973)
Donnachie, Ian & Hewitt, George: *Dictionary of Scottish History* (Glasgow 2001)
Duncan, A. A. M: *Scotland: the Making of the Kingdom* (Edinburgh 1975)
Ellis, Peter Beresford,& Mac A'Ghobhainn, Seamas: *The Scottish Insurrection of 1820* (Edinburgh 2001)
Fenton & Palsson (editors): *The Northern and Western Isles in the Viking World* (Edinburgh 1984)
Fraser, George MacDonald: *The Steel Bonnets* (London 1971)
Grant, I. F: *The MacLeods* (London 1959)
Grimble, Ian: *Clans and Chiefs* (London 1980)
Henderson, Isabel; *The Picts* (London 1967)
Henderson, J. *Scottish Battles* (New Lanark 2004)
Jackson, Kenneth Hurlstone (translator): *A Celtic Miscellany*: (London 1951)
Jones, G: *A History of the Vikings*, (Oxford 1968)
Keltie, John S: *History of the Highland Clans and Regiments* (London 1897)

Laing, L: *The Archaeology of Late Celtic Britain and Ireland c 400 –1200 AD* (London, 1975)

Lindesay, Robert Lindesay of Pitscottie: *The History and Chronicles of Scotland*, edited By Aenas J. G. Mackay, (Edinburgh 1899 – 1911)

Loyn, H. R: *The Vikings in Britain* (London 1977)

Mackay, W (editor): *Chronicles of the Frasers* (Edinburgh 1905)

Mackenzie, W. C: History of the Outer Hebrides (1903)

Mackie, R. L: *A History of Scotland* (Harmondsworth 1964)

McCorry, Helen: *The Thistle at War* (Edinburgh 1997)

Maclean, Fitzroy, Highlanders: A History of the Highland Clans, (London, 1995)

Marren, P., *Grampian battlefields: the historic battles of North East Scotland from AD 84 to 1745* (Aberdeen, 1990)

Matthew, Rupert, *England versus Scotland, the Great British Battles*, (Barnsley, 2003)

Menzies, Gordon (editor); *Who are the Scots?: A search for the origins of the Scottish nation* (London 1971)

Paterson, Raymond Campbell: *For the Lion: A History of the Scottish Wars of Independence 1296 – 1357* (Edinburgh 1996)

Phillips, Gervase, *The Anglo-Scottish wars 1513 – 1550: a military history, Warfare in history* (Woodbridge, 1999)

Prebble, John: *The Lion in the North* (London 1971)

Reid, Stuart: *Auldearn, 1645: the Marquis of Montrose's Scottish campaign* (Oxford, 2003)

Ridpath, George: *The Border History of England and Scotland* (Berwick 1858)

Rixson, Denis: *The West Highland Galley* (Edinburgh, 1998)

Robson, J, *Border Battles and Battlefields*, (Kelso, 1897)

Rogers, H. C. B., *Battles and Generals of the Civil Wars, 1642 – 51* (1968)

Sadler, J., Scottish Battles: from Mons Graupius to Culloden, (Edinburgh 1996)

Skene, W. F: *Celtic Scotland: A History of Ancient Alban* (volumes 1-3) (Edinburgh 1886 – 1890)

Smout, T. C: *A History of the Scottish People 1560 - 1830* (London 1969)

Smyth, Alfred P: *Warriors and Holy Men: Scotland AD 80 – 1000* (Edinburgh 1984)
Tough, D. L. W: *The Last Years of a Frontier* (Oxford 1928)
Wainwright, F. T (editor): *The Problem of the Picts* (Edinburgh 1955)
Warner, Philip, *Famous Scottish Battles*, (London 1995)

About the Author

Born and raised in Edinburgh, the sternly-romantic capital of Scotland, I grew up with a father and other male relatives imbued with the military, a Jacobite grandmother who collected books and ran her own business and a grandfather from the mystical, legend-crammed island of Arran. With such varied geographical and emotional influences, it was natural that I should write.

Edinburgh's Old Town is crammed with stories and legends, ghosts and murders. I spent a great deal of my childhood when I should have been at school walking the dark roads and exploring the hidden alleyways. In Arran I wandered the shrouded hills where druids, heroes, smugglers and the spirits of ancient warriors abound, mixed with great herds of deer and the rising call of eagles through the mist.

Work followed with many jobs that took me to an intimate knowledge of the Border hill farms as a postman to time in the financial sector, retail, travel and other occupations that are best forgotten. In between I met my wife; I saw her and was captivated immediately, asked her out and was smitten; engaged within five weeks we married the following year and that was the best decision of my life, bar none. Children followed and are now grown.

At 40 I re-entered education, dragging the family to Dundee, where we knew nobody and lacked even a place to stay, but we thrived in that gloriously accepting city. I had a few published books and a number of articles under my belt. Now I learned how to do things the proper way as the University of Dundee took me under their friendly wing for four of the best years I have ever experienced. I emerged with an honours degree in history, returned to the Post in the streets of Dundee, found a job as a historical researcher and then as a college lecturer, and I wrote. Always I wrote.

The words flowed from experience and from reading, from life and from the people I met; the intellectuals and the students, the quiet-eyed farmers with the outlaw names from the Border hills and the hard-handed fishermen from the iron-bound coast of Angus and Fife, the wary scheme-dwelling youths of the peripheries of Edinburgh and the tolerant, very human women of Dundee.

Cathy, my wife, followed me to university and carved herself a Master's degree; she obtained a position in Moray and we moved north, but only with one third of our offspring: the other two had grown up and moved on with their own lives. For a year or so I worked as the researcher in the Dundee Whaling History project while simultaneously studying for my history Masters and commuting home at weekends, which was fun. I wrote 'Sink of Atrocity' and 'The Darkest Walk' at the same time, which was interesting.

When that research job ended I began lecturing in Inverness College, with a host of youngsters and not-so-youngsters from all across the north of Scotland and much further afield. And I wrote; true historical crime, historical crime fiction and a dip into fantasy, with whaling history to keep the research skills alive. Our last child graduated with honours at St Andrews University and left home: I decided to try self-employment as a writer and joined the team at Creativia ... the future lies ahead.

Printed in Great Britain
by Amazon